Early Medieval History

J. M. WALLACE-HADRILL

Early Medieval History

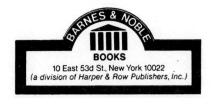

BARNES & NOBLE

BOOKS
10 East 53d St., New York 10022
(a division of Harper & Row Publishers, Inc.)

ISBN 0–06–497393–X

Contents

Preface

In a series of papers related in general theme but written over a span of twenty-five years changes in viewpoint are bound to occur. These I have neither attempted nor wished to conceal. All I have done is occasionally to correct a fact, modify a statement or add in a footnote a reference to a subsequent publication that I consider must not be overlooked. I have added two postscripts. In other respects the papers are as they first appeared, and I thank those concerned for their permission to republish in this form. One paper has not hitherto been published: 'Early Medieval History'.

I dedicate this book to Anne, in the year of our silver wedding.

ALL SOULS COLLEGE, OXFORD   J.M.W-H.

I

Early Medieval History*†

My predecessor but one, Sir Richard Southern, in his inaugural lecture, paid delicate tribute to earlier occupants of his chair. Of his
own distinguished tenure I feel inhibited from speaking, for he
teaches us all, still; but I will follow his example by remembering
my own immediate predecessor. Geoffrey Barraclough, *mox de
hieme in hiemem regrediens*, had ceased to be a medievalist before
his brief tenure of the Chichele chair. However, I think of him as
such. For two terms, when I was an undergraduate, I used to
journey from Corpus to Merton, where he was a junior research
fellow, for tuition in medieval history. (It was, as it happened, my
introduction to a college, to which I have since enjoyed the privilege
and pleasure of belonging for twenty-one years.) He may not remember those meetings in Grove Building as clearly as I do: it was
an electrifying experience—for one of us. I here and now record my
debt to him.

The public shape of the earlier Middle Ages, at least in the West,
is the only thing about them that we need not question. One could
put it this way: post-Antique to the seventh century and pre-
medieval to the tenth, or so I am told, the shape is determined by
collapse and invasion at the start and, at the end, by invasion and
collapse. It will never be much altered. Somehow these large issues
of upheaval can slacken their hold on the imagination, or at least on
the English imagination. One looks for life. Where is it?

What I would like now to discuss are largely matters of the mind,

* References for this chapter start on p. 18.
† An expanded version of an inaugural lecture delivered before the University
of Oxford on Guy Fawkes Day, 1974.

but they have a startling physical background in sheer want. Enslaved by circumstances, the tiny labouring population of western Europe contrived for centuries to feed their social superiors, and even themselves. Let me take you to the village of Brebières in northern France,[1] one of the many good gifts of archaeology to the historian. It lay some 5 km south of Douai on wet ground above the marshes of the river Scarpe. Even nearer lay the royal Merovingian villa of Vitry-en-Artois, and indeed it was to the villa that the hamlet seems to have owed its existence as a satellite-settlement of peasants who provided supplies of meat when the king was in residence, and perhaps when he was not. Some thirty hut-sites have been excavated. They have yielded some remains of pigs and oxen, horses, hens, goats, geese—and one duck, one wild boar and a few deer; also potsherds, some glass and bronze, a few knives, nails and combs, four fibulae, three rings, a pair of scissors and a wooden pestle, the quality of all of them very poor. Now this village flourished, if that is the right word, for something like two centuries. When the royal villa ceased to be used, the village was abandoned, the villagers apparently taking with them whatever utensils were usable. Perhaps it was a relief to take their rheumatism away from all that mud. Poor though they had been—and most of the interesting finds were confined to the three largest hut-sites—they may have counted themselves exceptionally lucky, as stock-raisers to the king. One would not normally expect to find much evidence of the consumption of meat. But that apart, they had little enough to show for two centuries of toil. Privation, disease and misery explain the tenacious hold of villagers everywhere on the only comforts that were left to them: the soothsayer, the wise woman, the medicine man, the gods of the countryside and the saint in his shrine. Men reduced to nothing will tend to draw together to make themselves something as a unit bent on propitiating the seen and unseen sources of their wretchedness. In the enslaved *rustici*, therefore, I detect what is entirely characteristic of the time: the capacity of the group to identify itself in a common purpose and to maintain its private privilege against the world of outsiders—in this case, the privilege of suffering. His kin, his neighbours and his gods lift my *rusticus* to membership of a little community which is itself and not any other community. How it lives is conditioned not only by hunger and exhaustion but also by its common view of good and evil, life and death, gods and demons; and of this we have abundant archaeological evidence. Moreover, its thinking on such matters has an extension in time. Periodical celebrations at the graveside witnessed to the abiding relationship of the dead with their surviving kindred. Everything else, and everyone else, was hostile until proved otherwise. More than that. If modern analogues mean anything, friendship within the village itself needed to be kept in repair by constant acts of propitiation and reassurance; women's tongues wag at the well, and men's in the field.

If we turn to the cities—poor collections, for the most part, of a few hundred inhabitants—we shall find other communities that identify themselves in much the same way. Their sense of solidarity against a hostile world was incapsulated in the person of the reigning bishop, heir to civil as well as ecclesiastical tradition. It was he in whose hands lay the city's peace, a peace as real as that of any kindred, and by no means extended to include adjoining cities. Alive or dead, the good bishop would protect his flock. Eutropius, ascetic bishop of the miserable see of Orange, promises to pray, when he is dead, for his Orangemen (*pro Arausicis meis*).[2] His responsibility for them will not cease at the grave but will rather increase as he joins his prayers with those of all his predecessors. But while he lives he is custodian of their lives, their morals and every thought of which they are capable. Such, at least, was the claim of one great bishop, Caesarius of Arles, who not unnaturally called himself their *superinspector*.[3] And again, the bishop and his flock will feel most at one at the shrine of the local saint. Today we are better able than we once were to assess the meaning of the saint; and this we owe to the labours of many scholars who have clarified the central position of the saint in local liturgy and broadened the approach to include something of the social significance of the cultus.[4] We begin to see the saint for what he really was: successor to the local pagan deity, some of whose attributes he might inherit. If anywhere, there is continuity here. Insofar as the Christian god was a reality to townsman or peasant, he was a distant one, little likely to interest himself in the affairs of one community. After all, he had to be shared with other communities, whose interests he might prefer to further. Gods have always been capricious. But the local saint was different. He knew his community—might indeed have lived in it during his lifetime—and if suitably placated with gifts would prove to be what every sensible community wanted: a patron. Here was the god at whose shrine one might reasonably pray for the birth of children or a good harvest, for recovery from sickness or deliverance from plague, or for a happy outcome to a marriage-deal. Moreover, it would pay the saint to listen, for there were ancient rivals to hand. The humble representatives of the ancient gods had not disappeared, even if the gods themselves had been down-graded to devils. It was after this fashion that a community of town or countryside might be integrated and controlled by a normally benevolent will. It is to the united flock that miracles will be publicly vouchsafed by their saintly patron; and in what other context could tradesman and rustic, landowner and professional man, lady and prostitute, ever be united? At this level a Christian community has meaning.

As with episcopal churches, so with monasteries. Inward-looking communities by their very nature, they were watchful of the stranger, to say nothing of the *gyrovagus*, here today and gone tomorrow. They open their gates on clearly-defined conditions; and the monk who goes away on the business of his house will feel lost in the outside world and unsafe till he returns. He will not even accept hospitality outside the gates unless, again, on clearly-defined conditions. He is part of a community that has one will, and his life can have no meaning if he is severed from it, even for a short time. At least until we reach the age of Charlemagne, a monastic Rule is one man's compilation, a fragment of personal legislation within a complex tradition; and it is not the less personal if, as is so often the case, the Rule is anonymous to us. The compiler will construct his Rule from other Rules known to him, adding and subtracting as he sees fit. What Rule could be more solidly in the tradition of monastic legislation and yet more personal than that of St. Benedict? It is the perfect separative instrument, the triumph of an age whose instinct was to arrange itself in communities. Now, the purpose of the Rule, as of all Rules, is the furtherance of the spiritual ends of monasticism. But St. Benedict's Rule does more than this: it makes the purpose possible of achievement. One should avoid the trap of supposing that this 'little Rule for beginners', as Benedict called it, was an easy option, easily entered upon; that was not what made it possible of achievement. Nor was it a convenient escape-route from the drudgery of cultivation or the horrors of battle: it offered a harder alternative. No man of the sixth or seventh century would lightly un-kin himself or his son, making him a pauper and a stranger to his natural friends. What was attractive, and what was sought, was alleviation from insecurity, from the inadequacy of the individual to face the seen and unseen worlds alone, and the happiness of finding identity in a common will. From the same motive the monk's kinsmen at home in his village made periodical escapes from self by dressing up at feasts and festivals to impersonate somebody or something else; a wolf, a bear, a goat or a horse. Of course, there were always monks who entered, and left, monasteries for quite other reasons; and monasteries could be very disturbed places, as was the convent of Ste Croix at Poitiers when a group of royal ladies took things into their own hands and kidnapped the abbess.[5] But to enter a monastery in the sixth century was not to enter Cluny or Cîteaux; many were desperately poor and many, also, failed to survive. Even if we allow, as we now should, that the *hemina* of wine allotted by St. Benedict to his monks was three-quarters of a litre and not one quarter,[6] the monk was in for a tough time. He had to be out in the fields, far from home, to earn his bread; so much so, that the *horarium*, *lectio*, meals and rest were necessarily rearranged to meet a new situation. The possibility of a monk's total exhaustion was a matter for serious consideration. Never once does St. Benedict legislate out of kindness but always with a view to his monks' capacity to achieve their objective. Many of his chapters end with a penal clause, a threat of punishment unspecified, where his great predecessor, the author of the *Regula Magistri*, ends on a more cheerful note, and is optimistic where Benedict is pessimistic. To accept the life of the monastery, then, was to enter upon a hard way. Yet thousands flocked to monasteries, and were accepted. Who can say how many were rejected? To become a monk was to join the one medieval community that, whatever it did, always knew what it ought to be doing.

It was the spiritual rather than the material benefits of such a community that first and forcibly struck the outside world. The founder was the link with place. It is his land that is alienated to sustain a religious house; he builds the house; and he and his heirs will not cease to be interested in what goes on there. They must protect it and add to its endowments if they can. In return they will expect to exercise some influence over the community, as in the election of abbots; and founder's kin elected to that office were not always unsuitable or unacceptable. The family will expect to be remembered in prayer, as a family. We do not have to question the religious motives of monastic founders to see that monasticism adapts itself comfortably to local and private requirements. A house so established is certainly cut off from the world at large but is very much part of the smaller world in which it stands; it serves a local need in good faith. Monasticism is monks; and what monks achieve is conditioned by experience of life outside the walls. *Ingeld* and *carmina* generally get in by the back door, here and there; which is no reason to dismiss monasteries as so many permanent sites for medieval pop festivals.

I am tempted at this point to consider several other shapes of community, people isolated by their occupation or by the hostility of others, as for example, slaves, warbands, guilds, even women— fifty per cent of the population designated the special instrument of the Devil by the other fifty per cent until the tables were turned by that splendid nun, Hrotsvita of Gandersheim. But I prefer to consider the Jews. Early medieval Jewry is a community in itself, tenacious and clear about its beliefs, practices and history, and pathetically sure of better times, as in Septimania under the Carolingians, when rescue by some eastern member of the House of David was spoken of.[7] But it seems more natural to think of the Jews as dispersed over Europe in many communities that lived and worked among Christians. We know that in towns, where their business was trade, they formed large minorities; in Narbonne, and spasmodically in Spain, possibly a majority. But they were also craftsmen, warriors and farmers, living under Roman Law and not normally distinguished by their clothing or place of dwelling from others. For this distinction we have to wait till the Fourth Lateran Council, though in the eleventh-century Cottonian manuscript, Claudius B iv, Jews already wear the caps that were to become so familiar.[8] The eleventh century is a watershed in Christian-Jewish relationships. It had never been the official policy of the Church to persecute Jews but to convert them by argument and to place practical disadvantages in their path if they chose not to be converted. Expulsion was one of them, though Gregory the Great opposed it. Persecution was normally a local matter. Now, local bishops were quite capable of a hard line on Jews: they knew that if conversion to Christianity was forced, conversion to Judaism was not—and it happened. Kings could take a line even harder than the Church advised, as in Visigothic Spain, where the large Jewish population endured persecution more terrible and more sustained than anywhere else at any time, except our own. But what specially sharpens the distinctness of these Jewish communities is the attitude of the population they lived among. In an encyclical letter of the year 417, Bishop Severus describes how he marched his flock across the island of Minorca to convert a Jewish congregation.[9] The Jews were ready to defend their synagogue with weapons of all sorts and their womenfolk hurled stones, apparently from windows, though not very accurately. There is a pitched battle and the synagogue is destroyed by fire. But not even with the help of the relics of St. Stephen was conversion an easy matter. The encounter called for leaders: the bishop on one side and the Rabbi Theodore on the other; but it is the *populous christianus* that settles the outcome. Long after this period, the Christian citizens of Toledo were inspired by the oratory of a visiting Dominican to drag the entire Jewish community from worship in their beautiful synagogue—now the Church of Santa Maria la Blanca—and throw them over the cliff's edge into the Tagus. Gregory of Tours relates how on Ascension Day the citizens of Clermont, excited by their bishop's attempts to convert the local Jews, rushed upon the synagogue and completely destroyed it. The bishop's comment was: 'I do not drive you by force to confess the Son of God.'[10] What he wanted was unity. Again, when King Gunthramn entered the city of Orleans, he took exception to the loyal shouts of the Jews, observing that it was simply done in the hope that he might order the rebuilding at public cost of their synagogue, destroyed some time ago by the citizens.[11] Such outbreaks of local violence might be whipped up by authority: but one has the impression that not very much whipping-up was called for. In part, this may be explained by jealousy, though all Jews were not rich and few, if any, practised usury so early. Rather more, I think, it must be explained by the distinctness of the Jews—a dogged community of belief and maddeningly prepared to suffer for it. It seemed a standing affront to Christian townsmen who most keenly felt their own identity at the great moments of religious observance, rogations and festivals. It was as if the Jews sought to benefit from the successful efforts of a trades union of which they were not members. Jews lived and prospered within walls that stood under the protection of such as St. Martin while propitiating him not at all—indeed, insulting him and all that he stood for, by denying him. You ought not at one and the same time to belong and not to belong. The contrast was too great to be endured. One understands and admires the constancy of the Jewish communities more easily than one grasps what it was that drove

Christian communities to acts of barbarism. Heretics and schismatics of many complexions were at hand to vex and challenge Christian orthodoxy and make it feel unsure of itself; but only the Jews, ordinary men and women, could rouse other ordinary men and women to frenzy; and this because the Jews, too, were a community—coherent, steadfast and, in a material sense, useful.

Thus far, I have been attempting to substantiate a very simple point; namely, that it is in the groups in which early medieval people arranged themselves that we find purposeful life that is worth pondering. It does not follow that individuality was always lost in such purpose, or that men were set so fast in moulds of thought and patterns of behaviour that it took the explosions of the eleventh century to release them. Was it likely to have been so in an age that calmly accepted the inexplicable and called it miraculous, that hourly expected the unexpected? Who could have anticipated Caedmon's outburst of song in a Northumbrian cowshed? Or the isolated shafts of philosophical insight of John Scottus Eriugena? Or the marvellously lifelike figures, adapted no doubt from some Antique exemplar, of the constellations in the ninth-century manuscript of Aratus, where Andromeda is so plainly a girl who has danced through the night and begun to feel the weight of her arms and feet?[12] Or how shall we account for the mausoleum of Theodoric at Ravenna, for which can be found no dominant root in any surviving architecture? Therefore I should like to go on to consider one or two quite extraordinary acts of initiative. They are the more remarkable when seen against the background that scholarship today presents of learning harnessed to *collectanea*, whether liturgical, literary or other.

My first initiator is Isidore of Seville. Jacques Fontaine, in his splendid book,[13] draws a parallel between Isidore's *Etymologiae* and contemporary church-building. One can see such a church as S. Juan de Baños, in northern Spain, or San Salvatore at Spoleto, poised transitionally between Antiquity and the Middle Ages. But to their builders and first users they were not transitional: they were original. As with church-builders so with Isidore: you have the re-employment of old, discarded material to make something useful and new; in the one case, Late Roman shafts and capitals, and in the other, quantities of traditional learning channelled through manuals and commentaries and collections, many no doubt derived from Africa. It is just this acceptance of the past that gives the *Etymologiae* their impersonal look; one feels that all is grist to such a mill. The reality is different.

Isidore's book is a compendium of knowledge for the literate of a new Spain—Spain of the Visigoths, recently converted to Catholicism. It is an interpretative compendium, carefully designed to be read and not merely referred to. Isidore is an etymologist. The heart of his culture is language, which he serves by exposing the meaning of words. In this spirit he takes his readers back into Antiquity, to the masters of classical learning, whom he fits into a Spanish framework, making the whole intellectually viable, and going some way along the road towards the definition of a barbarian-romanesque culture. It is no substitute for Augustine's *De Doctrina Christiana* but is still an impressive statement of Christian culture in terms of language, its principal tool, breaking down experience into words, and words into meanings. In the word, he says, lies the essence and original force of what it signifies. Not all words can be etymologized thus, but chiefly those that he classifies as words *ex causa, ex origine* and *ex contrariis*. So his way of thinking about words is quite unlike that of an orthodox grammarian. His concern is with language as revelation. So he makes his dignified way through the seven liberal arts: medicine, law and chronology; the Bible, the canons and the offices; the doctrine of man and God, angels and saints, the Church and the sects; languages, races, kingdoms, the army, citizens and kinship; the anatomy of man; the animal world and inanimate nature; town and country, stones and metals, weights and measures, agriculture and botany, war and justice, games and pastimes, ships, buildings and clothing, food and drink, furniture and much else. There is a plan. We pass from the formal structure of how we know things to God, and thence down again by way of angels and men and beasts to the material world, its parts and its elements. No section of the work makes sense unless the plan is kept in mind. I do not mean to bore you with further analysis but will simply indicate one or two characteristic treatments that strike the eye. Isidore devotes much space to grammar. He gives a faithful exposition of a useful, practical art that would not have shocked his predecessors; but upon this he superimposes another view of grammar as the mistress of method, the way to get at meanings, the weapon of intellectual analysis. The whole of his classification turns on this adjustment of grammar to ask the question 'why' not 'how'. The symbols of language are no longer

B

just parts of speech, but the significations of a mysterious truth. So marked a degree of originality might indeed have surprised his predecessors. Even on mathematics he manages to be himself. He reproduces what Cassiodorus teaches him pretty exactly but interprets mathematics metaphysically. Number he identifies with the essence of the world, unexpectedly and almost lyrically. 'Take away number', he says, 'and all perishes.' His etymologies of the names of numbers are fantastic but explicable. Quite unmoved by Cassiodorus' horror of infinity, he sees it as a symbol of the divine absolute and borrows an expression from St. Augustine to express his intense admiration of it. In brief, he starts with arithmetic as a series of technical definitions and finishes in arithmology, a mystical exercise in pure number or sacred pendant to arithmetic. It is no longer the great quantitive discipline of Antiquity. As for astronomy, names are once more a privileged means of access to knowledge of the nature of the cosmos and a path to a mystical interpretation of the sky. So he adopts a mythologizing approach to the seasons, planets and constellations. The stars seem to him the most splendid witness of God's creative power: *astrorum micantium splendentibus signis adornavit.* I have said enough to make my point, which is that Isidore is an original in a field where originality was least to be expected. We do not go to him for etymology in the accepted sense; we go to him for a view of how a national culture might be constructed.

I turn to a second original. Pope Gregory the Great alarms because he is emotional. Mental imbalance seems to threaten. He would not be pope today. The *Cura Pastoralis* would by itself constitute a claim to great originality: no westerner before him had looked as he looked at the work of a bishop, the art of arts, the art of the government of souls; or had traced a bishop's motives in accepting office, even to the roots of self-deception. 'The mind', as he put it, 'will often lie to itself about itself.' But the psychological insights of the *Cura Pastoralis* are as nothing compared with those of the great sermons on the Book of Job. At a rarefied level, they are biblical commentary as a means of action, and a treatise on the mystical life. A report reached him that Bishop Marinianus of Ravenna thought they ought to be read aloud at vigils: 'not on your life', said Gregory, *non est illud opus populare.*[14] And indeed it is not. The *Moralia in Job per contemplationem sumpta* belong to a tradition in social theology that goes back to St. Augustine, and reaches forward at least to Odo of Cluny, a theology more concerned with the nature of man than with that of the Church. But Gregory's mind was not Augustine's: Gregory's was a mind that felt in order to see. He takes the Book of Job and says he will comment on it, verse by verse, in a traditional manner. As it turns out, literal and allegorical interpretations bore him and he soon forgets about them. Instead he uses Job as a raft for exploring deeper waters: moral and spiritual progress towards the contemplative life. It is no exegesis but moral theology, sombre and passionate, almost Pascalian. One must wait a long time to hear again a contemplative groping through images of darkness and light to confront the God who eludes him. So he is also pessimistic; contemplation throws him back (*reverberata*) exhausted; and all is to do again. Perpetual action that perpetually fails, set among the horrors and ruin of sixth-century Italy, seems dreadfully appropriate. It is also appropriate that he is not really an intellectual, at least not in the sense that Augustine and Ambrose were intellectuals. He is a man of action and a moralist, exploring approaches. His originality lies in his grasp of human nature. He has watched men of all kinds and knows what they are; not merely the uprooted and the starving but substantial men who have made a good thing out of troubled times. He is never deceived, and can describe what he feels in language that can still stop the reader in his tracks. Let him stand for the dark introspection of the early Middle Ages, as Isidore for the making of a cultural barrier of security.

Both men, and all their contemporaries, took for their starting-point the Bible. A glance at Lowe's *Codices Latini Antiquiores* shows that vastly more early medieval manuscripts of the Bible and biblical commentary survive than of any other work. The thought-world of the Bible is, as you know, extremely various; it could embrace the illustrators of the Utrecht Psalter but also those of the Beatus commentary on the Apocalypse. Pope Gregory grasped its huge emotional range when he said that the Bible was like an inspired letter; or again, like a river at once deep and shallow, where the elephant swims while the lamb splashes, fit for children and for learned men; or a mirror in which we see ourselves. It conditioned more or less every man who put pen to paper; both what he said and how he said it. Now this is an extraordinary social phenomenon: men's minds are now in willing captivity to a revealed world of which their own existence is a mere projection. It provides norms and standards, warnings and examples, all within an unclearly differentiated past in which men, singly or in groups or in nations, struggled with the problem of the unseen; and it is the unseen, in its varying shapes of comfort and wrath, that stands between medieval man and his Antique ancestors; this, and not any material difference. Technology will not distinguish Cicero from Isidore; but the Bible will.

Now the Vulgate is in Latin, the language that Isidore was so concerned with. But what is medieval Latin? It is a curious fact that we acknowledge our difficulties in dealing with archaeological evidence, place-names, art and a host of other disciplines more readily than we acknowledge the existence of the problem of language. There were in fact several medieval Latins, each conditioned in its development by where it was used, and for what purpose it was used. They are specialized—one might almost say private— means of communication. There is no *koine*. For example, the Latin of the Church is something special, but yet subdivides into lesser Latins: there is stylistic evolution in the Latin of the canon of the Roman Mass, of the Psalter, and of the monastic rules, liturgy making its own special linguistic demands; Christian prose and poetry follow distinct linguistic paths; and all this without taking account of the individual contributions of such as Tertullian, Augustine, Jerome and Benedict to the language in which they expressed their complex thoughts. One can see at once that the relationship between language and religion will be intimate, that social and spiritual evolution will be conditioned by the language in which it is expressed. But the language of the Church is only one Latin. There is also the Latin of law. I recall the sorrow of Eduard Fraenkel that the Oxford School of Literae Humaniores paid no attention to the Corpus Juris Civilis. To do so would be a tall order; yet it is true that the legal Latin of the early Middle Ages—canon as well as civil—comes nearer to something the Golden Age might have understood than any other later Latin. Or rather, some of it does. When one enters the related field of the Latin law codes of the Goths, the Lombards and the Franks, one must be prepared for a Latin that is barbaric indeed; but it is attempting to express ideas that were alien to Roman Law. Barbaric, too, is the Latin of the vast corpus of charters—often, I suspect, the nursery of men who also wrote of other matters—and the Latin of the capitularies. Then there is narrative Latin, the language of the historians. Who shall say that he understands Bede? No medieval writer wrote clearer Latin than Bede; but where it is most limpid it is also most deceptive. And, as against Bede, there is Aldhelm; yet beneath Aldhelm's *exotica* lies a comparatively simpler language. These men of great intelligence think within frameworks alien to us, and to Antiquity.

Two writers of Latin prose have things so new to say, and audiences so new to address, that they well-nigh invent a new language for their special purposes. One is Gregory the Great, master of several styles, but especially master of a nervous, direct style adapted to the intelligent unlettered who faced with him the prospect of Armageddon. Even within his correspondence one can see him adapting his language to the recipient: it was one thing to write to Constantinople and quite another to castigate some benighted bishop who had blundered into error or simply gone to sleep. The other original was Gregory of Tours, who laments his *rusticitas* but does not admit that what he had to say could not have been said half so well in any other Latin—if, indeed, at all. He is not unaware of his literary distinction. He can handle the rhetorical *cursus* and is soaked in the language of the Bible, but his power in the use of a story and of dialogue is his own. The *sermo rusticus* is a new weapon. Auerbach has shown how he can tell a story that no classical writer could have told: the telling is conditioned by the language.[15] His inspiration is the bishop's direct pastoral contact with his flock, his interest is in the event as it happens, which he evokes directly and dramatically. Something of this urgent sense of conveying the immediacy of human relationships is already in St. Augustine, who begins to formulate the stylistic contrast between classical rhetoric and Judaeo-Christian literature. Gregory takes it further. Perhaps I do an injustice to Caesarius of Arles, with his vivid, direct, sermons. Add him, and we have a trio of writers of a new Latin—trenchant, mordant, and right for the job. We may look on to Alcuin, Einhard and Lupus—all great men with their pens—but we shall not again meet with a Latin that has so beautifully the feel of the early Middle Ages. And always one has to try to account for the Latin one finds. I wish I could account for the strange power of certain Visigothic writers, and particularly of Julian of Toledo's *Historia Wambae regis*. Perhaps we should look to Africa. Yet another language of which one hears nowadays is Anglo-Latin, by which is meant the Latin, and more particularly the religious Latin, of the Anglo-Saxons. I am unsure how far this Latin is distinct from its continental counterparts, but everything suggests that it would have its own characteristics. Vernacular will influence Latin, as Latin will influence vernacular. And here indeed one touches a new field: the interaction of spoken and written Latin and vernacular. Of Greek I say nothing, though strands of it continue to float through medieval Latin, and here and there a man will actually know some. In southern Italy under the Ostrogoths it is even possible to speak of a renaissance of Hellenism, however short-lived, and to see a link between Vivarium and the renaissance of the Carolingians.[16] Indeed, we are learning to take seriously the connections between East Rome and the western world. It surfaces not only culturally but politically and economically. Nevertheless, we should not be persuaded that the characteristic life and thought of the West are fundamentally indebted to Byzantium; not even through translation. If we except some patristic literature, Latin translations of any Greek were rare indeed at this early time. I am really saying that the westerners were barbarians: I feel all too much affinity with them. Barbarians because they failed to understand or to transmit much of the legacy of classical Antiquity, though, but for the Carolingian *scriptoria*, we should have very much less of classical literature than we do have. They were not immobilized in some intellectual equivalent of a Germanic swamp, but were a new admixture of people on an old ground, adapting what they had to fresh purposes and therefore frequently at cross-purposes. Nowhere is this clearer than in their handling of language—a disordered complex of group-communications that breathes life in every line.

From time to time I have referred to 'the early Middle Ages'—though I have not so entitled my lecture. The western centuries between the fifth and the tenth do share certain characteristics that distinguish them from earlier or later centuries; but that does not make them a clearly-defined period, as historians use that term. It is convenient, but no more, to see new beginnings with the large-scale Germanic settlements or with the conversion of Constantine or with the events of the year 476. But the western part of the Empire had long been familiar with barbarian settlers, and as for Constantine's conversion, it did not strike the circle of the Emperor Julian that something irreversible had happened. The real beginning, for the historian, is the birth of Christ. Neither the Roman pagan world nor, I think, subsequent historians of that world, ever found the phenomenon of Christianity easy to come to terms with; understandably, since it presented no common front. We face a kind of slack of the tide, with no clear set to what spins in its eddies; four centuries of instability of argument and emotion. Historians hate instability. By the side of this, it is no great matter to define the stages of the disintegration of imperial authority in the West: it disintegrated not on any one occasion or by any one act, but simply when people thought it had. Empires fall in the mind, and the Roman state had been falling thus for a very long time. It was in the surviving East, not the falling West, that Zosimus and John Lydus maintained that something important had come to an end: fortune had abandoned the Empire, the whole Empire.[17] I doubt if Justinian or Procopius would have agreed, nor even those western barbarian *filii* of the Empire who drew subsidies, received imperial marks of recognition or, when out of favour, fought pretenders backed by emperors and watched imperial fleets manoeuvring in western waters. But still it was possible to see things as Zosimus saw them. What one meant by Empire was equivocal. What one meant by Christianity was also equivocal, not in its substance but in what was made of the substance by argument and by mere misunderstanding—a process in which the tenacity of local ignorance played its full part. Archaeology confirms this on a massive scale. The late Antique funerary memorial will sometimes blend Christianity with one kind of traditional paganism, while the early Germanic grave will blend it with another. There are representations of Christ on Germanic gravestones that would do very well for Woden, and bits and pieces among the gravegoods that leave one wondering what on earth the pious kindred understood by Christianity.[18] The mixture persists and the shift in emphasis is slow. For these reasons I see no clean beginning for early medieval history.

As to the end of it, the situation is worse. The eleventh century indeed marks a beginning, but it does not mark an end. And near that point in time falls what we call the Carolingian Renaissance, the sounds of which reverberate today. Finally, then, I ask myself what I am to make of this phenomenon. We are almost forced to think of it in terms of schools, of *scriptoria*, even of scripts; and nobody who saw the bringing-together of so much that was splendid at the Aachen commemoration of Charlemagne can wonder that it is so. But there was much, also, that was not so splendid—enough to remind us that books matter for what they say. It was an experiment in education for a particular purpose. It had for its background, though not for its roots, an act of force; or rather, a series of acts, by which a Rhineland family disposed of its rivals, seized two crowns, obtained an imperial title and imposed its authority in a variety of ways as far as the fringes of western Europe. The family claimed a Christian basis for its authority and meant what it said. This is the establishmen that makes its voice heard in capitularies, the royal annals, Einhard, Hincmar, and elsewhere. There is also an anti-establishment. This too we can hear, even from the earliest days of the Carolingian rise to power. First it is local, sectional opposition to a dangerous family; but even then it reflects a dislike of uniformity and, soon, disillusionment and anger. The elaborate provisions of the capitularies are evidence of what should be done and what had not been done; not of what had been done. Furthermore, what was not done was seen against a background of extraordinary social disorder; of corruption, exploitation, famine, poverty, conspiracy, unrest, feud, desertion, sorcery, prognostication and a host of bad omens; in some ways, terribly like the fourth century. The moral atmosphere of the age of renaissance is lurid and even catastrophic; certainly it is not one of peaceful achievement in the field of learning. Now and again we think we spot a don and start with relief; Lupus of Ferrières pauses to explain accentuation. Yet he was a great man and not at all an Edward Casaubon lost among his Parerga. The lower lights are more characteristic: Notker, busy with his *Gesta Karoli Magni*; a weird monastic re-creation of Charlemagne as a half-legendary figure and ideal for his successors, which could not possibly have been contrived in any monastery during the previous century. His new Charlemagne is a man of iron—the image recurs—a traditional Frankish chieftain, quite unlike his byzantinizing successors. Notker is no biographer like Einhard but he knows his craft, such as it is. He dreams up a personality and appropriates a warlord for his monastery, St. Gallen, much as the *Gesta Dagoberti* appropriated a former king for St. Denis, and the *Vita Remigii* another king for Reims. There is nothing 'popular' about the *Gesta* or about its vivid anecdotes. In medieval manuscripts it will be found in respectable company. Fantastic yet respectable, it stands somewhere near the birth of the Carolingian legend, which was to flower, centuries later, in the Pseudo-Turpin chronicle, the literature of the pilgrim route to Compostela, and the court of Barbarossa. Already when Otto III wishes to identify his rule with Charlemagne's, he places on his seal the face of legend, bearded and ancient—*Blanche ad la barbe e tut flurit le chef*, a harbinger of the old man of the chansons de geste. Aachen, St. Denis, and Compostela were to be the poles between which this extraordinarily powerful fantasy revolved.[19] This in itself suggests a reason why there is no demarcation between parts of the Middle Ages. Life goes on: a nice mixture of ruthlessness and fantasy. Ruthlessness is highly prized. If you look at Ermold's poem on Louis the Pious or Nithard's history of Louis's sons, you will find an emphasis on martial qualities and deeds of iron that would have seemed entirely proper to Gregory of Tours. We have not got far, for all the ideals of Charlemagne's friends. These very writers are part of the Renaissance. They command attention often on grounds of literary quality; they know how to use information, how to hold attention, how to achieve effect; and what they have to say is, as often as not, chillingly barbaric.

A further aspect of this Renaissance was its wonderful variety. No part of life remains untouched. Once remove the directing hand of Charlemagne and it continues along divergent paths in centres far removed from each other. The pull of the local is never more in evidence. Indeed, if I were to pick out one centre of Renaissance that most clearly illustrates this tendency it would be a centre on the edge of the Carolingian world and sometimes hostile to it; the little kingdom of the Asturias, centred on Oviedo and tucked away in the mountains of northern Spain. Here was something the Arabs did not conquer. By existing, it constituted the beginning of the Reconquest of Spain. Consciously a continuation of Visigothic kingship, it harboured part at least of the great library of Toledo, and in its surviving buildings we can still see the power of an architectural and decorative style, not uninfluenced by the Carolingian, that might be called Neo-Visigothic. It was a kingdom geared to war from the beginning and founded on successful resistance. Charlemagne found it ready to co-operate in the field but no more willing than Offa or the Beneventans to accept imperial *auctoritas*. It even played with the heresy of Adoptionism, than which nothing was likelier to irritate good Carolingian churchmen. Remote, sophisticated and bellicose, the kingdom of the Asturias had its counterparts elsewhere—as, for example, in Brittany or in Italy. Let it stand for the intense localism that brought out what was individually best in these remote stages of European history. Localism; communities, societies, groups and sects bent on the perpetuation of what they were; and, against a backdrop of pot- and post-hole, fibula and scramasax, some rare inmates. I have glanced at Benedict, Isidore and Gregory. I might have chosen Bede and Aldhelm, Columbanus and Boniface, Alcuin, Hraban Maur or John Scottus, or indeed others. A rum lot; but a sizeable succession of men with this one claim to our attention: nobility of mind.

NOTES

1 See Pierre Demolon, *Le village mérovingien de Brebières* (Arras, 1972).
2 *Vita Eutropii, Gallia Christ. Nov.*, VI, col. 17.
3 *Césaire d'Arles, Sermons au Peuple*, I, ed. M. J. Delage (Paris, 1971), p. 270.
4 I think particularly of the work of Père Delehaye, Père de Gaiffier, and F. X. Graus.
5 Gregory of Tours, *Hist.*, IX, 39–43; X, 15–17.
6 *La Règle de Saint Benoît*, ed. A. de Vogüé and J. Neufville, II, (Paris, 1972), p. 677.
7 See Arthur J. Zuckerman, *A Jewish princedom in feudal France, 768–900* (New York and London, 1972), whose conclusions, however, should be treated with caution. A safer general guide is Bernhard Blumenkranz, *Juifs et chrétiens dans le monde occidental, 430–1096* (Paris and The Hague, 1960).
8 See Ruth Mellinkoff, 'The round, cap-shaped hats depicted on Jews in BM Cotton Claudius B. iv', *Anglo-Saxon England*, II (1973), pp. 155–65.
9 *Epistola Severi, Pat. Lat.*, 41, cols 822–32. I am grateful to Mr. Peter Brown for reminding me of Severus.
10 *Hist.*, V, 11.
11 Ibid., VIII, 1.
12 Illustrated on the dust jacket of *Karl der Grosse: Das geistige Leben*, ed. Bernhard Bischoff (Düsseldorf, 1965).
13 *Isidore de Séville et la culture classique dans l'Espagne wisigothique*, 2 vols (Paris, 1959).
14 *Reg. Greg. I*, XII, 6.
15 Erich Auerbach, *Mimesis*, ch. 4.
16 See Pierre Courcelle, *Les lettres grecques en occident* (2nd ed., Paris, 1948), part 3.
17 See Walter Goffart, 'Zosimus, the first historian of Rome's fall', *Amer. Hist. Rev.*, 76 (1971), pp. 412–41.
18 See E. Salin, *La civilisation mérovingienne*, esp. vol. 4.
19 This was the subject of a memorable set of lectures delivered at Oxford by the late Dr. Robin Flower in 1937. They were never published, and are now lost.

II

War and peace in the early Middle Ages*†

Men of the earlier Middle Ages knew what they meant by war
and peace. Their definitions are not hard to find, even though,
when found, they prove to be inconsistent. They knew that there
were just and unjust wars, good kinds of peace and bad, and they
could envisage war and peace as two poles of a single concept. My
intention is not to survey this large and ramshackle field but simply
to inquire how far some of the definitions tallied with the facts of
war and peace; and whether, at the end, the pressures making for
peace had affected the nature of war. To ask whether Western
Europe in the days of King Alfred and the later Carolingians was
more or less peaceful than it had been four centuries earlier is not
very meaningful, since an entirely new situation was created by the
attacks of the Vikings, Arabs and Magyars; but it is meaningful to
ask whether four centuries of additional experience had caused men
to look at war and peace in a different way.

As always with medieval attitudes, one starts with contributions
from a remoter past; and of three of these contributions—Roman,
Christian and Germanic—we know enough to identify them in the
medieval context. The Roman attitude, at least under the Empire,
was in theory unambiguous and in derivation Greek: every war
needed justification. The best reason for going to war was defence
of the frontiers, and, almost as good, pacification of barbarians
living beyond the frontiers. Outside these reasons one risked an
unjust war, and emperors had to be careful.[1] This at least was the
theoretical position, though practice could be very different. It may

* References for this chapter start on p. 35.
† *Transactions Royal Historical Society*, 5th series, vol. 25 (1975). Prothero
Lecture delivered before the Royal Historical Society on 20 September 1974.

in part explain why we have no Roman treatise on the theory of war, as we have, for example, a very enlightening treatise from the late fourth century on its practical application within the framework of saving manpower and taxation by means of technical innovations.[2] But even in *De Rebus Bellicis* one encounters a certain ambiguity: the purpose of war may be defence, but the technical innovations to which the author wishes to draw the emperor's attention happen to involve weapons of attack. Cicero, in *De Officiis*,[3] had already been clear about the difference between just and unjust wars; and he was not the only one. The Romans must be given more credit than medievalists usually allow them for their consistent belief that warfare ought not to be waged for offensive purposes; and among these they counted the pursuit of glory unaccompanied by further justification.[4] As for peace, the *Pax Romana* so ardently desired, it was significant that the goddess of peace was iconographically very like the goddess of victory.[5] In other words, peace was something to be sought for and won on the battlefield, something to be constantly defended when won. Peace, then, was not merely absence of war; it was a condition that in practice resulted from war, and which would always demand a warlike stance. In the words of Vegetius, leading writer on military matters, *qui desiderat pacem, praeparet bellum.*[6]

What for these purposes I call the Christian contribution comprises biblical and patristic strands. In brief, it ranges from the Old Testament to Ambrose and Augustine,[7] and is, on the whole, consistent. Warfare for God's purpose must be waged by God's people, and its justification will be peace. Peace is the supreme realization of divine law. It is not then surprising that the Bible seemed to join with Antiquity in urging the necessity for the military virtues. Indeed, it has rightly been said that the collective fury of God's war, the war of the Chosen People, was something more terrible than any act of individual heroism of Germanic epic. God was present in battle as leader of his people,[8] and his enemies could justly be sacrificed to him. There is more to it that that; but I content myself with isolating the strand in the Christian tradition that was to have significant bearing on early medieval practice: the justification for Christian warfare that overrode all obstacles was the achievement of God's purpose. One may sense in this a driving-force, perhaps also an absence of brakes, that could make Christian warfare something more formidable than its pagan imperial counterpart.

Thirdly, the Germans. It is not easy to distinguish their ancient and traditional views on war and peace from those that came to prevail when they were settled within the Empire. We lump them together, both the Germans and their views, in a way that the Romans did not, and by so doing risk dismissing them as uniformly and invariably warlike. As they come within the ken of the Romans they certainly look warlike—and inevitably, since war was the context in which the Romans knew them. All of them, so far as we know, had a warrior-class, armed and trained to fight, if not always very formidably; and they had leaders in war, as Tacitus tells us.[9] But they did not live for or by warfare. They were agricultural peoples, upon whom the necessity of getting a living was imposed. I am far from regarding the Germanic peoples as harmless farmers who somehow wandered, or were pushed, over the frontier into imperial territory. Indeed, I am not sure that we even yet understand the nature of their migration—supposing it to have been a migration. But they could fight for a place in the sun, successfully enough to be hired as mercenaries and settled as such. To this extent they had their contribution to make to the medieval pool of ideas about war and peace. But when we find them settled in Italy and Spain, Gaul and Britain, they have already in varying degrees absorbed something of the ethos of *Romanitas*, and even of Christianity.

At this point it may be well to distinguish the warfare of which I am thinking from feud, the process by which Germanic kindreds settled their differences. A good deal has been written about feud.[10] If it was private warfare (and it could be) it was conditioned by accepted rules imposed by custom, indeed by necessity. When first encountered in written sources, it is already deeply involved with the business of finding composition. In other words, the feuding process was amenable to settlement on agreed terms that were a substitute for bloodshed. Things did not always work out this way; indeed, we cannot tell what generally happened at any one time or place. But the composition-tariffs of the barbarian law-codes can only mean that composition was an accepted part of feud. A feud may of course be private warfare on a very large scale, as between kings. There are cases of this in Frankish and in Anglo-Saxon history, where wars between peoples, though caused by personal differences between kings, are yet waged in a manner indistinguishable from any other wars on the same scale. But when we speak of feuds we generally mean quarrels between families, involving the neighbourhood more or less. Such evidence as we have of these by no means suggests that the Germans took to fighting between families as a desirable occupation and proper outlet for bellicose instincts. Rather the opposite.

Which Germanic peoples can be considered essentially war-like and attuned to warfare as a national occupation? One thinks of the Goths. If we may believe Philostorgius, Wulfila decided not to translate the Books of Kings into Gothic lest the stories of war should inflame their warlike instincts.[11] Certainly he did not translate the Books of Kings. But when we see the Goths settled in Spain, we find a military caste indeed, generally ready for an outing, but some of them are quietly scraping a living out of the Meseta of Castile. Gregory of Tours had a low opinion of the Gothic warrior's courage,[12] but he may not be a reliable witness. I do not think we can call the Goths an exceptionally warlike people. The Lombards may be better candidates. Paul the Deacon, writing in the ninth century but using older material, clearly considered them warlike by nature; for them, war was a great tradition, and an occupation properly associated with ritual and sacrifice. Thus Alboin, besieging Pavia, vows that when it has fallen he will kill *universum populum*, which can reasonably be taken as a mass-sacrifice to his gods.[13] But it is another matter to equate the people with the *exercitus*. Liutprand indeed admitted that he could not eradicate the Lombard military instinct, though in the special context of the *iudicium Dei*.[14] Yet the Lombards, like all Germanic peoples of whom anything is known, had a clear concept of peace, or rather of various kinds of peace, some of them capable of steady extension. There is no need here to recapitulate the plentiful evidence for the peace of the Germanic homestead, well-attested as it is in Anglo-Saxon practice, nor yet of the general peace of a people, which, if Brunner is right, reaches back to Antique times.[15] As recorded, however, it is already associated with kingly authority, and certainly the special peace of the king's residence, his city, his servants and travellers seeking him, seems to owe little to Volksrecht. With the Anglo-Saxons, general recognition of the king as protector of the general peace seems to have been a hesitant growth before the eleventh century. In Maitland's words, 'the time has not yet come when the King's peace will be eternal and cover the whole land. Still we have here an elastic notion.'[16] But wherever we look, peace to the German never looks like an abstraction or a distant political ideal. It is rather a condition of non-hostility that a man or a group of men may grant and enforce, insofar as it affects him or them. Often it seems to imply a normal state of enmity from which, by special dispensation, some person or class of persons is exempted. Even to marry into another kin is to make of that kin a friend where before, as a matter of course, one had an enemy. Hence the procedural caution and care that characterize the Germanic marriage-negotiation and settlement. There are, then, varieties of Germanic peace, all of them implying absence of hostility within a specified context, and sometimes extendable by special arrangement. Obviously it is a concept vital to the conduct of the social life of any people, but it is nonetheless negative, resting as it does on the knowledge that the world at large, and especially the world just beyond one's own experience, is naturally hostile. One of the kinds of peace that are found quite early is the peace accorded to the Church, or to churches, which is not the same as the peace accorded by the Church. Churches and their officials need special protection from kings, and, as we know, they get it. No doubt the pagan shrines had also got it. But it raises the point that the evidence of peace-bestowal and peace-protection in the Volksrechte is already associated, however slightly to begin with, with Christian cultus.

We come thus to the Church that faced the Germans when they settled the Western provinces, and to its own notions of peace and war. St. Augustine's view was that war was the price of peace, and the just ruler will not be able to avoid it; it will be forced on him by his enemies. The fact that he will be fighting a just war is small comfort, for the cause of war will be the wickedness of his enemies. Behind warfare there is always wickedness. St. Augustine does not elaborate this idea of the regrettable just war, though the canonists were to do so;[17] the regret is his, the justness or unjustness is Roman. Isidore is less certain that warfare is regrettable. His section *De Bello et Ludis* (and it is interesting that he lumps them together, making of both a kind of festival), starts with a good Ciceronian definition of the just and unjust war.[18] A war, he decides, has four stages: battle, flight, victory, peace. *Pacis vocabulum videtur a pacto sumptum.* And *pax* will be followed by a *foedus*. In other words, peace is a technicality dependent on victory in the field. Isidore follows this up with a section *De Triumphis*, a concept dear to the mind of late Antiquity. A witness of much Gothic warfare, he has not concluded that to fight is incompatible with Catholic doctrine. Nor was there any reason why he should have done so. The community of all men under natural law, even when envisaged as divine law,[19] by no means obviates the need to fight in a just cause. The justness still remained to be determined from the Christian standpoint, and the Fathers had been clear that the profession of war was entirely compatible with Christianity. Lactantius, Origen, Tertullian and Ambrose had no doubt about it. Provided that the purpose of war was just, it could be waged; and peace, itself the justification for war, was the supreme realization of divine law. Thus there was nothing in the Christian tradition that need have caused the churchmen of the early Middle Ages to look upon the warring Germans as wicked because they fought. A just war was still perfectly acceptable, however saddened one might be by bloodshed and destruction.

But could the Germans be induced to fight just wars? Of their disposition to fight there could be no question. Warrior-classes trained in the mysteries of battle, cut off from their fellows by the exercise of a special craft, were not going to lay down their arms because they had become landowners in a Roman province. A young prince, not of weapon-bearing age, is buried at Cologne in the mid-sixth century. He is furnished with a complete military equipment. Some of it is of the right size for adults and the rest look like miniatures or toys. What they constitute is the symbolic or ritual equipment of the class into which he was born.[20] He was not a warrior; but a warrior was all that he could have become, or desired to become. He belonged to a hereditary fighting caste. For such a one, Frankish life *was* war.[21] And not of course Frankish life only, but the life of every German brought up in the military tradition of his people. Whether we should conclude that a whole people was thus dedicated to war is another matter. If we look at Frankish history over the Merovingian period we might indeed be tempted to reach just such a conclusion, for the Franks seem not often to have let a campaigning season pass without exercising their skills. However, a closer look will reveal that their campaigns were fought for a variety of reasons and in rather different ways. Gregory of Tours, surveying the scene between the accession of Clovis and his own time (late sixth century) has much to record of fighting, but most of it—*bella civilia* caused by fraternal disputes and feuds—falls outside any definition of warfare as a national occupation. National campaigns are fought outside Francia, against Alamans, Saxons,

Goths and Lombards, and though they are often inseparable from booty-raids, Gregory, a bishop, does not see them as unjustly aggressive. Indeed, they are the proper pursuit of Catholic kings, who should be extending the sway of the Church (and thus their own) by attacking the heathen. This is specially the case when attacking the Visigoths of Septimania and Spain, craven Arians who are hardly forgiven when their king Reccared accepts Catholicism for them. Gregory's well-known account of Clovis' campaign against Alaric[22] is an account of a Catholic hero fighting under the aegis of St. Martin and St. Hilary, with the full approval of the Eastern Emperor. Now, whether this account be fundamentally historical or not, it signifies that this is how a Gallo-Roman bishop of the later sixth century can best represent the matter. The Church has accepted the Franks and taught their kings what to fight for, and in which direction to expand their martial energies. There is no question of taming them. The tragedy is, as Gregory sees it, that the Merovingians of his generation have fallen short of Clovis' ideal and turned their swords upon each other. In other words, Gregory stands at the beginning of that process whereby the Church persuaded the Franks to extend their power by warfare associated with missionary objectives. There is nothing said of peace as a national objective but only of peace as the proper relationship of one Merovingian king with another. Neither in Gregory's History nor subsequently do we find kings going forth to righteous warfare as a matter of course with their people uniformly assembled behind them. Foreign campaigns are fought by armies that differ markedly in personnel, equipment, tactics and objectives. Not all Merovingian armies comprised even a majority of Frankish warriors; there were contingents of Burgundians, Aquitanians, Alans and even Saxons; their best generals were Gallo-Romans; their composition varied, according to the need, in the proportions of cavalry, infantry and siege-experts; and the Franks themselves might be city levies on any scale and also the followings of kings and magnates.[23] We cannot, then, say that the Franks of Gaul were a people habitually in arms; and it is not even certain that so much can be said of their great men, trained as they were for warfare. Yet the Franks are above all other Germans marked out as a warrior-people. Apart from their normally disastrous compaigns in Spain and Italy, to which Gregory and Fredegar often give a religious complexion, their less well-recorded campaigns in the Rhineland deserve attention for what they tell us of war and peace. The Merovingians stepped into Roman shoes to be defenders of Gaul against eastern pressures on the Rhineland. Whether against Frisians, Saxons, Thuringians, Alamans or Bavarians, the Merovingians saw themselves as defenders, not aggressors. True, defence could carry them fairly deep into Germany, as when Dagobert went for Samo's Wendish kingdom in Bohemia;[24] and the eastern emperors were not always happy about Frankish operations over the Rhine. But the general tenor of these operations was certainly defensive. They were campaigns to repel threats or to bolster up allies; and with them went Frankish settlements along the rivers flowing west into the Rhine; and with the settlements went the establishment of churches on a modest scale. Thus missionary work in Germany antedates the Anglo-Saxon effort by many years. Such limited aims are very different from those of the early Carolingians.[25] The first Frankish expansionist was Charles Martel, but the Frankish *Reihengräber* that stretch from southern Frisia to the Alaman territory belong to an earlier time and bear witness to piecemeal colonization in the marcher lands and approaches to the Rhine.[26] The Frankish lady who was buried among *Reihengräber* at Wittislingen in the mid-seventh century was a Christian,[27] and this argues at least an oratory. It amounts to this: however practical the motives that led to campaigning and settlement in the Rhineland and its northern and eastern approaches, the Merovingians could be represented quite reasonably as acting defensively and the Church went with them. It was the kind of activity that Gregory of Tours had longed for. The missionary work of such a one as St. Amand, among Slavs, Gascons and finally Franks and Frisians of the Lower Rhine, was precisely what he had had in mind; and it worked, then as later, just so long as Frankish military power was at hand to assist. St. Amand was a professional missionary: *docete omnes gentes* was his maxim.[8] Merovingian military might, when not turned in upon itself, was habitually employed in ways that answered fairly well to the Catholic requirements of just war.

I do not know that the Anglo-Saxons were much less militarily inclined than the Franks. Bede does not depict them as engaged in continuous campaigning, let alone crusading; but much of what warfare there was could be seen as Christian warfare, justifiable warfare. Even so, he can write feelingly of a time of peace in our own sense of the word, a time when ordinary folk could get on with their business undisturbed, and a woman and child walk safely anywhere.[29] This great peace—*tanta pax*—was the outcome of a good deal of righteous battle. Edwin had to win his crown and fight to keep it. A believer, his earthly power was increased, as that of Clovis had been, so that he ruled over Britain *ut quod nemo Anglorum ante eum*;[30] and so the prophecy was fulfilled that he should overcome his enemies and surpass in power all former English kings.[31] Thus, wars of territorial expansion could be just wars, Christian wars, just as much as those fought for national preservation. Equally justifiable was the rebellion, amounting to war, of those who supported Penda's son in Mercia against the foreign overlord, Oswiu; their courage won back for them their lands and their freedom. But, Bede goes on, they rejoiced to serve *Christo vero regi*.'[32] In other words, though the rebellion was easily explicable and justifiable as patriotic revulsion against foreign dominance, it could also be made to bear a religious overtone. But there were aggressive wars that bore no semblance of justice. Penda and Cadwallon could not be forgiven their attacks on Northumbria, nor Cadwalla for his treatment of the Isle of Wight, nor Ecgfrith of Northumbria for his unprovoked expedition against the innocent Irish, for which God exacted proper vengeance at Nechtansmere.[33] In brief, war was a natural condition for the Anglo-Saxons, as for the Franks and Lombards and Goths; so natural that it should be prepared for and anticipated by warriors trained and equipped in its service. Hence Bede's evident distress at the condition of affairs in Northumbria, as revealed in his letter to Egbert of York; young warriors, deprived of land for their upkeep by improper monastic foundations, are going abroad or living debauched lives instead of preparing themselves to fight for their country against barbarian aggressors.[34] Northumbria is open to invasion; she cannot fight a defensive war, as she should. Northumbrians both noble and simple ought to be training themselves in the art of war, not taking monastic vows; what the result will be, the next generation will discover.[35] Analysis of this kind one might well expect from a political bishop like Gregory of Tours, but it is remarkable indeed from a monastic schoolmaster, however able. The fact is, Bede was a man of his time: he could see the need for a warrior-class both in the political circumstances of Anglo-Saxon England and in the teaching of the Bible and the Fathers. Not for nothing did he comment on the Books of Kings. It was not difficult for him to see in Oswald the ideal of the Christian warrior, praying before battle for God's protection in a just war to defend his people: *iusta pro salute gentis nostrae bella*.[36] What could be more explicit? But successful defence merges without too much difficulty into successful aggression. Oswald's power was extended over all Britain.[37] How this came about we are not told. But the justification in Bede's eyes was clearly his Christian piety, which he owed to the teaching of Aidan. Once again, a pious king will have his reward here on earth, as well as hereafter. Not that worldly success, however justified, need always lead to victory: he died in faith, and he died *pro patria dimicans*;[38] and he died in battle, no longer the victor. King Sigeberht, too, was dragged to battle from his monastery in order to put heart in the East Anglian warriors whose distinguished commander he had once been. But this saintly king with his *virga* in his hand, was no longer the same man. He and his warriors were routed and killed by the 'pagans'.[39] Bede faces facts. But Oswald was right to extend his power by battle; Sigberht was right to join his warriors in the field; Oswiu was right to stand against Penda's larger army and defeat him with God's help, though it was a little awkward that he had first tried to buy the old savage off. An explanation was called for: *neccessitate cogente*.[40] It was better to fight, as Bede well knew. And of course there was encouragement for this view from higher quarters. Bede gives his readers Pope Vitalian's letter to Oswiu, in which he assures the Catholic king that 'all his islands' shall be made subject to him, as both he and the writer desire.[41] To seek the kingdom of God, to add a new people to the faith, is a way to win the apostolic promise: 'all these things shall be added unto you'.[42] Moreover, the Old Testament is cited in support. Isaiah had foreseen the bright future of the root of Jesse and the raising up of the tribes of Jacob.[43] The Pope does not in so many words equate Oswiu's people with the People of Israel; but the idea is surely present in his mind. When were the Christian peoples of England happiest? Bede is in no doubt; it had been during Archbishop Theodore's reign. Then had been the *feliciora tempora* of brave Christian kings: *cunctis barbaris nationibus essent terrori*.[44] One cannot quite call this aggressive, but it points to the need for a Christian society to be on its toes, armed and alert, ready to do battle. A king can do this and more provided he be sustained, like Wihtred of Kent, *religione simul et industria*,[45] which in context means piety and soldierly zeal. Perhaps one should add a gloss to what looks like a simplified picture of fighting rightly

and fighting wrongly. It might be the case that a Christian king
would employ pagans in his forces, and this happened with the
Franks, who used the Saxons; or again, that an unjustified attack
would bring about a desirable end, as when Cadwallon killed the
two apostate Northumbrians; or yet again, that a good man might
rightly be required to follow his lord to a bad war, which is the
poet's assumption when he makes Beowulf fight for Hygelac in an
unjustified attack on the Frisians.[46] In tricky cases excuses could be
found. Pope Nicholas I informed the emperor Louis II that there
was nothing wrong in making arrangements with pagan peoples if
it were for the security of Christendom or tended towards conversion, and he cited the examples of Solomon and Charlemagne.[47] The
end generally justified the means, so long as one was clear that the
right posture of Christians towards pagans was offensive; and so too
towards heretics and all enemies to Christian society's peace.
Reservations about war therefore do not amount to much. Old
English penitentials might brand killing in war as homicide, but
the penance was not heavy, and on the other hand there were
prayers in the liturgy for those who fought.[48]

But there is a related problem. Germanic pagan peoples had a
clear sense that war was a religious undertaking, in which the gods
were interested. At once one thinks of Woden as a God peculiarly,
though not exclusively, connected with warfare. Goths and Vandals
were well aware that victory depended on the gods and called for
sacrifice. A disobliging war-god stood some risk of being abandoned,
as Clovis abandoned his gods after Tolbiac.[49] But when the Goth
Totila addresses his troops and informs them that God only favours
the side that fights in a just cause[50] we are surely faced with Christian influence, for only a Christian would have allowed that God's
favour was not the property of any one people. Moreover, Totila was
chivalrous and mild with his enemies, as Goths went. Pagan and
pagan-transitional warfare, then, had its religious facet. Not surprisingly, Christian missionaries found this ineradicable, though not
unadaptable to their own purposes.[51] Christian vernacular makes
considerable use of the terms of pagan warfare. I am uncertain
whether the preferred terms are borrowed exclusively from the
vocabulary of the *comitatus*, nor, if they were, whether these terms
had no religious significance. But they were borrowed, and notably
by the Anglo-Saxons. We are told that the earliest use of *dryhten*
as a Christian term in any Germanic language is by Caedmon,[52] and

this was not long after the conversion of Northumbria. It was to become the standard Old English literary version of Christian *dominus*. Why, then, did the men who converted the Anglo-Saxons differ so sharply from Wulfila? The Anglo-Saxons were not less bellicose than the Goths. The answer may lie in the prudent spirit of accommodation shown by Gregory the Great. More than that, the pope was an ardent supporter of warfare to spread Christianity and convert the heathen,[53] and this last is, I think, the more important consideration. So far from rejecting the Germanic war-ethos the pope means to harness it to his own ends, and the evidence is that he succeeded. The barbarians may fight to their heart's content in causes blessed by the Church, and this is made clear not only in the matter of vocabulary. It is the position of the Church rather than of the Germans that had undergone modification. As Erdmann showed, the Church subsumed and did not reject the warlike moral qualities of its converts.[54] Who shall say that St. Michael of later days was not Woden under fresh colours?

The Anglo-Saxon fruit of so much teaching and experience was King Alfred, commander in a great war that was at once defensive, patriotic and Christian. In his actions and in his translations he reveals himself as a Gregorian, even an Augustinian, king. Under the high-kingship of God he fights God's battles, and he fights in the name of his *dryhten*, Christ.[55] From Orosius he learns that Christian wars, unlike those of an earlier time, are fought for justice, not for conquest; and he knows that mercy is proper to a king. This is very much how Asser saw him; that is to say, as a leader of *Christiani* against *pagani*, an indefatigable warrior who would rather have spent his reign in peaceful pursuits if he had not been compelled to defend his land and people. If he thus appears as a warrior *malgré lui* it is in part because of his remarkable gifts aside from generalship, in part because Asser leans towards an interpretation of a king's duties that sees fighting rather as a grim necessity than as a desirable occupation. Alfred plainly had a positive idea of the blessings of a state of peace; by which I mean that he knew what he would do if prolonged peace were ever his country's lot. Compare this with Einhard's picture of Charlemagne; as real a man as Asser's Alfred, but a different man. Charlemagne is no less interested in the intellectual life and the teachings of the Church than is Alfred and perhaps not much more of a campaigner. But he has a more positive attitude to Christian warfare. There are always justifications for his campaigns: he is defining a frontier, putting down revolts, carrying Christianity to pagans. But no one could deny that the Saxon wars were aggressive, involving as they did deep penetration in Saxony, mass-deportation and slaughter—some of it, as at Verden, done in cold blood. Alfred did nothing like this. Nor does Einhard think it necessary to justify the attack on Spain: he simply reports that, having garrisoned his Saxon frontier, Charlemagne attacked Spain with every man he could raise.[56] Similarly he went for the disobedient Bretons,[57] and then the Lombards,[58] and so on. Einhard is summarizing what he read in the annals, and all he seems to feel, though he does not even add this in so many words, is that you could do as you pleased with pagans and rebels. The upshot was that these wars of the *rex potentissimus* doubled the dominions that his father had left him.[59] It was plain annexation: *auxit etiam gloriam regni sui*;[60] his kingdom was extended *subigendis exteris nationibus*.[61] As to Viking attacks on Francia, here indeed Charlemagne was on the defensive, even if one cause of the attacks may have been earlier Carolingian offensives. But Einhard shows us a traditional Germanic warrior—*corpore . . . amplo atque robusto*[62]—whose perfectly serious Christian aspirations for himself and his people were best realized in conquest. No wonder that the inscription over his tomb at Aachen contained the phrase: *regnum Francorum nobiliter ampliavit*.[63] It is in Charlemagne, not in Alfred, in Einhard, not in Asser, that one sees the first real triumph of Catholic teaching on war. It can all be justified and held up as an example to a weaker generation. There is no sighing for peace; the *regnum Christianum* is the *regnum Francorum*. This of course is a one-sided view of a complex and fruitful reign, but it certainly protrudes positively as a reason for wonder and pride. Einhard insists that Charlemagne was a traditional man, liking Frankish dress and food, songs and habits. Traditional too, no doubt, was his training for and pleasure in war. But the ninth century is not the sixth, and Frankish bellicosity was not what it had been—which indeed may help to explain why Einhard shows what it should be. Not every magnate wished to be away in Italy or Spain for long months on his lord's wars. This leads me to suppose that the teaching of churchmen had hardened, that the lesson of the just war was more in need of activation than that of the just peace. Traditional Germanic prowess in war now demanded emphasis; and this is what the writers of the ninth century accorded it. But

they were lucky. If it took a little consideration to represent the
aggressive wars of the Carolingians as wars of religion, there was no
problem at all with their defensive wars. Charles Martel could quite
properly meet and defeat the Arabs on Frankish soil *Christo
auxiliante*;[64] and when the Carolingians had finished with the
Arabs, there were the Vikings. Ninth-century writings on Frankish-
Viking encounters were not only naturally couched in terms of
Christian defence against pagan aggression, but in my opinion justi-
fiably so.[65] It was as a Christian warrior that Louis III met and
defeated the Vikings at Saucourt, and his victory could be celebrated
in verse.[66] Whether or not we see the Viking assaults as the principal
cause of the disintegration of Carolingian power in Francia, that was
how they struck contemporaries: the besieged West was a Christian
West, and the wasting wars it was called upon to fight were just
wars of defence. It is all the more remarkable, then, to find that
Einhard's barbarically aggressive Charlemagne is accepted as a
model and an ideal. He appears in Notker's *Gesta* as the idealized
iron warrior, whose deeds should be better known,[67] a Christian ruler
indeed, but a Davidic figure of formidable power. So too, his son,
Louis the Pious, who as pictured by Notker, loved iron and weapons
more than gold.[68] This was the right model for the insufficiently
militant Charles the Fat. Equally aggressive is the outlook of
Ermoldus Nigellus' poem, *In honorem Hludowici*. He starts by
invoking Christ who opens the gates of heaven to good warriors
(*militibus dignis*),[69], which indeed was an inducement that popes
occasionally held out—as did Leo IV in 848. Anyone, he says, who
falls in battle and dies in faith shall by no means be denied entry into
heaven. Therefore let battle be joined, *omni timore ac terrore
deposito*.[70] Ermold goes on to describe the expedition of his hero,
Louis the Pious, against Barcelona, which he led as Charlemagne's
lieutenant. It is quite simply an expedition of destruction. Barcelona
is besieged by the Frankish army, while its Saracen commander
bewails the appearance of the besiegers: *fortis et armigera est
duraque sive celer*.[71] 'These men', he says with a deep sigh, 'pass
their lives under arms and are trained to war from boyhood . . . the
name of Frank makes me shudder, the very word "Frank" comes
from "ferus".'[72] Nevertheless he resists, thus putting the garrison
beyond the pale of Christian charity: they are not merely pagans and
rebels (the original reason for the attack) but resisters. So the siege
proceeds, with a great deal of taunting from both sides. When at

last Barcelona capitulates, we are not told what fate was meted out to the Saracen rank and file: *hostibus imperitant* could cover anything.[73] But the commander is taken back to Charlemagne, together with the spoils, which include buckles and cuirasses, clothing and crested helmets, and a horse with a golden bridal.[74] In brief, Louis has conducted a traditionally barbaric campaign and has returned victorious, laden with booty. If Christ has been with him, so too has Mars. Whatever they obtained, the Saracens had deserved no mercy and no warning. It would have been otherwise had they been Christians. Later on in his poem, Ermold describes a campaign against a converted king, when Louis sends an ambassador to warn him of what is in store for him, 'for he has received baptism and so we ought to give him due notice'.[75] There was a recognized procedure as between Christian combatants. One could even say that there were already the beginnings of something like an international law of war.[76] Of course it would be idle to suppose that the siege of Barcelona bore much resemblance to Ermold's description of it. But the outlines will have been right and also the sentiments; for the poem was intended for Louis himself, as an attempt to win back favour for the poet. This, then, was how the top echelon of Frankish warriors wished to be commemorated.

But it must not be thought that the Church that urged kings to war had nothing to say about peace and made no effort to secure it: I mean, peace as an immediate goal, as opposed to that distant peace which was the Christian justification for all fighting. For such peace was from time to time possible for the great nations of the West; they were not always denied it, as was the mountain-kingdom of the Asturias, a society that only survived because it was organized for perpetual war.[77] Carolingian campaigning did worry churchmen intermittently. If warfare were a Christian undertaking, its rules could to some extent be prescribed and thus its impact controlled. Charles the Simple found it necessary in 923 to attack the rebellious Robert of Paris on a Sunday. The Church was horrified, and at a subsequent synod at Reims imposed penance on both sides. It was a three-year penance during Lent, and during the first Lent the combatants were all to be treated as virtual excommunicants.[78] This was much severer than the three-day fast ordered by the bishops after the battle of Fontenoy: the combatants of 923 had fought, on a Sunday, what amounted to a civil war, one side employing newly-converted Vikings; and the result had been disastrous. Here then was a case of the Church penalizing warriors, if not preventing war. The more clearly one distinguished between warriors and others, the easier perhaps such penalization became. There was an *ordo* whose work was fighting, the *bellatores*, as opposed to the *oratores* and the *imbelle vulgus*, as the author of the Miracles of St. Bertin expresses it.[79] It is not the people who fight, but the professionals whose leaders might be induced to listen to their brethren the bishops. It was Archbishop Theodore who stopped the war between kings Ecgfrith and Æthelred,[80] and Archbishop Hincmar who saved his master by causing Louis the German to withdraw his army from West Frankish territory.[81] The peace and quiet of his kingdom was indeed the proper concern of any Christian king. As the Fathers at Toledo neatly put it, *sub [regis] pace pax servatur Ecclesiae*,[82] or, in a piece of earlier legislation, there should be *una et evidens pax* for all the king's subjects.[83] But then, of course, the upshot of peace and quiet at home was victory over the enemies of the people abroad.[84] The *bellatores* still had a job to do, and the Church would see that they did it. However, one must give some weight to a steady trickle of peaceful admonitions from churchmen of high standing and real influence; for the ninth century was one in which advice was listened to by men of action. Indeed, the wilder the time, the more insistently the lesson of peace was preached. It was preached by Alcuin and Agobard, by Jonas and Hincmar, by Sedulius and Rather of Verona, and it figures in the *arengae* of several imperial and royal diplomas and papal documents, as for example Gregory the Great to the Emperor Maurice in 595: no one can rule rightly *nisi noverit divina tractare, pacemque rei publicae ex universalis ecclesiae pace pendere*.[85] Charles the Bald can be praised by Sedulius as a peace-lover, if in a rather equivocal context: *Lilia pacis amas, bellorum mixta rosetis*.[86] In poetry and in liturgy, in history and in letters, war and peace remain linked as a pair.[87] It is the Christian warrior who is most often reminded of the blessings of peace; but it is the same warrior who is encouraged to make war. There should be limitations not only on the reasons for fighting but on its seasons. Thus, Pope Nicholas I warns the Bulgarians that though there should not be fighting in Lent, or indeed at any other time, *si nulla urgat necessitas*, nevertheless, if necessity does urge it, fighting is not merely permissible but right, even in Lent.[88] A further step is taken by the council of Charroux in about 989 when it proclaims the Peace of God to protect non-combatants; and to this are joined three special interdicts and anathemas, one of which covers *agricolae ceterive pauperes*.[89] What is new is not the protective sentiment but that the delimitation of war should be enacted as Church law and sanctioned by ecclesiastical punishment. It is the beginning of a long and complex process of definition and intervention, and really marks the end of the early medieval phase of war and peace.

I would conclude that the chances of a peaceful life in the year 900 were somewhat less than in the year 500. The investment in war was greater, and its reach commonly more extensive. The Church had not exactly let Woden out of the bottle, but it had certainly not secured the stopper. Warfare had been canalized in directions suitable to the Church, but not very efficiently. This in its turn encouraged churchmen to preach peace, to limit the proper occasions of war, and to protect non-belligerents and special places and occasions. One is surprised at the measure of their success.

NOTES

1 I have to thank Professor P. A. Brunt and my son Andrew for advice on the Roman view of warfare.
2 The text of *De Rebus Bellicis* is edited and translated by E. A. Thompson, *A Roman reformer and inventor* (Oxford, 1952).
3 *De Officiis*, ed. C. Atzert (Teubner, 4th edn., 1963), I, 34–40; I, 80–2: II, 18; III, 46, 88.
4 According to Giulio Vismara, 'Problemi storici e istituti giuridici della guerra altomedievale', *Settimane di Studio del Centro Italiano di Studi sull' Alto Medioevo*, XV, ii (Spoleto, 1968), p. 1162, the Eastern Empire clung to an imperial doctrine that all war was legitimate if initiated by the emperor; but this needs qualification.
5 I here follow Gina Fasoli, 'Pace e guerra nell'alto medioevo', ibid., pt. i, to whose paper I am generally indebted.
6 *De Re Militari*, ed. N. Schwebel (Strasbourg, 1806), III, prol.
7 See e.g. Deut., 7: 21; 9: 1; 20: 16; 28: 47; Numb., 21: 14; I Chron., 10: 11, 27.
8 Deut., 20: 4.
9 *Germania*, ed. J. C. G. Anderson (Oxford, 1938), 7, 1.
10 Cf. my 'The bloodfeud of the Franks', in *The Long-Haired Kings* (London, 1962).
11 Cf. D. H. Green, *The Carolingian Lord* (Cambridge, 1965), p. 279.
12 *Libri Historiarum*, ed. B. Krusch and W. Levison, *Mon. Germ. Hist., Script. Rer. Mero.* (Hanover, 1951), II, 27.
13 *Historia Langobardorum*, ed. G. Waitz, *Script. Rer. Germ. in usum schol.* (Hanover, 1890), II, 35.

14 *Leges*, cap. 118, *Die Gesetze der Langobarden*, ed. F. Beyerle (Weimar, 1947).

15 *Deutsche Rechtsgeschichte* (2nd ed., Berlin, repr. 1958), II, sections 65, 66.

16 F. Pollock and F. W. Maitland, *The History of English Law before the time of Edward I* (Cambridge, 1895), II, 452; see also I, 22, 23.

17 *De Civitate Dei*, ed. J. E. C. Welldon (London, 1924), XIX, cap. 7.

18 *Etymologiarum sive Originum Libb.*, ed. W. M. Lindsay (Oxford, 1911), Bk. 18.

19 Cf. Vismara, *ut sup.*, p. 1152.

20 J. Werner, *Settimane di Studio*, XV, i, 101.

21 See the discussion by J.-P. Bodmer, *Der Krieger der Merowingerzeit und seine Welt* (Zürich, 1957).

22 *Lib. Hist.*, II, 37.

23 Bernard S. Bachrach, *Merovingian Military Organization, 481–751* (Minneapolis, 1972) discusses the composition of Frankish armies but makes too much of local levies.

24 Fredegar, *Chronicorum Libri*, ed. B. Krusch, *Mon. Germ. Hist., Script. Rer. Mero.*, II (Hanover, 1888), and J. M. Wallace–Hadrill (London, 1960), IV, 68.

25 On the contrast see Rolf Sprandel, *Der merovingische Adel und die Gebiete östlich des Rheins* (Freiburg im B., 1957).

26 Cf. A. Bergengruen, *Adel und Grundherrschaft im Merowingerreich* (Wiesbaden, 1958).

27 J. Werner, *Das alamannische Fürstengrab von Wittislingen* (Munich, 1950), pp. 75–7.

28 See Wolfgang H. Fritze, 'Universalis gentium confessio', *Frühmittelalterliche Studien*, 3 (1969), pp. 88 ff.

29 *Ecclesiastical History*, ed. and trs. B. Colgrave and R. A. B. Mynors (Oxford, 1969), II, 16.

30 Ibid., II, 9.

31 Ibid., II, 12.

32 Ibid., III, 24.

33 Ibid., IV, 26.

34 *Baedae opera historica*, ed. C. Plummer (Oxford, 1896), I, 415.

35 Colgrave and Mynors, *Eccl. Hist.*, V. 23.

36 Ibid., III, 2.

37 Ibid., III, 6.

38 Ibid., III, 9.

39 Ibid., III, 18.

40 Ibid., III, 24.

41 Ibid., III, 29.

42 Matth. 6: 33; Luc. 12: 31.

43 Isaiah, 11: 10.

44 *Eccl. Hist.*, IV, 2.

45 Ibid., IV, 26.

46 On which see J. E. Cross, 'The ethic of war in Old English', *England before the Conquest*, ed. Peter Clemoes and Kathleen Hughes (Cambridge, 1971), pp. 277–8).

47 *Mon. Germ. Hist.*, *Epist.* VII (*Karo. Aev.*, IV), no. 54, p. 351.

48 Cf. Cross, *ut sup.*, pp. 280–1.

49 Gregory of Tours, *Hist. Libb.*, II, 30, 31.

50 Procopius, *Gothic War*, ed. H. B. Dewing, VII, xxi, 7–11.

51 See Green, op. cit., esp. pp. 279–97.

52 A. H. Smith, *Three Northumbrian Poems* (London, 1933), pp. 12 ff.

53 *Gregorii I Registri*, *Mon. Germ. Hist.*, *Epist.* I, no. 73, p. 93.

54 *Die Entstehung des Kreuzzugsgedankens* (Stuttgart, 1935), pp. 16 ff.

55 Cf. *King Alfred's West-Saxon version of Gregory's Pastoral Care*, ed. and trs., Henry Sweet, Early English Text Society, vols. 45, 50 (London, 1871).

56 *Vita Karoli Magni*, ed. O. Holder-Egger, *Scrip. Rer. Germ. in usum schol.* (Hanover, 1911), ch. 9.

57 Ibid., ch. 10.

58 Ibid.

59 Ibid., ch. 15.

60 Ibid., ch. 16.

61 Ibid., ch. 17.

62 Ibid., ch. 22.

63 Ibid., ch. 31.

64 Fredegar, cont., ch. 13.

65 I defend this position in 'The Vikings in Francia' (Stenton Lecture, Reading, 1974). See below, pp. 217–36.

66 By the poet of the *Ludwigslied*.

67 Ed. H. F. Haefele, *Mon. Germ. Hist.*, *Script. Rer. Germ.*, N.S. xii (Berlin, 1959).

68 Ibid., p. 87.

69 *Ermold le Noir*, ed. Edmond Faral (Paris, 1932), p. 2.

70 Mansi, *Sacrorum conciliorum nova et amplissima collectio*, XIV, 888.

71 *Ermold le Noir*, p. 32, line 369.

72 Ibid., lines 376–9. The same etymology is in Isidore, *Etymol.*, IX, 11, 101.

73 Ibid., line 563, p. 44.

74 Ibid., lines 572–5, p. 46.

75 Ibid., lines 1322–3, p. 102.

76 Such is the contention of Vismara, *ut sup.*, p. 1199.

77 See C. Sánchez-Albornoz, 'El ejército y la guerra en el reino Asturleonés', *Settimane di Studio*, XV, i, pp. 293–428.

78 See the account in A. Eckel, *Charles le Simple* (Paris, 1899), pp. 123–7.

79 *Mon. Germ. Hist.*, *Scriptores*, XV, 513.

80 Bede, *Eccl. Hist.*, IV, 21.

81 *Pat. Lat.*, cxxvi, cols. 9–25.

82 *Concilios Visigóticos e Hispano-Romanos*, ed. José Vives (Barcelona-Madrid, 1963), I, Toledo XIV, xii.

83 *Mon. Germ. Hist.*, *Leges* I, ed. K. Zeumer (Hanover, 1902), II, 1, i.

84 Ibid., I, 2, vi ('Quod triumphet de hostibus lex'). Cf. P. D. King, *Law and society in the Visigothic kingdom* (Cambridge, 1972), pp. 33 ff.

85 *Greg. I Reg.*, pp. 320 ff. See H. Fichtenau, *Arenga* (Graz-Cologne, 1957), pp. 76 ff.

86 *Mon. Germ. Hist., Poetae Aevi Caro.*, III, ed. L. Traube (Berlin, 1896), p. 181 (*Ad Karolum regem*, line 41).
87 Cf. Gina Fasoli, *ut sup.*, p. 45.
88 *Pat. Lat.*, 119, col. 998.
89 Cf. Erdmann, op. cit., pp. 53 ff.

III

The graves of kings:
an historical note on some archaeological
evidence[1]*

Every historian of the earlier Middle Ages must come to terms with archaeology. He has been offered material out of which something very like a reconstruction of his picture of early medieval society seems possible. He marvels at the exquisite techniques of his archaeological colleagues and he pauses while they make initial historical sense out of their own revelations. Moreover, he accepts the archaeologist's claim to be neither more nor less than an historian[2] and if he feels that the archaeologist is sometimes guilty of trying to carry him over-far along the road of hypothesis, he in his turn should feel some guilt for the state of the texts to which the archaeologist must turn for narrative background. The truth is, that the worst gaps in early medieval scholarship are still philological, not archaeological. We have not got very far along the road to understanding the fearsomely complex course of the Latin language as it wends its way from the Fathers to Bede and beyond.

Thoughts such as these have been quickened in the post-war years by the interpretative work of British archaeologists upon deposits of the magnificence of Sutton Hoo and of St. Ninian's Isle, as well as by the completion of Édouard Salin's notable synthesis of Merovingian archaeology and history. Grateful though he must be, it would be possible for the historian of an older discipline to ask more questions than he does about the interpretation of archaeological evidence of this nature, and even to inquire whether joint enterprise in relating archaeological to written sources might not sometimes prove rewarding.[3] Here, I am only concerned

* References for this chapter start on p. 56.

to consider archaeological evidence on a narrow front: the burial
or commemoration of kings. Not of all possible burials or com-
memorations, but of some to which attention has recently been
drawn. I am well aware that I am leaving out of account not a
few important burials that may be classified in a general way as
princely[4] and can only hope that it will become clear why I have
done so. My concern is with kings. The two problems that have
been in the forefront of my mind as I studied the archaeological
evidence have been, first, how we are to distinguish a king's grave
when we see one; and, secondly, how far it is worth distinguishing
a king's grave from that of any other chieftain or man of wealth
or power.

At Sutton Hoo we have the cenotaph[5] of one who was wealthy
and powerful, whatever else he was not; and for twenty years
we have been taught to regard him as royal. The first publication
about the discovery, the composite paper published in *Antiquity*
vol. XIV (1940), contained a cautious assessment of the evidence
for royal rank from the pen of the late Professor H. M. Chadwick.[6]
This assessment is, so far as I know, the only considerable statement on the matter to which any historian has committed himself.
Upon it have been erected edifices of hypothesis which might have
surprised the writer very much, not least when one recalls his
warning that 'it does not necessarily follow that the person buried
or commemorated was himself a king'. The arguments of Professor Chadwick and others will need to be considered; but it
may be said at once that the most compelling, as it is also the
least susceptible of proof, is simply the difficulty of believing that
anything so fine should commemorate anyone but a king.

Unless I am mistaken, there are three reasons for holding that
Sutton Hoo is royal: the magnificence of the deposit; the symbolism
of certain objects in the deposit; and the relation of Sutton Hoo
to Rendlesham and to the coastline of East Anglia. I propose
to examine each reason in turn, while allowing that the order in
which one asks questions of so complex a piece of evidence must
to some extent affect the conclusions at which one arrives.

I

When we say that the treasure of Sutton Hoo is magnificent, we
mean that in quantity and quality it surpasses what is known to

us of Dark-Age treasure found in comparable circumstances. We mean, too, that it includes certain fine pieces which to us are either extremely rare or unique. Can we go further and say that it surpasses either in quality or quantity what the makers of Sutton Hoo, and their contemporaries elsewhere in Europe, would have expected to see in the grave or the cenotaph of any chieftain not a king? The question is difficult for two reasons. First because the treasures of the royal graves with which Sutton Hoo might be compared in magnificence have, with hardly an exception, come down to us incomplete; and secondly, because written accounts of royal grave-goods do not get us very far. So far as the latter go, no historian or chronicler leaves us a detailed account of the funeral of such a man as may be inferred from the grave-goods at Sutton Hoo. The poet of *Beowulf*, however, does provide something akin to what we seek. In the words of Professor Dorothy Whitelock, 'one result of this new find is that we need no longer charge the poet with inaccuracy on account of the richness of the equipment in the burials he describes, nor even make allowance for poetic exaggeration'.[7] In other words, Sutton Hoo casts some light upon the *Beowulf* funeral scenes. But what light does *Beowulf* cast upon Sutton Hoo? Not very much, beyond a general air of authentication. Nor should it be expected to do so, since *Beowulf* is a poem, not a history.[8] So far as I am able to tell, *Beowulf* does not help us to say whether the Sutton Hoo cenotaph was magnificent enough for a king. A more serviceable idea of royal magnificence, even if unassociated with burials, may be obtained from continental accounts of the doings of kings and of others of royal blood; and these will at least help us to form some estimate of what constituted wealth on a royal scale. Would Sutton Hoo have seemed royally magnificent to the men of King Chilperic, who watched him send off his daughter Rigunthis to her future husband with treasure that filled fifty waggons;[9] or to the associates of the Ostrogothic princess Amalasuntha, whose fortune, when packed for shipment, amounted to 2,880,000 *solidi* (that is, 40,000 lb. of gold);[10] or to the Visigothic King Sisenand, who bribed King Dagobert with an immense gold *missorium* from the royal Gothic treasure that weighed 500 lb. and was ultimately redeemed in gold *solidi*;[11] or to King Dagobert himself, whose embellishment of the abbey-church of St. Denis with gold, gems and much else that was precious was a cause of astonishment to the Franks?[12] Would it have seemed magnificent to

D

Queen Brunechildis, who could make a present of a specially-wrought golden shield?[13] Plainly we lack the evidence to speak of the quality of these gifts; but we can say something about their size and quantity, and it would be unwise to dismiss these or any other early medieval figures as nonsensical except where they are demonstrably false. Far too often we are told that early medieval figures may be ignored, when what is really meant is that they fit awkwardly into some preconceived picture. Barbarian kings were often astonishingly rich, whether through looting, gift, subsidy, inheritance, taxation or trade; and we may add that some of their subjects, whether laymen or clerics or mere adventurers, were also astonishingly rich. In general, I could not assert that wealth was concentrated in royal hands in any exclusive sense. Sutton Hoo is indeed a notable treasure, but its splendour consists more in the quality of the goldsmiths' work than in quantity of gold or other treasure, though this is considerable enough. It is not to be supposed that any of the barbarian kings and princesses whose treasures have been mentioned could have failed to be delighted with the Sutton Hoo treasure; but whether they, or, let us say, the men who buried King Penda,[14] would have considered it sufficient for a royal grave, is a question that it might be safer to leave open.

With what royal graves, then, may Sutton Hoo be compared in terms of magnificence? With those of the Swedes, plainly. The royal burials at Old Uppsala were cremations and the grave-goods recovered too incomplete to afford an accurate idea of their original splendour. But those at Vendel and at Valsgärde (not however demonstrably royal) were not cremated, the latter being practically untouched. May it not, however, be begging the question to assume that kingship meant the same thing in England and in Sweden in the seventh century? This question needs to be faced before a satisfactory comparison can be made between the magnificence of such graves of the two regions as are claimed to be royal, though in the meantime particular objects among Swedish grave-goods will naturally continue to be compared with similar objects from Sutton Hoo. For the moment, there may be something to be said for taking our eyes off Sweden and broadening the field of comparison. From Merovingian Gaul we have a few burials, Christian and pagan, that are either certainly or probably royal. Added to this, the present evidence for comparing seventh-century Anglo-Saxon with Frankish kingship is documented in a way in which the evidence for an

Anglo-Swedish comparison is not. The Merovingian grave-goods have not been destroyed by cremation but on the other hand they have suffered greatly from robbers. The grave of Childeric I, buried in Tournai in 481 or 482, was laid bare by a workman, Adrian Quinquin, in 1653. The story of that celebrated discovery has often been told, though never better than as told first by the antiquary and physician Jacques Chiflet, largely on information supplied by his son Jean Chiflet, canon of Tournai, who was an early visitor to the scene of the excavation.[15] The Tournai excavation resembled Sutton Hoo at least in this, that from the first moment it attracted publicity and became a subject of debate in the world of learning. In every other respect—in the manner of the excavation, the preservation of the grave-goods and their evaluation—the fate of two treasures could scarcely have been more different. The Tournai treasure was scattered to the four winds at the moment of its discovery; and even such part of it as eventually reached the Cabinet des Médailles in Paris suffered further from pilfering in 1831. No scholar knows now, and no scholar ever knew, the nature and extent of King Childeric's grave-treasure; and here is an insurmountable disadvantage when one attempts to compare its riches with those of Sutton Hoo. But this much at least we can tell, either from what survives or from early descriptions: King Childeric was laid to rest, two centuries before Sutton Hoo, with magnificent war-gear, a cloak embroidered with some three hundred golden 'bees', a fine gold bracelet and buckles, a crystal globe and a miniature bull's head in gold (perhaps talismans), the severed head of his war-horse caparisoned in precious materials, a signet-ring bearing his name, a purse containing one hundred gold coins and a box containing two hundred silver coins. Nor is this a complete inventory. Nothing that survives of the Tournai treasure is of the quality of Sutton Hoo; but there is enough of it to focus attention on the variety and quantity of possessions that could go to the burying of a comparatively unimportant Frankish kinglet of the period preceding the conquest of Gaul by Clovis. Childeric was no savage; he had his contacts with the authorities of Roman Gaul and had played his part in its military history; and his seal-ring was engraved in Latin characters.[16] Plainly he had had his reward. But it is not likely that he enjoyed the opportunities for amassing wealth of a Clovis or of an Anglo-Saxon *Bretwalda*. Nor do I discern anything specifically regalian about his grave-goods.[17] Indeed, some would say that even his seal-ring,

allowing it to be genuine, is no indubitable proof of the presence of
his body, since royal seal-rings are known on occasion to have been
entrusted to referendaries or other royal officers. Tournai could thus
be a referendary's grave. But this is surely going too far. It will be
enough, perhaps, to draw attention to the treasure in coins which
his kindred thought appropriate to the burial of the king of the
Franks of Tournai. It was not a fortune, but it must have represented a sacrifice much beyond the forty *tremisses* of Sutton Hoo. To
this I shall return.

Happily, Tournai is not all our Merovingian evidence. The abbey-
church of St. Denis, lying a little north of Paris, had become by the
middle of the seventh century an acceptable resting-place for the
Frankish royal house. M. Salin has recently been able to undertake
excavations under the floor of the present church and has discovered
evidence of burials stretching far back into the Gallo-Roman period
and forward into the Middle Ages.[18] A number of these are Frankish
and at least one is claimed as royal Merovingian. Burial no. 16,
distinguished by M. Salin as 'une sépulture princière',[19] was contained in a sarcophagus that had suffered disturbance and pillage.
However, the goods found with the skeleton comprised the remains
of some fine war-harness and an elaborate belt (the latter robbed of
its buckle), traces of leather dyed purple and gilded, evidence of
rich embroidery and three gold rings—one, of particular splendour,
containing the only sapphire hitherto found in a Frankish grave.
These and other objects had been overlooked by the robbers; but
they are enough to give us some idea of the splendour that was not
overlooked. M. Salin considers the skeleton to be that of a young
man and the grave-goods datable to the seventh century. The most
suitable candidate among the Merovingians would be Chlotar III,
who was buried at St. Denis in the spring of 673. We cannot, of
course, on grounds of a largely inferred splendour, firmly identify
this burial with royalty, let alone with any particular king. There is
no one object in the grave that speaks of kingship. There is no
inscribed seal-ring, as at Tournai. What turns a possibility into a
likelihood is the site of such a burial in the seventh century, and the
presence of certain pagan usages in a Christian milieu: for a strong
element of paganism permeated Merovingian kingship to its last
days. Here, contemporary with Sutton Hoo, is a burial the richness
of which speaks for royalty because it is found in a specifically royal
burial-ground. The same has been claimed for Sutton Hoo, but

whether with the same degree of assurance is perhaps open to question till the whole site of Sutton Hoo has been explored. St. Denis, like Sutton Hoo, stands in urgent need of further excavation.

Dom Bernard Montfaucon has left us an account of the discovery of the tombs of King Childeric II and of his wife Belechildis, together with that of their child, the infant Dagobert.[20] In 675 the king and his queen were assassinated in the Forest of Livry[21] and buried at St. Vincent, later St. Germain-des-Prés. Their tombs were discovered in 1656 and Dom Jacques Bouillart leaves the earliest account of them in his *Histoire de l'abbaye royale de Saint Germain des Prez*, published in 1724. Dissatisfied with this account, Montfaucon went to the trouble of interrogating certain old men at St. Germain who remembered something more of the celebrated incident. What emerges is that the tombs had been 'visitez' in 1645, when the burials had been disturbed, and then opened a second time in 1656. On the last occasion, those present had reported seeing 'un grand passement d'or en forme de couronne' on the king's head, and furthermore 'un morceau de toile d'or qui lui couvroit le visage, des éperons, et que sa ceinture qui paroissoit entière et d'un pouce de largeur, étoit enrichie d'espace en espace de quelques boucles et ornemens d'argent'. These and other objects were removed by the monks and sold. Queen Belechildis, as found in 1645, 'avoit encore ses habits roiaux et un coussin d'herbes odoriferantes sous sa tête,' though by 1656 all was 'des cendres et des ossemens ... un bâton de coudrier rompu en deux, et quelques herbes odoriferantes'. Montfaucon adds that 'au dedans du tombeau à l'endroit où reposoit la tête de Childeric étoit gravé son nom ainsi CHILDR. REX'. Inscription, tomb and contents have all disappeared. Whether or not the inscription was contemporary with the burial, there can be no reason to question its accuracy. Here, then, is another Merovingian contemporary of the Sutton Hoo man. We recognize him by an inscription, and to this we add, but only as confirmation, the vestiges of rich grave-goods. The 'grand passement d'or' may be termed kingly decoration, perhaps suggested by former imperial regalia. In the circumstances it has significance. It cannot be taken as an essential emblem of kingship, but it would be surprising to find it in the grave of one who was not of royal blood. We can identify the tomb of King Childeric II but we cannot even guess at the riches it contained.

Tournai, St. Denis and St. Germain help us in different ways to form a picture of royal barbarian burials, both pagan and Christian, against which to assess the royal magnificence of Sutton Hoo. I may briefly mention one burial as representative of a class that does not help us. In 1842, a workman digging on the bank of the River Aube near Pouan (arr. Arcis-sur-Aube) uncovered a human skeleton and grave-goods of exceptional richness and quality. These grave-goods are now in the museum of Troyes, where they have recently been studied by MM. Salin and France-Lanord.[22] Following Peigné-Delacourt, who first published a study of this treasure,[23] these scholars hold that the Pouan grave could well be that of the Visigothic king Theodoric, killed in 451 at the battle of the Catalaunian plains while in alliance with Aetius against Attila. The grounds on which the claim is made are, first, that the site of the battle cannot have been far distant from Pouan, and secondly, that the magnificent grave-goods do in fact belong to the earlier part of the fifth century. The grave yielded a longsword of fine workmanship with a gold-worked sheath of rare mastery; a scramasax with a gold-covered grip and a fine sheath; buckles, a bracelet and a torque of gold; and a gold ring, inscribed 'HEVA'. The site of the battle has been endlessly sought, from one end of Champagne to the other; and I incline to the view of Professor E. A. Thompson that it has been sought in vain.[24] If, however, we accept Moirey as the likeliest site,[25] then we must allow that Theodoric was carried well over thirty miles to his burial. In some circumstances such a distance could be negligible; but not in these. There is no single piece of the treasure that identifies the warrior as a Visigoth, let alone as a Visigoth king; and certain features of the burial are distinctly un-Visigothic. We know from Jordanes that Theodoric's body was retrieved by his son, Thorismund, on the following day and was buried;[26] and that is all we know, unless we attach significance to the ring. MM. Salin and France-Lanord prefer to say nothing of this awkward piece of evidence, though M. Babelon, also believing the grave to be Theodoric's and perhaps following Peigné-Delacourt, explains the inscription as having reference to a woman, *Eva*, and supposes that Theodoric was wearing his wife's ring when he was killed.[27] This is not inconceivable; other warriors have been buried with their wives' rings; but we do not know the name of Theodoric's wife, and *Heva* may be a man's name. The balance of probability is that the Pouan grave is the grave of a warrior named *Heva*. What lies behind the belief of MM. Salin and France-Lanord that Pouan is Theodoric's grave is plainly stated in these words: 'il s'agit bien d'un roi car, à cette époque, pareille richesse exige la qualité royale'.[28] It lies equally behind the belief that Sutton Hoo is royal. Magnificence is a relative term, and such evidence as chance provides still leaves me uncertain about the degree of magnificence that 'exige la qualité royale'. In southern Germany alone are three burials that on grounds of richness are properly claimed as burials of important folk: Gammertingen, Ittenheim and Wittislingen; and the last in particular contains treasure that any queen would have been glad to possess.[29] Yet nobody has claimed that they are royal on that account.

2

The symbolism of early medieval kingship defies any attempt at definition, let alone classification. This is not for want of evidence or for failure to look at it,[30] but because the barbarian kings were themselves uncertain, and, I sometimes suspect, indifferent. In practice, *signa barbarorum* varied enormously; so that it is quite possible to claim almost any item of war-gear or apparel or ornament as royal in a particular case or group of cases. What is not so easy to prove is that a king wore or bore a particular object because he was a king.

In the case of Sutton Hoo it could be claimed that the person commemorated was royal because his cenotaph contained noble war-gear. But in fact the claim is advanced for quite other objects; the whetstone namely, and the iron stand. Upon these two objects much turns, and this has been explicitly stated by archaeologists. The whetstone is not the first to be found in comparable circumstances; they have been found elsewhere in Britain and are not uncommon in Sweden. But this is the biggest. It is two feet in length and is made, except for the extremities, of unpainted stone. It is unused and perhaps unusable. Sir Thomas Kendrick wrote of it: 'It is a unique, savage thing; and inexplicable, except perhaps as a symbol, proper to the king himself, of the divinity and mystery which surrounded the smith and his tools in the northern world.'[31] And Mr. Bruce-Mitford: 'Of the whetstone little need be added to what has been said elsewhere. Whether one calls it a "sceptre"—an object normally held in the hand—or prefers the word "mace"—normally carried in front of an official—it is clear that in it we have a

symbolic and ceremonial piece, and also one that is in the highest
degree striking and unusual. It obviously has the character of a
whetstone; but it is equally obvious that it is more than a whetstone.
That is the real point.'[32] The real points, I think, are three. First,
that it is a whetstone; second, that chance not having revealed to us
others like it, we run some risk in judging it unusual to the barbarian world that made such things; and third, that there is no
supporting evidence, literary or other, to justify us in calling it
monstrous or savage or ceremonial or symbolic or royal. I do not
think that there is any reference in classical or medieval literature to
the symbolic employment of the whetstone; at least, I have searched
fairly widely and found none. Wilhelm Berges and Adolf Grauert
have seen in this particular whetstone a symbolical staff, of a kind
that would normally be made of wood but that, made of stone,
might well possess added magical significance. In it would be
incapsulated the special powers that underlay the good fortune of
the royal dynasty that owned it, just as Odin's divine power was
incapsulated in his spear.[33] Yet there is no true parallel. Staffs are
not whetstones; stone is not wood, neither is it metal; and carved
faces that look impressive to one man look commonplace to another.
Objects not quite similar exist all over the Germanic world; and the
trying little discrepancies remain. Short of supposing that, in some
distant Valhalla, the weapons of the dead man might require shar-
pening, I see no explanation for the whetstone. If it must be symbolic, then we might as properly explore its potential symbolism in
some other field, e.g. that of religion, as in kingship; and the same
may apply to the iron stand. In our search for the thought-world
of the Germanic peoples we are nowadays ready to see symbolism
in almost any object among their grave-goods. Sometimes we are
right. But where we have to do with a rare object, and an object in
itself obscure, like the Sutton Hoo whetstone, it would be best not
to confuse interpretation with speculation.

The iron stand of Sutton Hoo is 1.95 metres in length, pointed at the bottom and surmounted with an iron ring on which
perched a small bronze stag. Below the ring was a square iron
grille with supports beneath and sharp, inward-sloping points
like bulls' horns at the corners. It has been suggested at various
times that this iron stand was a flambeau; a lampstand for small
float-wick lamps; a portable weapon-rack; or a *segen*, like that
which was placed high over Scyld's head in *Beowulf*. There is

something to be said for and against all these suggestions. A more widely-held interpretation sees in it a banner or standard such as Bede says was sometimes carried before King Edwin of Northumbria.[34] Yet it is not like any standard, Roman or barbarian, of which we have exact knowledge from literary or archaeological evidence; and the standards that appear on Roman coins are many and various. Meditating upon the reconstructed object that is now in the middle of the King Edward Gallery in the British Museum, I have wondered whether it might not be a rack for holding or suspending heads or scalps. What did barbarian warriors do with these particular spoils of war? They were more numerous and more prized than is sometimes appreciated and cannot for ever have dangled from saddle-bows, as we can see them doing on the golden vase of Nagyszentmiklòs.[35] But this is one guess among many; and there is little enough to choose between any of them. The stag is a great rarity and the iron stand, as we have it, unique. Unique, that is to say, to us: not necessarily to the Germanic world that used it. The object should surely remain an iron stand. We do not know what it was for and accordingly can infer nothing whatsoever about the rank of the Sutton Hoo man from its presence in his cenotaph.

This is all the symbolic evidence that exists for the view that Sutton Hoo is royal.

3

Four miles north of Sutton Hoo, on the east bank of the River Deben, lies the hamlet of Rendlesham. Bede refers to it in the following passage: Sigeberht was succeeded as king [of the East Saxons] by Seaxbald's son Swithhelm, who had been baptized by the same Cedd in the province of the East Angles, in a royal *vicus* called Rendlesham, that is to say "Rendil's dwelling"; and Aethelwold, king of that same people of the East Angles and brother of their king, Anna, accepted him for godson as he rose from holy baptism.[36] That is all Bede says: he is not very communicative on the history of East Anglia, and there is rather much that we do not know and cannot guess about it. A *vicus regius*, such as Bede here refers to, may be taken to denote a royal estate or farm, no doubt furnished with wooden buildings and a stockade. It may have had a hall, or even a complex of halls, after the fashion of the halls of Yeavering in Northumbria, the post-holes of which archaeology has so lately revealed.[37] In the next few years, archaeologists may well present us with the timber support-holes and ground plans of other such halls. But investigations at Rendlesham have not yet, to my knowledge, revealed any such thing. What reason have we, then, to suppose that Rendlesham was a *vicus* of special importance to the East Anglian kings? Place-names give no decisive clue. Barbarian kings moved about freely among their widely-scattered estates. This I say even bearing in mind the occasional interesting find from the Deben valley. In about the year 1690, a crown weighing 60 oz. was found at Rendlesham; it was promptly sold and melted down. Edmund Gibson, Bishop of London, who first mentions it in the 1722 edition of Camden's *Britannia*, says 'it was thought to have belonged to Redwald or some other king of the East Angles'. (Perhaps with this in mind, M. R. James included it among the three crowns that figure in his ghost story, *A Warning to the Curious*.) Local antiquaries of Gibson's time were intrigued by Redwald the *Bretwalda* and even tried to explain Rendlesham as Redwald's-ham, which is out of the question. One would not expect a seventh-century English king to wear a crown. Indeed, for crowns or diadems of any sort one would have to look either some way forward or else back to priestly regalia of the Romano-British period, such as were ploughed up not long ago at Hockwold in southern Norfolk; though on the continent one could find other parallels. Are we, then, on grounds of a crown that can scarcely have been seventh-century Anglo-Saxon and of a royal hall that has not yet been found entirely wise to picture Rendlesham as 'a principal centre of the Uffingas, possibly even the principal one in the seventh century'? Why must it have been 'considerably more than just one of the "country houses" of the Uffingas which happened to get a mention in Bede?'[38] Still less can I find justification to picture there buildings of an important seat or manor, including a temple or church, after the pattern of Uppsala. Bede does not speak of a church. There is no reason to suspect that Rendlesham was specially important to the royal house of the Wuffingas or Uffingas; and therefore Rendlesham casts no light on the importance to them of Sutton Hoo.

The only feature of the Sutton Hoo treasure that is held to provide a firm date for the cenotaph is the small collection of Mero-

vingian *tremisses* from the magnificent purse. These coins enable
us to date the cenotaph to the middle of the seventh century. Now
coins, as Mr. Philip Grierson has warned us, do not always tell
the truth; but the Sutton Hoo coins may be able to offer us something besides a date. In the first place, they tell us that the Sutton
Hoo man did not mint his own coinage. He was content to
use the Merovingian gold coinage that dominated north-western
Europe. What this reveals about commercial relations between
Merovingian Gaul and East Anglia is not a matter on which agreement will soon be reached; but relations of a social and religious
kind were frequent enough and are far better documented than
any relations between East Anglia and Sweden. Whether or not,
then, the Sutton Hoo man had business dealings with Merovingian
Gaul, he used Merovingian *tremisses*, and those who commemorated
him thought it no slight to leave a handful of these coins in his
purse. King Childeric was buried with three hundred coins; the
Sutton Hoo man was commemorated with forty. It would be
folly to deduce that the Sutton Hoo man was therefore not rich
enough to be royal. Wealth in gold was not always or necessarily
calculated in terms of coinage. I imagine that the Sutton Hoo
cenotaph could easily have been furnished with a much larger
collection of coins, had that been considered appropriate. But
the coins would still have been Merovingian. Dr. C. H. V. Sutherland has shown that gold coins were being minted in England
in the early seventh century.[39] There was a London and an
East Saxon gold coinage by this time; Penda's sons had a Mercian
gold coinage in the period 656–700; there is a possibility of West
Saxon gold coins of an even earlier date. 'Though the stimulus
came from abroad, this new English gold was independent in
its outlook and instinct; English design is conspicuous, and English
innovation could be bold and satisfying.'[40] There is even the
possibility of itinerant English goldsmiths. Why, then, not in
East Anglia? Dr. Sutherland's answer is that East Anglia lay
outside the zone of early English gold minting and might be
expected to be dominated by Merovingian gold.[41] This is as much
as to say that no East Anglian gold of the period is known to numis-
matists. The answer is perfectly satisfying until one recalls the
splendour of the gold treasure of Sutton Hoo. This has been claimed
to be native East Anglian and to reveal a level of local artistic
achievement such as had never been suspected before. Why,

therefore, does not the craftsman who made the great gold buckle of Sutton Hoo also provide his master with a gold coinage? In Merovingian Gaul and elsewhere, the work of the goldsmith and the minter went hand in hand, as the career of St. Eligius of Noyon exemplifies. In Kent there is evidence of a very early connection between the two. To cite Dr. Sutherland once more: 'It will be unnecessary to emphasize the importance of the Kentish concentration of coins in relation to the Kentish concentration of jewellery.'[42] Are there any special reasons why this should not have been so in East Anglia? Was East Anglia so dominated by Merovingian trade as to be unwilling to risk a gold coinage of its own? There is no evidence that this was so.[43]

It has not been my business to argue that the Sutton Hoo cenotaph is English or foreign, for this must turn upon an expert knowledge of the work of the craftsmen employed. I merely observe that the experts do not agree; and, in the light of the evidence they adduce, this can hardly be surprising. I will go further and say that if, at Sutton Hoo, we have the cenotaph of an East Anglian king in the centre of his power, surrounded with the work of his native goldsmiths, the absence of any trace of an East Anglian gold coinage needs a word of explanation. It does not necessarily follow that any king should have his individual gold coinage but only that an English king of the mid-seventh century employing such goldsmiths might have been expected to encourage some manifestation of Dr. Sutherland's 'independence' and 'innovation'.

Why does it matter so much to be careful about asserting that a grave or a cenotaph is royal when nobody doubts that it concerns an important person? Why be over-scrupulous in disinguishing kings from other chieftains? The answer is, in part, that if, on some such general ground as wealth, we allow a particular grave to be royal, it follows that we shall next be tempted to see royal symbolism in our hero's grave-goods and shall, some other day, claim some other grave as royal because it contains identical grave-goods. This is no theoretical temptation: important graves still yield a rather large number of (to us) unique objects. Any of these may strike us as symbolic because they are unique and obscure; and any of them may occur again in circumstances equally baffling. This is no plea against speculation. The duty of the archaeologist is to make sense of what he finds. But making sense need not entail the proposition: 'This is the best sense I can make of the evidence. If you cannot make better sense, then admit that I have guessed the truth.'[44] It is one thing to say 'this must give us a fair idea of how great men like kings and chieftains were buried or commemorated', and quite another to say 'this is a king's cenotaph or grave on general grounds of probability, therefore on particular grounds we can go on to assert that this object and that are specifically and symbolically royal though we do not know what they are'. The hunt for a royal candidate then ensues, which it would be churlish to deny is good fun.

But danger of another order lies in overlooking the fact that the kings of the age which we have been considering held a perfectly definite rank. They were no more nobles and chieftains than they were bishops; and it was not only, or always, wealth that distinguished them from their followers. Had it been so, the Merovingians would have lasted a century less than they did. They were distinguished from other great men by rank and by function. The world of Liuvigild, Liutprand, Dagobert and of the kings known to Bede was a world of kings whose authority, however unsure we may be of its symbolism, had roots in the Roman as well as the Germanic past, and an active model, honoured if remote, in Byzantium. Contemporary writers are careful to distinguish them from other great men who were merely powerful or rich. They were nearer in function to the anointed kings of the eighth century than to the war-lords of the migration period. I do not imply that they were not warriors but only that the best of them were something else in addition. The East Anglian royal dynasty of the seventh century, whether its family links were with Scandinavia or Merovingian Gaul or neither, must be seen in a European context. If we assert on present evidence (and there is still much to learn) that a member of that dynasty lay buried or was commemorated at Sutton Hoo, we prejudge an important issue. If we assert the contrary, we prejudge it no less.

POSTSCRIPT

Since this paper was written, fifteen years ago, much work of the highest sophistication has been done on the contents of Sutton Hoo. The site has been examined afresh, though the neighbouring barrows (greater in number than was once thought) remain largely un-investigated. A further group is due for examination in 1975. No one can tell whether further changes in general interpretation may then prove necessary.

What I wrote in 1959–60 may well have been *überspitzt*. If it was so, it was in reaction against an unduly rapid settling of the climate of opinion; or so it seemed to me. Some of what then seemed possibilities have now become certainties, while others have been abandoned as a result of patient archaeological research. It is pre-cisely this changing picture—which may change yet again—that impels me to republish my paper. It affords an opportunity to re-assess my own position and to present it side by side with what I originally wrote. It is not my purpose to assess in detail the archaeo-logical findings of the intervening years, much less those in the wider field of Anglo-Saxon and continental archaeology to which Sutton Hoo belongs. For this we await the publication of Dr. Bruce-Mitford's definitive study, the first volume of which is due to appear in 1975. I wish merely to indicate the respects in which my views have been modified. My argument is not, and never was, that Sutton Hoo was not, or could not be, royal or East Anglian or of the seventh century. Indeed, in a recent publication (*Early Germanic Kingship*, pp. 69ff.) I have supposed a situation in which it could be all three. What matters is the nature of the proof.

1   *The magnificence of the deposit*

The East Anglian kingdom was clearly a one-horse show when compared with some of its neighbours, to say nothing of the major continental kingdoms. Therefore any substantial deposit of this kind in East Anglia is surprising, even if it would not have surprised a Merovingian or Lombardic king. That it is magnificent in any respect was hardly to be expected. It is a point I had overlooked. It rather tends to support the case for the royal nature of Sutton Hoo than otherwise. It is another matter to determine what should be understood by 'royal nature'. Forty-two gold coins, blanks and ingots may in the circumstances be considered rather more than a handful, particularly since Professor Philip Grierson and Dr. Kent have cast serious doubt on Dr. Sutherland's dating of early Anglo-Saxon gold coinage. It now seems unlikely that any Anglo-

Saxon gold coins were available within the accepted dates for Sutton Hoo. The attempt to introduce such coinage in Kent *c.* 600 did not catch on, and there is a gap till its revival some fifty years later. The number of the coins and the presence of the blanks may well have special significance.

2 The symbolism of Sutton Hoo

Much still turns on the interpretation of the standard and the whetstone. Inasmuch as I cast doubt on the symbolism of the standard, I was right; for the stag has since been demoted from its dominant position on the standard, which can now be considered a utilitarian object, an iron stand for whatever purpose. On the other hand, the stag is now transferred to the whetstone, which thereby gains in importance. I would recognize the whetstone as a symbolical object—though symbolical of what I do not know. It may be worth looking afresh at the Scandinavian evidence. Attention has been drawn (by S. L. Cohn, *Speculum*, July 1966) to the association of the whetstone with the sacrificial cult of Thor, and also (by H. R. Ellis Davidson, *Frühmittelalterliche Studien* 3, 1969, p. 218) to Snorri's tale of how Odin disguised himself as a craftsman with a wonderful whetstone in order to enter into the service of a giant. If we consider, then, that the Sutton Hoo whetstone was, in origin at least, associated with Scandinavian rites, the problem arises of whether it was a relic of the Wuffingas or of someone else.

3 Rendlesham

Though, to my knowledge, no further work has been done on the site, it is nonetheless true that the East Anglian kings did pay special attention to this southern district of their kingdom. I consider that I underestimated the evidence for this, as assembled by Dr. Bruce-Mitford. That Bede should refer to Rendlesham at all is of significance, since places that he mentions have a way of turning out to be important. The evidence of the ninth century is also relevant. My pupil Dr. Alfred Smyth argues in a forthcoming book on the common origin of the Scandinavian kingdoms of York and Dublin that it was in the Rendlesham-Sutton Hoo area that King Edmund met his death at the hands of that *paganissimus rex*, Ivárr the Boneless, in 869. Edmund had been staying at his *palatium* at (un-identified) *Haegelisdun* when Ivárr advanced on him from Thetford with the demand that he hand over a share of his 'ancient treasures' and accept the position of a tributary king. The demand was refused and the king was ritually slain. We no longer identify *Haegelisdun* with Hoxne, in the north of the kingdom. It probably lay much nearer to Sutton; and it is to be remembered that the East Anglian archdeacon Hermann, writing in the eleventh century but using local traditions (*majorum relata*), reported that Edmund's body was first buried beneath a temporary structure, *in villula Suthtunc dicta, de prope loco martyrizationis* (*Memorials of St Edmund's Abbey*, I, p. 27). If the district was important to Edmund in the ninth century, it is unlikely to have been unimportant earlier.

4   *The body*

If, as now seems most probable, a body did indeed lie along the keel-line, we can abandon the hypothesis of a cenotaph, which never was attractive despite the ingenuity spent on it. The discovery removes one of the planks of the early phase of interpretation. I continue to keep an open mind about the identity of the body—a matter, indeed, on which it may never be possible to be certain. If I were told that the body was, for example, that of Redwald, I should be in no position to deny it, or to wish to deny it. But I should look to the proof. Nor am I wholly convinced that the burial (if such it is) can be securely dated from the accompanying objects—though, as to their individual dating, I happily follow the experts. But let Sutton Hoo, in its East Anglian setting, be magnificent enough to be 'royal'; let the whetstone have an undetermined symbolism; and let the district be important to the East Anglian kings.

NOTES

1 *Studi Medievali*, 3rd series, I, i, (1960), 177–94. The matter of this article has been discussed with many friends over the last ten years, to my great benefit. In particular I feel my debt to my colleague, Dr. Ida Gordon, though she would not accept all my views.

2 This claim has been made by implication many times but has found its clearest statement in the inaugural lecture of C. F. C. Hawkes, *Archaeology and the History of Europe* (Oxford, 1948).

3 One instance of an historian losing patience with archaeology in a promising field for co-operative work is provided by Charles Verlinden, *Frankish Colonization, a new approach, in Trans. R. Hist. Soc.*, 5th series IV (1954).

4 Cf. Hans Zeiss, *Fürstengrab und Reihengräbersitte*, in *Forschungen und Fortschritte*, XII (1936).

5 I provisionally accept the current explanation that Sutton Hoo is a cenotaph, because it seems not to be grave; and I can think of no other explanation. It is unnecessary here to enumerate the contents of the cenotaph or to recount the circumstances of its discovery since both are sufficiently fresh in the minds of scholars.

6 The already extensive literature on Sutton Hoo has been summarized by F. P. Magoun in *Speculum*, 1954. Attention may be drawn to the contributions of Mr. R. L. S. Bruce-Mitford, and particularly to his *Provisional Guide* (published by the Trustees of the British Museum in 1947 and reprinted in 1951); his two articles, *Saxon Rendlesham* (*Proceedings of the Suffolk Institute of Archaeology and Natural History*, XXIV, part III; centenary vol. for 1948) and *The Sutton Hoo Ship-Burial, recent theories and general interpretation* (ibid., XXV, part I, 1950); and his extensive appendix to the third edition of R. H. Hodgkin, *A History of the Anglo-Saxons* (Oxford, 1952).

7 *The Audience of Beowulf* (Oxford, 1951), p. 83.

8 A tendency to overlook this point may be detected in some recent commentaries, e.g Miss Rosemary Cramp's otherwise excellent *Beowulf and Archaeology* in *Medieval Archaeology*, I (1957), pp. 57–77.

9 Gregory of Tours, *Historiarum Libri*, VI, 45; 'nam tanta fuit multitudo rerum ut aurum argentumque vel reliqua ornamenta quinquaginta plaustra levarent. Franci vero multa munera obtulerunt, alii aurum alii argentum nonnulli equites plerique vestimenta et unusquisque ut potuit donativum dedit' (ed. Krusch and Levison, p. 318; ed. Buchner, II, p. 80).

10 Procopius, *De Bello Gothico*, II, 26–28 (Loeb ed., III, p. 22).

11 Fredegar, *Chron.*, IV, 73 (ed. Krusch, pp. 157–8; ed. Wallace-Hadrill, pp. 61–2). Mr. Philip Grierson has pointed out that Fredegar's figure of 200,000 *solidi* is impossibly high for the price of redemption since the bullion value of a gold object weighing 500 lb. would only come to 36,000 *solidi* (*Commerce in the Dark Ages*, in *Trans. R. Hist. Soc.*, 5th series, IX (1959), p. 133). However, compensation for the insult sustained by Dagobert in having his reward vetoed by the Goths must also be taken into account. Mr. Grierson's article conveniently summarizes many instances of barbarian wealth. See also R. Doehaerd, *La richesse des Mérovingiens*, in *Studi in onore di Gino Luzzatto* (Milan, 1949) vol. I.

12 Fredegar, *Chron.*, IV, 79 (ed. Krusch, p. 161; ed. Wallace-Hadrill, p. 67).

13 Gregory of Tours, op. cit., IX, 28; 'regina iussit fabricari ex auro ac gemmis mirae magnitudinis clepeum ipsumque cum duobus pateris ligneis quas vulgo bacchinon vocant eisdemque similiter ex gemmis fabricatis et auro, in Hispania regi mittit' (ed. Krusch and Levison, p. 446; ed. Buchner, II, p. 278).

14 Bede reports that, shortly before his death, Penda was not deflected from

E

his hostility towards Oswiu by the latter's offer of 'innumera et maiora quam credi potest ornamenta regia vel donaria' (*Hist. Eccl.*, III, 24: ed. Plummer, I, p. 177).

15 *Anastasis Childerici I Francorum regis sive Thesaurus sepulchralis Tornaci Nerviorum effossus et commentario illustratus* (Antwerp, 1655), especially, pp. 36–49. Further literature on the subject is extensive; mention must be made of the abbé Cochet's *Le tombeau de Childéric Ier, roi des Francs* (Paris, 1859) and of Ernest Babelon's *Le tombeau du roi Childéric et les origines de l'orfèvrerie cloisonnée* (Mémoires de la société nationale des Antiquaires de France, LXXVI, 1924). The last is a spirited defence of the authenticity of the royal grave against attacks that go back as far as that of James Douglas in 1793. Modern studies of the grave-goods include K. Böhner, *Das Langschwert des Frankenkönigs Childeric*, in *Bonner Jahrbücher*, 1948; H. Arbmann, *Les épées du tombeau de Childéric*, in *Meddel. fron Lunds Universitets Hist. Museum*, 1948; and E. Salin, *La Civilisation Mérovingienne*, I, 107, 181, 183, 233; II, 123, 232, 248, 251, 270–3, 288; III, 18, 43, 56, 93, 110, 212, 239, 240, 241; IV, 25, 96, 98, 169, 181–2; 424.

16 This ring was stolen and melted down in 1831. But there can be no serious doubt that it was found in the grave; and extant impressions taken from it suggest a ring which is authentic even if unusual in some ways. Such doubts as exist were ably summarized by Maurice Prou in his preface to P. Lauer and Ch. Samaran, *Les diplômes originaux des Mérovingiens* (1908), p. VIII, and were answered, to my mind convincingly, by Babelon. Chiflet immediately grasped its significance: 'ac ista quidem cuius aut aevi essent, aut personae, difficile fuisset atque impossibile iudicare, nisi una cum his repertus annulus aureus Childerici Francorum regis fecisset indicinam' (op. cit., p. 39).

17 Babelon, op. cit., p. 47, thinks that Childeric would have been buried with his diadem. It is unlikely, though not impossible, that he had a diadem. At all events it does not survive and was not described by Chiflet, who was rather of the opinion that the golden bees were the distinguishing mark of his kingship (op. cit., chap. XII).

18 *Les tombes Gallo-Romaines et Mérovingiennes de la basilique de Saint-Denis (fouilles de janvier-février 1957)*, in *Mémoires de l'Académie des Inscriptions et Belles-Lettres*, XLIV, 1958.

19 Ibid., pp. 35–45.

20 *Les Monumens de la monarchie françoise*, I (1729), pp. 173–5.

21 Fredegar, *Chron. cont.*, chap. 2 (ed. Krusch, p. 169; ed. Wallace-Hadrill, p. 81).

22 *Sur le trésor barbare de Pouan*, in *Gallia*, XIV (1956).

23 *Recherches sur le lieu de la bataille d'Attila en 451* (Paris, 1860). I have not seen this book.

24 *A History of Attila and the Huns* (Oxford, 1948), p. 141.

25 Cf. R. Latouche, *Les grandes invasions et la crise de l'occident au Ve siècle* (1946), p. 111.

26 *Getica*, XLI (ed. Mommsen, p. 113).

27 Op. cit., pp. 56–8.

28 Op. cit., p. 75.

29 Cf. Joachim Werner, *Das Alamannische Fürstengrab von Wittislingen*, in *Münchner Beiträge zur Vor-und Frühgeschichte*, 11 (1950).

30 See in particular P. E. Schramm, *Herrschaftszeichen und Staatssymbolik*, 1 (1954), (Schriften der Monumenta Germaniae Historica, XIII/1).

31 *British Museum Quarterly*, XIII (1939), 128.

32 *The Sutton Hoo Ship-Burial*, p. 8.

33 In Schramm, *Herrschaftszeichen*, I, esp. pp. 238–80.

34 *Hist. Eccl.*, II, chap. 16 (ed. Plummer, I, p. 118). Cf. D. E. Martin-Clarke, *Significant Objects at Sutton Hoo*, in *Chadwick Memorial Studies* (Cambridge, 1950), pp. 109–19. But the voice of caution has been heard once at least, for Professor Norman Davis writes 'have we yet, indeed, enough evidence to conclude that the iron stand is a military banner like that of the Romans? It seems too inconspicuous, scarcely taller than a man, and the figurine only three inches high' (*Review of English Studies* (1952), p. 64).

35 And as reported by Ammianus, *Rer. Gest. Lib.* xxxi, 2, 21.

36 *Hist. Eccl.*, III, chap. 22 (ed. Plummer, I, p. 174).

37 Brian Hope-Taylor, *The Listener*, 25 October 1956, p. 650, where the site is identified with King Edwin's *villa regia* mentioned by Bede, *Hist. Eccl.*, II, chap. 14 (ed. Plummer, I, p. 114).

38 Bruce-Mitford, *Rendlesham*, p. 236.

39 *Anglo-Saxon Gold Coinage in the Light of the Crondall Hoard* (Oxford, 1948).

40 Ibid., p. 71.

41 Ibid., pp. 67 ff.

42 Ibid., p. 25.

43 The way in which numismatic evidence may be used to point the existence of maritime commerce between any two regions is exemplified by the treatment of Sutton Hoo in A. R. Lewis's *The Northern Seas*, Princeton, 1958, pp. 120–7, 146 ff. But from the same evidence it would be possible to reach entirely different conclusions.

44 In this matter of weighing probabilities, the general historian labours under some disadvantage in not having available a sylloge of his country's significant archaeological Dark-Age material. Without this, and lacking the facilities to hunt through innumerable local journals, how can he know what lies behind the archaeologist's quantitative and qualitative assessments?

IV

Bede's Europe†

This famous church is an English church. A year ago, Dr. H. M. Taylor drew attention to structural and other features that it shared with some, though by no means with all, English churches of the same period. He mentioned, however, as a specially important factor, that 'in all seven kingdoms the churches were serving a single faith under a single supervision from Canterbury and ultimately from Rome'. In other words, St Paul's, Jarrow, is also a European church. In Bede's Jarrow we should expect to meet with something of what is familiar in the larger context of Bede's Europe. In fact, we do so. To take one instance, the inscribed stone of the *conditor*, Abbot Ceolfrith, recording the dedication of the church on this day, April 23, in 685, in the fifteenth year of King Ecgfrith's reign, recalls other dedications, not of the Anglo-Saxon world. It will recall, perhaps, that curious stone altar of Ham, near Coutances, in Francia, with its long verse inscription to tell us that that church was built and consecrated by Frodomund, Bishop of Coutances, on land given by Theuderic III in the sixth year of his reign (679), who also surrounded the property with a wall. On this stone an English pilgrim, it has been supposed, saw fit to scribble his name: *Dumkbertus subscripsi*—and more to that effect which has perished. Or it might recall something further afield, in Visigothic Spain: the dedication stone of the little remote church of San Juan de Baños in Palencia erected by King Reccasvinth to the honour of St. John the Baptist: 'lover of your name, I have built, dedicated and endowed this church at my own expense and on my hereditary land in the year 699'

† Jarrow Lecture, 1962.

(= 661). Ham, 679; Jarrow, 685; Baños; 661: they are very near in date, if otherwise far apart. Their inscriptions have no direct connection with one another, but their inspiration is common and their execution not without points of resemblance. They speak of a common civilization and so, inevitably, tell us something about each other. Jarrow belongs to Europe.

To the modern observer, Bede's Europe looks an exciting place. It would not be going too far to say that, in or round about Bede's lifetime, changes took place in the social structure of Europe not less momentous than those following the barbarian invasions themselves. The Saracens completed their conquest of the southern shores of the Mediterranean; they threatened Constantinople herself and caused the Byzantine emperors to redress their losses of Mediterranean territory by looking to their possessions in Asia Minor; they overthrew the Visigoth kingdom of Spain; and they shook the complacency of Francia and of Italy. The popes, deserted by Byzantium and menaced by Lombards, looked north for help. A looking north, indeed, may be thought to characterize the age of Bede in Europe. It has been seen as a turning-away from the Mediterranean world of Late Antiquity, and as the beginning of the opening-up of a new, northern Europe, an Atlantic Europe, whether in compensation or through processes that were coincidental. A northern civilization was emerging as surely as an Arabic civilization of the Mediterranean.

Bede, then, a man observant and alive beyond the usual run of men, might be supposed to have watched some of these dramatic developments with a keen eye. Probably he did. We must remind ourselves, however, that Bede was not the historian of Europe, on the confines of which he knew he lived, except in so far as Europe impinged on his England. All his writings, historical and other, could not together yield a coherent picture of the Europe of his day; nor is there any reason why they should. It is not so much, however, in the 'facts' of recent European history that he records that he betrays his awareness of Europe and of England's place in Europe, as in the slant of his mind, the assumptions that he shares with others. What is unique in Bede is his clear-headed mastery of the techniques of historical scholarship, not his outlook, which was compounded of reading and of observation of a kind that he had in common with his contemporaries on the continent. What I wish to attempt, therefore, is not to string together the 'facts', in order to find out how much

Bede knew of Europe; this could reveal little of interest. I wish
rather to inquire why it is that Bede made assumptions about his
Europe that we do not make, and why the nature of his writings
suggests a scene not at all to be comprised within the formula
'death of the Mediterranean world and birth of Atlantic Europe'.

Naturally, we should not expect from Bede a rosy outlook on the
contemporary scene, English or European. You will know from his
Ecclesiastical History and from his *Letter to Egbert* that he was
disturbed about the state of the Northumbrian Church in the closing
years of his life, and he gives good, practical reasons for his fears. The
Northumbrian Church, like churches everywhere in the West, was
passing through a difficult stage, brought about by its increasing
landed wealth and the relationship this implied with the great, and
especially with kings. For better or worse it was part of the Establishment. We should not ignore this, any more than Bede did. But
the roots of Bede's pessimism lay deeper. We have to look for them
in his Christian scholarship. The closing chapters of his *De Temporum Ratione*, completed in 725, and the chronicle (the *chronica
majora*) appended to it, illustrate the point. There he is at pains to
correct those who think they have any sure means of calculating the
time of the coming of Antichrist and the Day of Judgement; the end
of the world is not thus to be calculated; but it will come, just the
same, and the elect will know the signs of its coming. Bede followed
good precedent when he built his longer chronicle round the concept
of the Six Ages of the World (he entitled it *De sex huius saeculi
aetatibus*), in the sixth and last of which he deemed himself to be
living; he followed good precedent, but what makes the concluding
part of that chronicle impressive and moving is the restrained passion
with which he handles what he so evidently believed in: namely, the
Sixth Age itself, then the reign of Antichrist, the Day of Judgement
and the coming of the Eternal Kingdom, *illa aetas semper amanda
speranda suspiranda fidelibus*. He begs those who have benefited
from his little book, *de volubili ac fluctivago temporum lapsu'*, to
remember him in their prayers. Here then, as also in the preceding
sixty-fourth chapter of *De Temporum Ratione*, on the mystical
significance of Easter, we see a mind unfolding that is unlike our
minds, not in quality merely but in assumptions that must affect any
view of contemporary history. It is the mind of a theologian, as
Wilhelm Levison pointed out long since. It is a mind, we may add,
perfectly attuned to its age. There is nothing to startle contem-

poraries in *De Temporum Ratione* and its chronicle, nor much to give them hope in the doings of nations.

Some ten years before Bede's birth, there appeared in the western Mediterranean the by then uncommon sight of a Byzantine emperor on the warpath. Worsted by the Arabs and unpopular at home, Constans II decided to make himself felt in Lombard Italy and to check the Arab advance into the central Mediterranean; and this he did from headquarters at Syracuse, in Sicily, which he probably meant to be permanent. Syracuse was not far from Carthage; and from Carthage his grandfather, the great Heraclius, had set out to rescue Byzantium from the menace of Persia. There is little record of his six years in the West; the chronicler Fredegar may well have intended to write about them (*chron.*, IV, 81) though, if he did, he never succeeded; but they made some stir there, as can be inferred from Bede's story (HE. IV, 1) that the Franks delayed Abbot Hadrian on his way to England until they were sure that he had no *legationem imperatoris ad Brittaniae reges adversus regnum* (*sc. Francorum*). Though—perhaps because—they were familiar with pilgrims, the Franks were touchy about foreign travellers and foreign contacts of their own countrymen. So too were the Visigoths, whose seventh council of Toledo, in 646, made special mention of the trouble that arose when men fled to foreign courts. They thereby lent moral support to the legislation on treason published by King Chindasvinth three years earlier. Had they but known it, the Franks need not have feared the intrigues of Constans II, for he was hit on the head and killed with a silver ewer almost at the very time that Hadrian and Archbishop Theodore were reaching England. That was the end of personal imperial intervention in the West, though other emperors would have liked to intervene and Justinian II, in particular, passionately wished to do so. The possibility that they would was in men's minds at least as late as the early eighth century. We may note Bede's lack of interest in Constans' doings. The Byzantine emperors were no longer wanted in western Europe, whether in Italy, Spain or elsewhere; though, in contradistinction, Byzantine ways and manners still had their attractions, even to some extent in Archbishop Theodore's England. Why the emperors were not wanted, even by those with some knowledge of Roman history, is no question for a short answer, but it certainly had to do with disapproval of imperial involvement, at one time or another, in monothelitism. The suspicion that the emperors were unorthodox was not quickly allayed. They were not at once looked to as the welcome shield of the West against Islam; and this calls for some explanation.

We may say, first, that the speed of advance of Islam from its home in Arabia into Syria, Persia, Egypt and Roman Africa, did not strike western contemporaries as it strikes us. Far as we are from these events, we are struck, as they were not, by their rapid sequence. We string them together, not unjustifiably, in this manner: 632, the death of Muhammed; 635, the surrender of Damascus; 636, the battle of Yarmuk and the loss of Syria; 637, the defeat of the Persian army and surrender of the Persian capital, Ctesiphon; 643, the Arabs reach Baluchistan on the borders of India; 641, the surrender of Alexandria; 648, the subjugation of Tripolis; 664, the expedition against Sicily; 698, the fall of Carthage; 711, the crossing into Spain; 717, the great siege of Constantinople. It was very much, in less than a century, but, stated in this manner, it conceals certain truths that were obvious enough at the time. It conceals the widely differing nature of the expeditions involved, which ranged from haphazard raids to carefully prepared campaigns; it conceals the disarray of the Arab-Berber world in terms of objectives and even some disunity in religious practices; it conceals the strength of the Persian resistance on land as well as that of the Byzantines—much more efficacious—by sea; it conceals, finally, a multiplicity of reactions among the subjugated populations to the Arab overlords. We cannot, then, be surprised if Bede did not quickly see the Arab campaigns as the irresistible advance of a New World that could destroy the religion and culture of the Old. Neither did Fredegar, the Burgundian chronicler, who lived nearer the events than did Bede and was chiefly struck by their episodic possibilities.

Bede was born when the Arabs were pressing along the coastline of Proconsular Africa; the crossing into Spain occurred at a time when he was hard at work on his biblical commentaries; he died three years after the Frankish victory at Poitiers (or Tours) and at the very time when Charles Martel was embarked on his campaigns against the Arabs in the Midi. About the victory he has a word to say, and I shall revert to what he does say. The events of the day in which he wrote have some bearing upon his references to Arabs of his own and of an earlier time. In what is probably his earliest composition, *De Arte Metrica*, he shows awareness of the *Mauri* (by which he presumably meant Arabs) and no love of them: *Vae, dativus et accusativus sequi debent: ut, Alius vae populo Maurorum!*

Vae populum Maurorum! His *De Locis Sanctis*, composed between 702 and 709, furnishes another very early example. This travel-book or pilgrim's guide to the Holy Places was put together largely from a similar guide-book, also named *De Locis Sanctis*, written by Adamnan of Iona between 683 and 686, and seen by Bede in the 690's. Adamnan had his story from a Frankish bishop, Arculf by name, who had made the pilgrimage between 679 and 682, but had been shipwrecked off the coast of Britain on his way home. Curiously enough, Bede tells us more about Arculf than Adamnan does, and, as usual, is not content to copy his source; he modifies the text before him to suit his own tastes and standards, and is master of his material. The tale as told by Adamnan and Bede is unusual enough, even judged by the general run of early medieval *Itinera*; but what makes it arresting as well as unusual is the circumstance that between 679 and 682 a western bishop, with no official support that we know of, could quietly visit Christian Holy Places in Arab hands and return to dictate a common-sense account that Adamnan and Bede treated as the basis of a practical guide-book for others intending to make the same journey. This argues a remarkable liberalism in the Arab rulers of the Levant. In fact, the ruler chiefly responsible was the caliph of Damascus, Mu'āwiyah, effective founder of the Umayyad dynasty and so the first, and in many ways the model, Arab sovereign. He ruled in Damascus from 660 to 680. His reign saw a great extension of Islamic power, and it would be a mistake to suppose that he did not regard Christian Byzantium as his natural foe. Nonetheless, his tolerant shrewdness taught him not to alienate the Christians over whom he ruled, and hence we find him relying heavily on Christian Syrians in the building up of something quite new, an Arab State, and encouraging the hellenistic culture that he inherited. We are told that the Arab chroniclers dwelt upon the sense of loyalty which the people of Syria cherished towards their new chief. No wonder that Constans II found him so formidable—though it was in fact during the succeeding reign of Constantine IV (Pogonatus) that Arculf travelled in the East. Adamnan reports from Arculf a miracle that happened in Jerusalem concerning the shroud or cloth that covered Christ's head at his burial. It became an object of dispute between what Adamnan represents as believing and unbelieving sects of Jews, whereupon the Saracen king Mavias (that is, Mu'āwiyah) invoked both parties, casting the cloth in a fire in his courtyard with the words 'now let Christ the Saviour of the

world, who suffered for the human race, who had this shroud
(which I now hold in my arms) placed on His head in the sepulchre,
judge by the flame of the fire between you who contend for this
cloth'; and the cloth, rising from the flames, fluttered to rest *ad
partem Christianorum*. Bede shortens this account, though he adds,
characteristically, to the words *Mavias Sarracenorum rex* the explan-
atory phrase, *qui nostra aetate fuit*. He also follows Adamnan in
describing (though in his own words) the Saracens' quadrangular
mosque at Jerusalem and in alluding to another mosque at Damascus. It may be of interest that, whereas Adamnan writes of this
latter as *quaedam etiam Saracinorum eclesia incredulorum* Bede has
*Saracenorum rex cum sua sibi gente aliam [ecclesiam] instituit
atque sacravit*. He feels no need to belittle the unbelievers, and is as
discreet about them as he is cool about the Eastern Emperors.
Sensing, perhaps, the early rumblings of the iconoclast controversy
that would have escaped Adamnan, he omits Adamnan's long
accounts of George the Confessor and of the Image of the Virgin
at Constantinople; nor does he feel the attraction of Constantinople
to the extent that Adamnan felt it. There is no great loss here,
though we may well wonder how Bede could have resisted Adamnan's delightful account of Arculf in Egypt, watching the Nile
crocodiles and finding out if he could walk through Alexandria in
one day. Of the two books, Bede's is the more practical pilgrim's
guide. Detachment towards the Islamic world is still apparent in
the geographical glossary appended by Bede to his commentary on
Acts, completed soon after 709, some six years later than *De Locis
Sanctis* (from which indeed he quotes). Geographical surveys of
this kind were not new, and books on cosmography were sought
after. King Aldfrith was prepared to give eight hides of land for
such a book (*mirandi operis*, says Bede) belonging to Wearmouth or
Jarrow. Bede relied heavily on the surveys of Orosius, Isidore and
Jerome, though the glossary is still characteristically his own. For
his note on Arabia, he takes a little from Orosius and one sentence
from Isidore, and this is what results:

> *Arabia: regio inter sinum maris rubri qui Persicus et eum qui
> Arabicus vocatur habet gentes multas, Moabites, Ammanitas,
> Idumaeos, Sarracenos aliasque quam plurimas. Arabia autem
> sacra interpretari dicitur eo quod sit regio turifera odores creans;
> hinc eam Graeci* εὐδαίμων, *nostri beatam vocaverunt.*

The Saracens he thus inserts in their Arabian context, but along with the Moabites, *aliasque quam plurimas*. We are not to guess that they were the challengers of Byzantium or the enemies of Christendom. For *Syria*, he is content to quote from Orosius without comment or addition; and under *Damascus*, after a phrase from Jerome, he consults *De Locis Sanctis*. This is what he writes:

> *nunc Sarracenorum metropolis esse perhibetur, unde et rex eorum Mavvias famosam in ea sibi suaeque genti basilicam dicavit, Christianis in circuitu civibus beati baptistae Iohannis ecclesiam frequentantibus.*

All the same, he is not quite so detached in the body of the commentary to which the glossary is appended; for here he says, commenting on Acts 7, xliii, *significat autem Luciferum cuius cultui Sarracenorum gens ob honorem Veneris erat mancipata*. But the radical change in Bede's outlook seems to follow, and may be a consequence of, the Saracen invasion of (or rather, intervention in) Spain in 711. Commenting on I Samuel 25, i, he at last sees the Saracens as enemies of the Church—*quae Sarracenos specialiter adversarios ecclesiae cunctos generaliter describunt*—though he seems to feel that as descendants of Ishmael they had little chance to be anything else. This was in 716. Four years later, commenting on Genesis, 16, xii, we find this uncompromising statement:

> *Significat semen eius [sc. Ishmael] habitaturum in heremo, id est, Saracenos vagos, incertisque sedibus, qui universas gentes quibus desertum ex latere iungitur incursant, et expugnantur ab omnibus: sed haec antiquitus. Nunc autem in tantum manus eius contra omnes et manus sunt omnium contra eum, ut Africam totam in longitudine sua ditione premant, sed et Asiae maximam partem et Europae nonnullam omnibus exosi et contrarii tenent* (Plummer; 'teneant' Giles).

Bede has come a long way. We shall not be surprised to find an echo of the same sentiment in the longer chronicle with which he concludes his *De Temporum Ratione*, in 725. Here his source is the *Liber Pontificalis*. From this he knows of the Saracen attack on Sicily and the haul of booty with which they returned to Alexandria. He knows from the same source of the stormy relations of Justinian II and the Saracens and of their struggle for the upper hand in Roman Africa; but he adds, of the events of 695–8, *quae* [*provincia*] *fuerat tenta a Sarracenis, ipsa quoque Carthagine ab eis capta et destructa.* He needed no written source to tell him that the fall of Carthage was momentous for the future of the Empire. The same instinct prompts him to give due attention to the great siege of Constantinople in 716 and 717. The author of the *Liber Pontificalis* writes: *Constantinopolim biennio est a nec dicendis Agarenis obsessa.* Bede is not interested in the *nec dicendis*; instead he adds a fact: the Saracens besieged Constantinople *cum immenso exercitu,* but he substitutes *triennio* for *biennio.* He goes on to recount how the prayers of the citizens brought hunger and pestilence upon the besiegers, who finally retreated, only to become involved in an engagement with the Bulgars. He closes this entry with the story that the Lombard king, Liutprand, came to hear that the Saracens had depopulated Sardinia and defiled the place where St. Augustine's bones had been brought to safety from Africa; so he purchased the bones *magno praetio,* and had them translated to Pavia. I do not know the source of this story. Paul, the historian of the Lombards, also has it, but has it from Bede. Wherever it comes from, Bede's decision to include it confirms the impression that his views of the Saracens were no longer as detached as they had been, twenty years earlier. There is more disposition to see in them a disruptive force, though little enough to give credit to the emperors who fought them on the high seas and kept the Mediterranean from becoming a Saracen lake. It is arguable that the hardships of what has been likened to a Byzantine economic blockade of the Mediterranean ports hurt the western world as much as it hurt the Saracens. If this is so, it may in part account for Bede's coolness towards the emperors of his day, though doubtless the iconoclasm of the greatest of them, Leo the Isaurian, must be a nearer cause.

The western kingdoms of Bede's day needed no emperor, though they were all debtors, great or small, to the traditions of imperial Rome, and could scarcely have challenged Byzantium's legal right to rule them as Rome's successor. One after another, the historians of the new and Christian states looked at the scene before their eyes and traced the story of the arrival and settlement of Germanic peoples in Roman provinces. We can read these accounts for Ostrogothic and Lombardic Italy, Visigothic Spain, Frankish Gaul and Anglo-Saxon England, and we may note that they have a certain amount in common with each other. This is partly, but not entirely, because for the history of the ancient world they used the same sources, and also because they read one another's writings. The writings themselves had some effect in shaping the development of the kingdoms. Bede, for his part, was proud of being an Englishman; he liked his lazy countrymen, *inertiae consulendum ratus* (*Expl. Apocal.*, pref.); and there is an unmistakably English, not to say insular, flavour about his writings as a whole. The Franks, too, were proud of being Franks, and even boastful. The pride of Isidore of Seville in being a Spaniard was no less; and we find the same pride reflected in the *Vita* of St. Fructuosus (whose canons were known to Egbert of York). We may well think that national feeling was not uncommon in the seventh century. Not unconnected with this, a new type of king was emerging. More than one of the Northumbrian kings came near to it, if Bede's judgement is anything to go by, while other kings did a little better. There was, for example, Liutprand, king of the Lombards. A Catholic (*catholicus princeps*, he calls himself) he was no friend of Rome; a promulgator of law—his *Leges* comprise 153 articles—he was no friend of Byzantium; an ally of Charles Martel, he was no friend of Islam. But he was near to being a great Italian king. He felt his Italian personality, as also the God-given nature of his kingship. A predecessor, King Agilulf, had summed this up in the phrase, very surprising for the times: *gratia Dei vir gloriosus rex totius Italiae*. Only in Bede's day were the English kings beginning to style themselves *gratia Dei* or the equivalent. The historian of the Lombards, Paul the Deacon, admitted that Liutprand was illiterate, but never mind—he was *nutritor gentis, legum augmentator*. He stood for Italy, or a good deal of it, just when iconoclasm alienated Italian sympathy from Byzantium. Bede, too, knew about him, as witness the story of St. Augustine's bones. Just such another king was the Visigoth, Reccasvinth, who died in the year of Bede's birth. Here was a lawgiver whose code, the *Liber Judiciorum*, was a systematic survey of all fields of law for his Spanish people; he no longer admitted a distinction between Goth and Roman. It is the greatest by far of all the barbarian law codes; and its strongly moralizing inspiration is ecclesiastical. Through Christian terminology it gropes for a working definition of those qualities of good law and good rulership that will together bring happiness to a people disposed to obey their king, *in civibus rector et in hostibus victor* (*Leg. Vis.*, I ,2, 6). Kings are most kingly when helping bishops. Bede, author of the letter to Bishop Egbert, would have applauded this sentiment; it finds another and closer echo in the Frankish Formulary of Marculf (I, 5). We should not wonder that kings of the quality of Reccasvinth and Liutprand had no further use for Byzantine overlordship: the western *regna* could stand alone. Bede in effect recognized this. For him, there was a beginning and also an end of the Roman Empire in the West. The great Constantine could be held up, in the *Ecclesiastical History* (I, 32) as the model that Pope Gregory once commended to King Aethelberht of Kent, if only to the extent that he was the prototype of a royal convert who prospered. But the cult of the first Christian emperor was, in the nature of the case, unlike that of any other ruler; and no subsequent emperor attracted Bede as model or overlord. He wished the Northumbrian kings to be masters in their own house; masters and warriors, doers of justice and rewarders of the faithful, and principally, therefore, loyal followers of Christ the King. His careful picture (HE. III) of the sanctified kingship of Oswald, who died *pro patria dimicans*, shows one such king. There is, then, a King over kings, who is not the Roman Emperor; and there are bishops and others who must expound His purposes to earthly kings. It was on the Kingship of Christ that Bede's thoughts dwelt at the last: *anima mea desiderat regem meum Christum in decore suo videre*. Something of the potential political significance of such a relationship of God with the kings of the earth had been grasped, centuries earlier, by Bede's particular master, St. Augustine of Hippo.

Italy contained not only Lombard kings but also popes. Bede's popes (some of them easterners by birth) were concerned to define Christian dogma, for they lived in a world of monothelites and iconoclasts, a world where Arianism was not yet extinct and heresy seemed a present danger. Bede himself, a teacher of monks, was accustomed to wrestle with problems of doctrine. In his longer chronicle he records the holding of the sixth oecumenical council (680) in Constantinople. He probably took this record from the *Liber Pontificalis*, to parts at least of which he had access. He goes on to summarize the five preceding oecumenical councils. A shorter summary will be found in the declaration of orthodoxy of the English Church at the Council of Hatfield of 679 (HE. IV, 17), later transmitted to a Roman council which itself preceded the oecumenical council. Eddius tells us something of this in his *Life* of St. Wilfrid. Bede himself did not fail to read the canons of Pope Martin's Lateran Synod on monothelitism (649) which John the

Archchanter brought to Wearmouth for transcription some thirty years later (HE. IV, 18). One must be struck, as Bede was, by the initiative of the popes in the defence of doctrine. This was nothing new in itself, but it was increasingly combined with other initiatives: in the field of law, for example. The unique juristic position of the pope happens to owe much to a famous document, the *Epistola Clementis*, which Bede himself cites, as Dr. Ullmann reminds us, in his explanation of the episcopates of Augustine of Canterbury and Laurence (HE. II, 4). The popes seem to speak for the West. To the Irish monk, Columbanus, writing to Pope Gregory the Great a century before Bede's time, the pope had been 'the most honoured flower of all Europe in her decay'. Papal power, as distinct from authority, grew by practice rather than by planning or speculating. It was couched in the language and thought of the Bible, and must be viewed religiously, not politically, as Lortz has pointed out. The correspondence of St. Boniface shows how successive popes met the demands of a growing northern church for guidance, and, without meaning to, increased their own direct responsibility. Two of these popes bore the name of Gregory. Recalling their great namesake's mission to the English, they may have felt a special sympathy for St. Boniface's English mission to the Germans. However alluring this possibility, the policies evoked by that name would be, first, the courageous upholding of the rights of the Church of Rome in Italy and the faithful custodianship of St. Peter's bones, attractive now to royal, not imperial, pilgrims; and secondly, the duty of the popes to save souls, by exercise of the jurisdictional *auctoritas* that each directly derived from St. Peter. The feeling that time was short, that apocalyptic zeal must burn in men, did not directly result from the advance of Islam and the difficulties of the Eastern Emperors: it was inherent in the Gregorian idea of papal rule and in Gregorian eschatology. This, and not the over-shadowing of Islam, accounts for the spiritual climate of Bede's times, and for Bede's own outlook as evinced in his comment on St. Mark 3, xx, that the faithful should:

non solum ab appetitu carnalium voluptatem verum etiam nonnunquam ab ipsa quoque panis quotidiani perceptione praepediant.

Or again, commenting on Nehemiah 5, i:

Atque utinam aliquis diebus nostris Nehemias, id est consolator,

*a Domino adveniens, nostros compescat errores, nostra ad amorem
divinum praecordia accendat.*

Bede felt that Christians should be outcasts, whether they sought a
foreign land like the Celts or stayed at home like himself: *inter
insidias hostium peregrinamur in terris* (Hom. on St. John, 16, xxiii-
xxx).

One of the momentous events of Bede's lifetime was the loss to
Christian Europe of Spain. It was the loss, in the first place, of a
great tradition of Christian scholarship, upheld first by the Church
of Seville and then by the Church of Toledo throughout the seventh
century. No man of his time more nearly approaches the depth and
sweep of Bede's scholarship than does Julian, Archbishop of Toledo.
The two scholars could have talked very happily together about the
Six Ages of the World, and doubtless Bede could have agreed with
Julian that if the Sixth Age was characterized by imperial rule, it
was neither coterminous with it nor particularly blessed by it: *sicut
enim in principio nihil Romano imperio fortius et durius fuit, ita in
fine rerum nihil imbecillius* (*De comprobatione aetatis sextae*, I, 21).
Julian's Toledo was the capital of the Visigothic kings, and the conjunction, here, of kings with archbishops emphasizes the Christian
side of the new kingship emergent in the barbarian successor-states.
This is apparent in the legislation of the later Visigoths, and apparent also in the unique series of conciliar canons, owing so much to
the political thinking of Isidore of Seville, that were issued from
Toledo. Here were Christian kings whose intense nationalism did
not prevent them from continuing to learn from the hated Byzantine emperors who, as late as 700, were planning a naval expedition
to recapture Spain; and here, too, were Christian bishops proud of
their *Landeskirche* but careful to cherish their link with Rome.
Isidore had foreseen a great future for Spain. Modern scholarship
fastens on the differences that arose between the Visigothic kings
and their magnates, and on the weakness inherent in the elective
nature of Gothic kingship; but neither of these was unknown to
Isidore or proved him wrong. Bede grasped something of the significance of the Arab invasion of 711; which is remarkable, since the
Arab grip on Spain was uncertain till the arrival of Abd-ar-Rahman
I in 755. The Arabs had been surprised at the ease of their military
conquest and were not ready or willing to exploit it systematically.

Moreover, there was serious Visigothic resistance to the Arabs in northern Spain; in Asturias, under Pelayo, from whose victory at Covadonga in 718 the Reconquista has been judged to begin; later, under his son-in-law, Alfonso I of Cantabria; and under Garcia Ximenez among the Basques. The walls of Mérida held up the Arabs for a whole year. Such happenings possibly led observers to look upon the situation in Spain as a mess rather than a menace. Visigoths had let the Arabs into Spain; some, now, withstood them, while others contentedly accepted their rule.

But Bede's sangfroid wore a little thin when the Arabs struck nearer home and entered France. His reference (HE. V, 23) to the *gravissima Sarracenorum lues* and to the devastation it wrought is in fact inserted as proof of the efficacy of comets as harbingers of disaster: there had been two comets in the year 729. (We may note, in passing, the *gravissima lues* of Gregory of Tours, *Hist.*, V, 34, certainly known to Bede.) It seems reasonable to associate this report with the Arab sortie in the direction of Tours in 732. Nonetheless, they had been campaigning in Visigothic Narbonensis since 714, had attacked Toulouse in 721, had taken Carcassonne and Nîmes in 725 and had sacked Autun in the same year. The venture as a whole was a *gravissima lues*, first and foremost for rich churches and monasteries. It was made the more serious by the inclination of some local magnates of Aquitaine and the Rhône valley, with no loyal feelings towards the Franks but with natural interest in Spanish affairs, to temporize with the Arabs. It would be idle to blame these fiercely independent men, who principally knew the Franks as ruthless overlords. The Carolingians, indeed, as much as the Arabs, proved to be the *gravissima lues* south of the Loire, as may be inferred from the account of the continuator of Fredegar, a contemporary. To these early years, and probably to 732, one might ascribe Boniface's letter (No. 27) advising the English nun Bucga to delay her pilgrimage to Rome on account of the *rebelliones et temptationes et minae Sarracenorum quae apud Romanos nuper emerserunt*. Was he perhaps referring to the *Romani* of the Midi, through whose lands the lady's course would lie? From 732 till his death in 741, Charles Martel was repeatedly engaged in campaigns against the Arabs, or their supporters, in Aquitaine and in the Rhône valley. There was something heroic about his struggle; but Bede did not live to witness much of it. His attention as an Englishman was in any event more readily caught by Carolingian campaigns in German territory, since these

F

were linked up with the missionary work of Englishmen. He was proud of his fellow-Northumbrian, St. Willibrord, and devoted much of two chapters (HE. V, 10–11) to his work among the Frisians. He does not mention the setback to Willibrord's work in the years 715–719. Of St. Boniface, on the other hand, he seems to have known or cared nothing. The reason for this lies partly in the comparatively late flowering of St. Boniface, who did not become an archbishop till 732 or thereabouts, and was unable to make much of the German Church till after the death of Charles Martel in 741. Nonetheless, he had been prominent enough since 719 for Bede to have heard of him, and to have addressed inquiries, had he so wished, to their common friend, Bishop Daniel. It is plain, from Bede himself, apart from other sources, that Willibrord was trusted by the Carolingians. They trusted him not merely in Frisia proper but in territories of more longstanding interest to the Frankish rulers—round Antwerp, for example, and in Echternach, which they probably meant him to use as a base for missionary work in Thuringia. They trusted him as they also trusted another foreigner, St. Pirmin, missionary in the vital area of Alamannia, where St. Boniface was unwelcome. An earlier instance of this same determination of the Franks to be masters in the Upper Rhineland was the offer of the see of Strassburg to St. Wilfrid by Dagobert II in 679. Though supported by Rome and protected officially by Charles Martel, St. Boniface was unlike Willibrord and Pirmin in that he never felt sure of the Frankish court. A note of insecurity persists through his correspondence into the time of the friendly Carloman and the tolerant Pippin III. The trouble may have been that the Franks considered the Saxons their enemies, while to the English the Saxons were kindred. St. Boniface's interests among them (cf. his Letter No. 46) may not always have coincided with those of the Carolingians, nor even, in consequence, with those of Rome. Bede perhaps knew something of the struggle between St. Boniface and the Rhineland bishops for the control of the German churches of Hesse and Thuringia. It was so much easier for him to approve of St. Willibrord's creation of the Frisian church, for this had full Frankish protection and backing. Bede, in sum, foresaw no more than did any of his contemporaries the creation of medieval Germany. Neither did he foresee the outcome of the naval struggle for control of the Mediterranean between emperors and caliphs, nor the road that the papacy was to take. Yet critical events in all these fields fell within his own lifetime. This is no reflection upon his perspicacity as a historian and an observer of his own times. It merely warns us that what Bede was looking for, and what he found, was not the unfolding of the story of the Byzantine *Imperium*, nor yet, at least directly, of the Christian *regna gentium* of western Europe; nor even of the papacy; it was the story of the Sixth Age, the *Ecclesia Dei*.

I should like to thank Professor Dorothy Whitelock for commenting on this paper at an early stage in its composition.

V

Bede and Plummer*†

There is in Corpus Christi College, Oxford, a large pen and ink cartoon, dated 1905. It shows the Fellows of the College processing to High Table. This they do above the caption *Nos miseri et egentes homines* (the first words of the College Grace before dinner). The only one of them who could be thought to look even remotely *miser et egens*—he was in fact a sumptuous host—happens to be the penultimate in the queue. It is Charles Plummer: a frail, stooping little figure, with a determined face, a high brow, a strong nose, and a jutting black beard. A firm but reticent man, one might guess, who would not wish posterity to know more about him than could be inferred from his published writings. Nor are we likely now to know more than will be found in the final pages of R. W. Chambers' lecture on Bede,[1] and in the British Academy memoir by P. S. Allen, Sir Frank Stenton and R. I. Best,[2] a trio that in itself is striking witness to Plummer's scholarly range. He does not appear in the *D.N.B.* However, anyone who has lived at all long with Plummer's edition of and commentary on Bede's *Ecclesiastical History*[3]—I say nothing of his other writings—will be clear that it tells him a good deal about Plummer, and about how Plummer conceived of his task. For there is nothing impersonal about a good commentary: it is the work of one man's mind, with all the selection, rejection and emphases that this implies. To comment on Bede is not merely to lighten dark places: it is to make a statement about Bede. The purpose of this paper is to discuss some aspects of the statement Plummer made.

* References for this chapter start on p. 93.
† A paper delivered at a conference held in Durham in September 1973 to celebrate the twelfth centenary of Bede's birth.

Much turns on the fact—and it did not escape Sir Frank Stenton—that Plummer was a humane man. He was interested in people, not in society, and had no marked taste for the technical adjuncts of Anglo-Saxon history, though he was not unaware of them. In this he was strangely unlike his Corp's tutor, Sir Samuel Dill, who saw the early European scene in terms of societies, groups and cliques, usually in decay. They can by no means be said to have cross-fertilized one another. But Plummer's humanity, heart-warming as it is, caused him to some extent to identify himself with Bede. One could almost say that Bede becomes Plummer; becomes, that is to say, rather like a nineteenth-century scholar and divine. 'A somewhat prolonged study of Bede's works', he confesses, 'has produced in my mind such a personal feeling towards their author, that I am well content that some trace of my own personal feelings and circumstances should remain in what I have written about him.'[4] And again: 'It is no light privilege to have been for so long a time in constant communion with one of the saintliest characters ever produced by the Church of Christ in this island.'[5] Bede's character, insofar as we can see it, was indeed attractive; and Plummer was not the first to have found it so. Stubbs had already fallen to its charm, and so too Bright; and the writings of these two scholars were congenial to Plummer in a marked way. The fact remains that Bede was no don.

I must not go further without acknowledging the great range of Plummer's equipment as a commentator; great, and in some ways, astonishing; for his work was completed in 1896. Subsequent technical advances in knowledge should not blind us to this. In the first place, he was aware to a unique degree that Bede as historian could not be appreciated outside the sum total of his writings. He saw that chronology was basic to Bede's thinking. Poole,[6] Levison,[7] Jones[8] and others[9] have taken the matter further than Plummer, but Plummer was the pioneer. He had an intimate knowledge of Bede's exegetical work, bad though the editions were that he had to use. Repeatedly he will cite a passage of biblical commentary that throws light on Bede's history; and he can look beyond Bede to Gregory the Great and other masters in that field. Soaked in all Bede's writings, he had a grasp of the writer's style—which nobody, since, has shown any keenness to investigate. For example, he notes Bede's use of *peto* construed with a double accusative,[10] of *vel* and *sive*,[11] of the infinitive of purpose,[12] of *bene venisti* in the sense of 'bienvenu',[13] and the stylistic difficulty of the chapters on St. Æthelburh.[14] He was keenly alive to the changing senses of technical words as well as to the possibility of textual corruption. I wish he had examined Bede's borrowings from Canterbury (to which he drew attention) from the stylistic point of view. Not only with St. Æthelburh but with the Life of Fursa (and others) Plummer can show how Bede treats a source, even on occasion obscuring its sense.[15] He can also spot difficulties in the division of books and chapters and knows that later additions can throw out the balance of the narrative. He is keenly alive to Celtic sources, and reasonably so to Scandinavian, following to some extent where Rhys and York Powell led him. (I am uncertain when he became friendly with Vig-fússon.) What he says about the Irish can plainly be corrected and expanded, but no one could accuse him of dismissing the Celtic world as a fringe to the Anglo-Saxon. He envisages the whole Anglo-Celtic scene. Often he reminds us that Bede was the first in a pro-gression of English historians: what Bede writes he will compare with the corresponding passage in the Old English translation of the *Ecclesiastical History*, in the *Anglo-Saxon Chronicle*, in William of Malmesbury or Florence of Worcester. A future commentator on Bede's *History* might feel less generously disposed, but he would also miss something. Plummer's citations from Browning and Ten-nyson, Kingsley and Rossetti, Froissart and Dante, do not, as H. A. L. Fisher observed in his review of Plummer, 'materially advance our knowledge of Bede';[16] but they came to him naturally. He saw—and this was real insight—that Bede's Anglo-Saxons showed no community of political sentiment; no more than Bede himself did Plummer see Alfred and Athelstan on the horizon. He was not to be taken in by J. R. Green. The dawning unity he did see was ecclesiastical, though a scholar who appreciated, as he did, the slow-ness of the movement of the Early Church away from Judaic practices[17] was unlikely to overestimate the speed of ecclesiastical development anywhere at any time. His commentary contains a wealth of what may be called special notes on technical subjects. Apart from the famous excursus on the Easter question, there are long notes on subjects as varied as the rite of baptism, church music, exorcism, symbolism, monophysitism, visions, and poetry. A note on *Ad* in place-names shows him painstakingly at work on a subject not at all near his heart.[18] Not many cared for place-names in 1896. Finally, he could use charter-evidence where it was relevant. All this I say in praise of Plummer, and could say more. His com-

mentary was and is a masterpiece. A revised edition of it—if indeed
one should ever revise a masterpiece—would in many ways be a
blessing. There is so much more (for example, in the field of archaeology) that now has to be taken into account. It would be a bulkier
volume than Plummer's, since apart from the incorporation of
the results of Bedan research over the last seventy years, not much
of Plummer's own solid researches could be discarded. Nevertheless,
Plummer's approach to Bede's objectives in the *Ecclesiastical History*
may not in all respects be that of historians who will soon be writing
about Bede.

Of Plummer's personal identification with Bede I have said almost
enough. He believed that Bede was the same type of 'saintly scholar-
priest' as R. W. Church and H. P. Liddon.[19] These were very considerable men. Nonetheless, Bede was something more than a saintly
scholar-priest. His learning was a route to objectives that scarcely put
us in mind of the Victorian scholar, however enlightened.

One such objective was Bede's intention to write ecclesiastical
history. *Historia Ecclesiastica* can be translated 'History of the
Church'; and this, at its lowest level, is what it is. Thus we may
speak of Bede's 'History of the Church of the English', meaning the
story of the foundations consequent upon St. Augustine's mission,
Theodore's reorganization and so on: a story of bishoprics and to a
lesser extent of monasteries. At this level it was entirely relevant to
include Arculf's description of the Holy Places in Palestine.[20] Levison remarked that Bede, like Rufinus, planned much of his history
in terms of episcopal succession, while not breaking down his
material into continuous blocks of diocesan history in the manner of
William of Malmesbury.[21] Within this framework the deeds of kings
could be exhibited as conducive or detrimental to the well-being of
the Church. But there was another level and a subtler sense of
ecclesiastical history, familiar since the time of Eusebius: history,
that is, as a record of salvation,[22] the proof of God's providence at
work. The English past could be presented in this way. Both senses
are plainly operative with Bede, conditioning what he said, how he
said it, and what he did not say. Plummer was not fully aware of this
deeper sense, possibly because he had little interest in Bede's fore-
bears and near-contemporaries in the art of writing ecclesiastical
history. He sees Bede as the father of English historiography, not as
heir to an ancient, if only spasmodically practised, tradition in European historiography. Levison, a master of continental sources, did

better than this, but even he was apt to confuse the techniques of writing (notably of chronology and hagiography) with the purposes. Let me give an example of what I mean. Bede's treatment of Romano-British history presents, in one sense, very little of a problem. We know most of his sources and can be tempted to see his account as little more than a medley. It is there to introduce our island story, completed with some geography and a selection of interesting local detail. This is roughly how Plummer sees it. But in fact Bede has taken from Orosius and others rather more than a selection of material useful to this end. His Romano-British history also exhibits a great preliminary: national disaster in the face of divine displeasure; for the Romano-British had had their own ecclesiastical history, and it was a bleak one. Gildas was right: how could such a people prosper? They started off well enough; the curious tale of Lucius and their conversion shows that Bede accepted that a proper beginning for Christianity in Britain was by papal mandate to a king. And they continued on their Christian course under Diocletian's persecution, bound to Christendom at large in martyrdom. He concludes: *Denique etiam Brittaniam tum plurima confessionis Deo devotae gloria sublimavit*,[23] and goes on to his long account of the martyrdom of St. Alban, hailed by Venantius as 'faithful Britain's child', as Bede notes. Alban thus decisively links Britain to the great church tradition of martyrdom, and through martyrdom to miracles. Next comes Arianism, which Plummer, following Bright, thought unduly emphasized, though a people's reaction to heresy is a very natural issue in ecclesiastical history. And after Arianism, Pelagianism,[24] and the terrible moral decline consequent upon the withdrawal of the Romans, the guardians of religion as well as of frontiers. Bede's reconstruction raises many problems. On one, Bede's ready acceptance of Gildas' picture of British luxury and vice, unchecked by God's warnings in the form of plague, Plummer makes no comment; indeed, no real collation of any kind of the views of Bede and Gildas. So we reach God's final judgement—the Saxons. These fourteen Romano-British chapters are in one sense 'political' history, but they are also Bede's interpretation of the British and their Roman involvement within the framework of ecclesiastical history. Here, as always, what Bede took from his sources was not allowed to lie inert. It became *his* history.

Let me turn to another major issue in the *Ecclesiastical History*: the conversion of the Anglo-Saxons. Bede does not consider it necessary to explain what paganism was. Whatever he knew or could know (and it was far more than we know) seemed irrelevant; and if we add to his chance references to paganism in stories involving conversion whatever can be had from later literary sources, archaeology and place-names, we still know rather less about Anglo-Saxon paganism than about the paganism of St. Boniface's Germans. Why is the content of paganism irrelevant to Bede? It did not seem so to Paul the Deacon, whose Lombards were remorselessly pagan. The answer lies in the purposes of ecclesiastical history. Speaking generally, the ecclesiastical historian conceived of the content of paganism, and especially of Germanic paganism, unseriously. There was no need to define its objectives, still less to distinguish its facets. It might indeed be tenaciously held, for which reason its adherents had had to be humoured or eased over the hurdle of conversion; but theologically it afforded no springboard into Christianity. However barbarous and bloody, its mere innocence protected it from serious consideration. Theologically at least, the pagan Germans seemed to offer western Christianity an unresisting field for missionary work. If Bede had been writing a history of the English people, as distinct from their ecclesiastical history, he could scarcely have avoided some treatment of their paganism as part and parcel of their life, not only past but present. As it was, he could and did avoid it. Gregory of Tours, who also wrote ecclesiastical history, also avoided it for the Franks. Plummer might perhaps have been more explicit on this point. It is right that we should know at least that Germanic paganisms were warband-religions and kin-religions, whereas Christianity was neither; and moreover, that pagan cultus as practised by warriors shared ethical concepts with the warrior's fighting-creed, from which indeed the Church borrowed some meaning-laden words when it faced the task of expressing Christian doctrine in the vernacular. Coifi's naive equation of pagan honour and success with Christian salvation was the reaction of a high priest whose congregation was a royal court of warriors.[25] Plummer was, of course, alive to the fact of paganism. In his notes to Book I, chapter 30, he considers at some length the approach of missionaries to it. However, this is not quite the same as considering what it was that missionaries were approaching. How did missionaries deal with paganism? Plummer is able to marshal a number of examples from papal correspondence, reports of English missionaries abroad, the council of Ratisbon, Theodore's Penitential and so on. There is more, but his assortment is a fair one. Moreover, he can point to Bede on conversion in other contexts: in his exposition of the Acts of the Apostles and in *De Temporum Ratione*. He knows that Christianity was 'contaminated' by paganism—in other words, that there was a degree of 'religious syncretism'—and that conversion was a slow business. But he does not ask whether the slowness, or indeed relapses, were in any way due to the nature of paganism itself. It was enough that paganism should yield to the demonstration of Christianity in action: first, the demonstration that victories in battle proved the power of the Christian god, and secondly that the teaching of Christianity was irrefutable. Teaching, indeed, was very much in Bede's mind: Æthelberht was taught and Edwin was taught, just as Clovis had once been. They were open to instruction. This in itself tells us something about paganism, as well as of the Christian attitude to conversion. Bede is clear that the conversion of the Anglo-Saxons had been mainly a matter of persuasion and teaching, not of compulsion. Was it still so in his own day—in Germany, for example? It had been Coifi, not Paulinus, who had desecrated the pagan shrine at Goodmanham;[26] by contrast, it was Willibrord and Boniface, not renegade high-priests, who went for the pagan shrines of the continental Germans. But the tradition of persuasion was a respectable one. The young Augustine of Hippo had been no friend of coercion[27] nor, to judge from his popular sermons, had Caesarius been. Bishop Daniel, too, was all for a reasoned presentation of Christianity,[28] which did indeed take some account of the facts of paganism. The conversion of the countryside—and not only of the countryside—was still a living issue in Bede's time. We must suppose that Christianity was presented to village communities in something of the spirit of St. Pirmin's *Scarapsus*; in brief, it was a matter of simple teaching, of weaning rustics from pagan junketings and offerings, from soothsayers, medicine men, and so forth. Certainly it cannot have been presented to them as the religion of victory, so efficacious with kings, nor as the religion of penitence, appropriate to substantial folk with uneasy consciences, some of whom were not above enjoying *Ingeld* in their monasteries. Bede, then, looked back on the history of the conversion and decided that the content of paganism was better ignored, whether in the raw state or as in part subsumed into current Christian practice. But heresy was quite another matter, and understandably worried him much more than did paganism. The conversion of heretics and schismatics could indeed be a matter of coercion; and here, too, Bede had Augustine of Hippo behind him. Into this context falls Bede's obsession with the issue of the date of Easter. You will recall Plummer's words: 'we cannot help feeling that the question occupies a place in Bede's mind out of all proportion to its real importance ... but the holiest men have their limitations'.[29] In other words, Bede overdid Whitby. But our business is surely to decide why the date of Easter assumed the proportions it did assume in his mind. Two consecutive Easters at one royal court were no doubt embarrassing to King Oswiu and his entourage but can hardly have moved Bede so greatly, over half a century later. Nor will it quite do to claim that a master in chronology would have been shocked by untidy thinking about dates, whenever it occurred. It is not even enough that Bede's view of Petrine primacy was engaged (and it may be observed in passing that it was Peter the doorkeeper, not Peter the bishop of Rome, for whom Oswiu opted). A deeper reason may lie in Bede's view of the unity of the Church, a portion of whose history he was writing. Unity of discipline, as of doctrine, were for Bede a condition of survival for the Church; even the well-loved Celtic clergy were rightly sacrificed to its claims. For Bede—and I do not think that Plummer quite saw this—knew the western Church for what it was: a confederation of churches, often fissile, divergent, ignorant, and passionately local.

I come to another major preoccupation of Bede's History on which Plummer has much to say, *more suo*. Miracles are widely distributed through the History. Levison, too, had much to say of Bede's miracle-stories, to the extent, indeed, of deciding that hagiography, like chronology, was a backbone of the whole undertaking.[30] In other words, Bede grew out of these technical studies into something bigger. One could add biblical commentary as a study at least as important on Bede's journey to history. However, Levison does fill out Plummer's picture by showing how Bede used hagiography and what of it was available to him. Following Karl Werner[31] he drew attention to certain hagiographers whose work influenced Bede—for example, Venantius Fortunatus; and particularly he emphasized Bede's debt to Gregory's *Dialogues*. This was a real service. But fundamentally Levison was not saying anything very different from what Plummer had already said. It amounts to this: Bede, a man of his times, must be expected to record miracles; we should be thankful that they so often include interesting

historical fact and not bother ourselves about their role in an otherwise carefully thought-out history, for they do not really affect
the rest of the matter. Yet it is not so clear why they were relevant,
nor what canons of criticism apply to miracle-stories that do not
apply to the remainder of the History.

Bede's miracle-stories make varying demands on modern credulity.
Some can be explained as possible on grounds of normal experience;
some are impossible on the same ground; some are partly possible.
How they are vouched for is a separate issue. In what sense Bede
himself accepted them is an important question. Dr. Hunter Blair
has written that Bede included miracles in his *History* because 'it
was part of the function of history to record what ordinary people
believed'.[32] This is certainly what Bede thought, and St. Jerome
and others thought the same. But there is a further consideration.
Bede, for these purposes, was himself an ordinary person, since he
too accepted the miracles he recorded. Plummer also may occasionally
have done so,[33] though on the other hand he accepted that Herebald's
riding accident could be rationally accounted for. 'In the story as
told by Bede', he comments, 'there is nothing distinctly miraculous.'[34] Nor is there. For some of the miracles attributed to St.
Cuthbert a rational explanation is possible; for example, the cure
of the young man with a diseased eyelid,[35] or Bede's own recovery,
referred to elsewhere, from a tongue complaint.[36] St. Cuthbert
shared with St. Martin the ability to look after his own, and to this
I shall return. I shall not be the only one present who has heard how
St. Cuthbert shrouded his city in impenetrable fog on the night
when German bombers were detailed to destroy it. Take another
sort of miracle: Dryhthelm's vision.[37] How much of it was really
Dryhthelm's? Bede calls it a *miraculum memorabile* but adds that
it was *antiquorum simile*. It followed a well-known pattern and
was undoubtedly the better for it. But what are we to say of a partly-
possible miracle-story such as that of Imma?[38] Let me remind you
of it. At the battle of the Trent, a Northumbrian thegn named
Imma was struck down. On regaining consciousness he bandaged
his wounds and made off, only to be taken prisoner by a Mercian,
to whom he represented himself as a peasant. He made a good
recovery and was then shackled to prevent his escape; but his fetters
fell off, not once but several times. His captor, discovering that he
was in fact a thegn, and moreover suspecting him of using pagan
litteras solutorias, sold him to a Frisian in London. The fetters con-

tinued to fall off. So he was allowed to ransom himself through the good offices of King Hlothere of Kent. Thence he returned to Northumbria and visited his brother, who was abbot of Tunna-caestir. The abbot revealed that he had been saying masses for him, believing him to be dead. The falling-off of the fetters had generally coincided with the celebration of a mass. Bede is clear about the moral: masses are efficacious for the deliverance of the souls of dead kinsmen—and, he could have added, for the bodies of live kinsmen, too. What was Bede's source? 'This story was told me by some of those who heard it from the very man to whom these things happened; therefore since I had so clear an account of the incident, I thought that it should undoubtedly be inserted into this *History*.' How are we to comment on this? The story is overwhelmingly circumstantial: no one will question that Imma actually had the adventure that is described. We might go on to speculate that in reality the Mercian sold him to the Frisian because he would fetch a good price, and the Frisian accepted his ransom because the Kentish king was prepared to find it, thus yielding him a quicker and better return than he might have obtained by selling him as a slave abroad. We may explain things thus, or in other ways. But what of the fetters so repeatedly falling off? They were presumably suggested by a Petrine parallel.[39] Someone, perhaps Imma himself or his brother, had recast the adventure as a miracle-story. Yet to Bede no part of the story is less reliable than any other part, and the miracle is the point of it, the only thing that makes it worth recording. I instance this particular story because of the combination of what we readily accept with what we tacitly reject, or accept only at a different level. There are, of course, other miracle-stories in Bede, and countless more in other writings of the period, that raise the same issue. Their narrators are living in a world where the miraculous can at once be interwoven into accounts of happenings and accepted on the same terms. I suppose that Bede was perfectly aware of this, and I therefore think that we should look carefully at the reasons behind his interweaving of the two strands of a story such as that of Imma. For it is the same mind and the same pen that report both and blend them into a narrative of ecclesiastical history. Plummer does not give us much assistance here. I do not of course mean that Bede falsified facts but only that we should consider with some care our own interpretation of what, in such a context, Bede thought facts were for; or, put another way, be sure of the

level at which we choose to appreciate his history. He was pheno-
mentally 'factual' for a man who lived in a world of invention that
could perpetrate straightforward forgery, with the best of intentions.
Consider his world. Scarcely more than century after Bede's death
we have the greatest of all medieval forgeries—Pseudo-Isidore—
and that was not the first. What is remarkable in the forgers is the
conjunction of forgery with high religious sense, though no theologian gave any justification for it. It seemed to them to be an
inspired action to reveal God's purpose by providing in writing what
ought to have existed but did not. Bede was no forger, but he does
bring the same high religious sense to his history—I mean, his
history as opposed to the facts out of which it is constructed. What
this signifies for the historian could be further explored.[40]

To take another instance: how should we comment on the story
of the healing of the wife of the gesith named Puch?[41] She suffered
for weeks from a severe illness. According to Bede's informant
(Abbot Berthun, who was present), Bishop John sent some holy
water to the woman, which she drank and washed in, and at once
rose from her bed, cured, and served the company at dinner. 'In
this', Bede concludes, 'she imitated the mother-in-law of St. Peter.'[42]
Indeed she did. Plummer notes that very similar stories are told of
St. Cuthbert and draws attention to Bede's comments on relevant
biblical passages. Colgrave adds a note of the building of *Eigen-
kirchen*, which has some relevance to the story. And that is all. Now
it so happens that Bede, while avoiding a direct statement, is fairly
clear about one aspect of the role of miracles in ecclesiastical history.
They are *signa*,[43] signs of God's intervention in the affairs of men,
demonstrating the sanctity of his chosen servants. At a time when
martyrdom was rarely available as the route to sanctity, the working
of miracles was a fair substitute. A miracle, then, at any time, and
whether performed before or after death, was irrefutable evidence of
something very special: God's power to override the normal course
of nature for a particular purpose. This had been the lesson of
Gregory's Dialogues, the burden of which was that, as in biblical
times and since, so still God continued to intervene miraculously in
the life of Italy. It was not lost on Bede. Plummer observed that
Bede's other writings contain clues to his view of miracles; as, for
instance, that miracles were relative to a certain state in the development of the Church, that the cessation of miracles should be attributed in part to man's sin, and that some men are permitted by

divine intervention to recover part of this lost heritage;[44] in short, that God was and is always prepared to intervene miraculously. Such interventions are characteristic of the life of the Church, having a cumulative force. Beyond that, they reveal and prove the presence of saints. One could say that Bede's Church functioned at more than one level. It was at one and the same time a *signum*, a spiritual manifestation of God's business, and a *res*, a visible institution, a human instrument if not an instrument of the state. Dr. Markus has ably discussed this duality in relation to St. Augustine.[45] It applies also to Bede. One is always aware of Bede's Church as an institution of men and women, meetings and buildings, and especially as a bishops' Church. He describes the Church at this level in a cool, even detached, manner. It is evidently a *res*. The Church at the higher level is principally revealed for him in the lives of its saints; and here there could be little room for detachment. What he really feels about it is revealed in his treatment of St. Æthelthryth. He starts with an account of her life;[46] of her perpetual virginity through two marriages, her entry into religion, her austerities, her death, and the discovery of her uncorrupt body sixteen years later, including the witness of the physician who had treated her. The chapter ends with a brief reference to miracles associated with her coffin, and with a note on Ely. Bede then inserts a hymn on the saint which he had composed many years before. He does this, he says, 'imitating the method of holy scripture in which many songs are inserted into the history'.[47] There is, then, a biblical analogy; but it is not the reason for the insertion. Nor is the reason instructional, since the hymn contains no information on the saint that is not already in the preceding chapter. In a learned note on serpentine elegiacs, in which the hymn is written, Plummer mentions other practitioners of the art: Ovid, Martial, Sedulius (whose work was known to Bede), and Paul the Deacon. The hymn is also alphabetic, and for this too Plummer cities other examples. The subject is virginity. It also attracted Avitus and then Aldhelm, whose poem Bede is not known to have seen and, earlier, Venantius Fortunatus, whose work he certainly did see. Plummer confines himself to noting that the virgins commemorated by Bede are also commemorated by Aldhelm, except for Euphemia, and suggests that the metre would be improved if Bede had substituted Eugenia (also known to Aldhelm).[48] He notes, too, that both Euphemia and Eugenia occur in Venantius' *De Virginitate*. But there is more to it

than that. Venantius' poem is the greatest of the early medieval state-
ments about virginity. Its subject is not the nun's vocation but the
visionary world that virginity conjures up, where the bride of Christ
sees the heavens opened and dreams of her union with Christ. For the
poet it is an ecstasy of song and light, flashing gems and brilliant
flowers; a vision that points straight to medieval mysticism. Now this
goes a good deal further than Bede. Moreover, Venantius' poem is
much longer and the metre is different. Yet it has something fundamental in common with Bede's poem. Incidentally, there are linguistic
parallels. For example, both writers use the verb *beare*, rare (except
as *beatus*) in classical and early medieval Latin; and they use it once
only, in these poems.[49] It is true that it is also used by St. Augustine
and by Sedulius and, very rarely, elsewhere; but the coincidence of
its use in two poems on the same subject is striking. Similarly, both
writers use the word *hydrus* once only,[50] and this, too, is a rare word.
But to return to what is fundamental, Bede sees virginity as Venantius saw it. What, Bede asks, has a great lady to do with earthly
marriage who has Christ for her groom? Is she not affianced to the
Lamb in heaven? Does she not court him with new songs on her
harp in heaven? This is precisely Venantius' approach, tender and
imaginative, if less erotic; altogether, one would say, inappropriate
to any historical narrative. Yet there it is. The reason once again
is that Bede is writing ecclesiastical history. It is no more irrelevant
to Bede the historian to hymn virginity in Latin than it was to
report that Caedmon praised God in the vernacular. But there is this
difference: Bede merely reports the miracle of Caedmon, whereas
his song to virginity is his personal contribution. And it is a contribution to history, Bede's spiritual justification for what he describes
more prosaically on other occasions: namely, the highest calling of a
royal lady, which is either not to marry, or, if married, to remain
virgin; it was best to enter the service of God as Christ's spouse.
It seems to have implications that invite comment.

Any Church bent on the conversion of a Germanic people to
Catholicism faced the problem of what it called evil spirits. Their
activity was never denied; they were everywhere. Not for nothing
did Germanic burials continue to be furnished with amulets, charms,
phylacteries, and talismans, long after formal conversion had taken
place. Indeed, I have the strong impression that in western Europe
generally those in authority were much more worried by attention
paid to evil spirits, in high places and low, in the ninth century than

in Bede's century and earlier.[51] Pagans had their ways of dealing
with such spirits. The Church for its part had always practised
exorcism. We have in the *Ecclesiastical History* a very instructive
case.[52] A man, Bede tells us, was possessed by an evil spirit: *subito
a diabolo arreptus*. The correct procedure was followed. A priest was
summoned, who pronounced the exorcisms provided for such an
occasion. Indeed, he worked hard at it; but nothing happened. Bede
expresses no surprise. Gregory of Tours provides a comparable
instance.[53] He says that a woman possessed by a spirit of prophecy
made a good living out of proclaiming the whereabouts of thieves
and what they had done with their loot, to the extent that people
thought there was something divine about her. The bishop had her
arrested, diagnosed an evil spirit and conducted an exorcism. Again,
nothing happened. The woman made off to another part of the
country. And again, Gregory expresses no surprise. I think it would
equally not have surprised Caesarius, who often preached to his
people of Arles about evil spirits, nor yet Martin of Braga. It was
possible for exorcism not to work, and this was a serious matter at
a time when the Church had to demonstrate the efficacy of its procedures to a semi-pagan population. But Bede has more to say, for
the failure of exorcism occurs in the course of a story that makes a
different point, since it provides a substitute for exorcism. The man
with the evil spirit was cured by something different: the mere
presence of some soil that had been moistened by the water used to
wash the bones of the saintly Oswald; in other words, a miracle was
performed by a saint. In itself, this was nothing out of the way.
What is remarkable is the juxtaposition of the efficacy of an English
saint and the failure of the traditional method of expelling an evil
spirit. Plummer has an excellent note on exorcism, so far as it goes.
He points out that there was more than one kind of exorcism and
can site Isidore, Theodore's Penitential and Bede's own works,
including a curious personal reminiscence from his commentary on
St. Luke.[54] What he misses is the significance of the juxtaposition. I
suppose he did so because, though he saw well enough that Bede's
age was one of transition from paganism to Christianity, he was less
impressed by the extent of the Church's own reactions to what the
Germanic mind could take. The Christianity of the missionary
Anglo-Saxon Church was experimental in important respects. Bede
here reveals one of these respects.

Bede's book was an ecclesiastical history of the whole English

G

people but it is not without a local slant. Like Plummer, Bede was a Bernician. Perhaps even more, he was a Northumbrian. The slant was not such as to worry Canterbury, which had to some extent inspired the work and contributed to it a little more extensively than Plummer thought, though it cannot on this account be said to have been written for Canterbury. However, a copy, *ad transscribendum*, may well have reached Canterbury within a year of its completion.[55] One might expect the Canterbury material to be handled in a way satisfactory to Canterbury, and doubtless it was. As for the rest, it had to satisfy a critical audience nearer home. We may ask, then, what sort of picture of Northumbrian history Bede created, and also ask what Plummer made of it. Despite his 'innumerable witnesses' to the Northumbrian past, Bede's account is selective and purposive. Modern scholarship has deepened our knowledge of this past and revealed something of what Bede does not record. As to what he does record, it seems to me that he means to emphasize the unity or at least the entity of Northumbria and to say no more than is necessary about the distinct traditions and rivalries of Bernicia and Deira, which he shows were real enough. His royal heroes were expansionists, men who not only controlled both parts of Northumbria but pushed her influence yet further afield. The division that seemed more critical to him was between Northumbria and Southumbria.

There is a religious side to this unsteady process of Northumbrian unification. It may be that we, and possibly Plummer, make too neat a distinction between Celtic Bernicia and Roman Deira. Wilfrid himself, Roman as he was, had much of the Celtic ascetic in him and was trained in a severe monastic tradition; and it is Bede, not Eddius, who gives us the epitaph of the *magnus praesul*, ending with a prayer that his flock might tread the same path.[56] On the evidence of the *History*, Bede was not as anti-Wilfrid as Plummer was. Bede's reservations about Wilfrid were less about the moral aspects of his life and rule than about his disruptive relations with kings and others: bishops and kings could not afford to live on a hostile basis. We all know that Bede venerated Aidan for his moral qualities; and these so captivated Plummer that he may have overestimated his importance, which was not lasting. The man who did have a future was St. Cuthbert. He brings together not merely Lindisfarne and Rome in his career but Bernicia and Deira in his cult. Plummer had remarkably little to say about him, however much he might be attracted to the story of Cuthbert and Herbert of

Derwentwater. Plummer's text makes it perfectly clear that Bede is drawing on his own version of Cuthbert's Life, itself based on an earlier anonymous Life. But it was left to Bertram Colgrave to indicate something of the literary background to the Lives as a whole.[57] In particular he showed that the Anonymous and Bede, and possibly Cuthbert himself, were indebted, whether directly or indirectly I am uncertain, to the Life of St. Martin by Sulpicius Severus. (There is so much of Sulpicius in Venantius' Life of St. Martin that it may be from Venantius that the material was derived.) At all events my strong impression is that both the Anonymous and Bede had access to that material, and that Bede used it more extensively than the Anonymous.[58] The debt was in fact greater than Colgrave recognized. Of course, Cuthbert may actually have been like St. Martin, though I doubt it. Nevertheless, the literary figure of Cuthbert seems fairly closely modelled on that of St. Martin, the greatest patron saint in western Europe, St. Peter excepted; patron most notably of the Merovingian dynasty since its beginnings under Clovis, and so of the Franks as a new people. The national hero of the Franks was the ascetic monk-bishop *par excellence*. Cuthbert, then, is cast in something of this mould. More specifically he is cast in Martin's role as miracle-working protector. Was Cuthbert designed to do for the Northumbrians what Martin did for the Franks? Was Lindisfarne to be Northumbria's Tours? It is no accident that Bede ends Book IV with a long account of the career and death of Cuthbert in 687 but yet includes the saint's translation in 698 and his miracles. Cuthbert in this respect shares a distinction with Gregory the Great, the account of whom marks the division between Books I and II.[59] There were several routes by which Northumbria could have acquired a copy or copies of Sulpicius. One—and I suspect not the most likely one—was direct from Ireland. Professor Brown has recently discussed one manuscript-link between Ireland and Lindisfarne.[60] It was real enough, but rather circuitous. Another link would be with Francia direct, which may, of course, be another way of saying with Ireland indirect. If we need to look for particular intermediaries we might think of Willibrord or Wilfrid, both of whom were well aware of St. Martin, or possibly the Church of St. Ninian, *Ad Candidam Casam*. Eddius himself seems to have known and used Sulpicius' Life.[61] Nor is it at all unlikely that Lindisfarne had a copy of Jonas' Life of St. Columbanus, itself influenced by Martin. But this is not the occasion to pursue these questions in detail. The fact remains that Bede's Cuthbert is a recognizable type of monk-bishop of ascetic stamp with a potential role in the making of a people. Whether or not Cuthbert modelled himself on St. Martin, his career could be described in words that often come from Sulpicius.

Finally, and in no pejorative sense, Plummer's approach to the continent is insular. Where Bede points directly to the continent Plummer will follow and will often find material to illuminate what Bede has said; and even occasionally when he does not: as, for example, when Plummer spots a Frankish parallel to Redwald's polytheism in Gregory of Tours or draws attention to Childebert I's *carta* abolishing idolatry. But the fact is that it was no part of Bede's plan to correlate the closely parallel development of the English and Frankish Churches. We have to do that for ourselves, and ought to do it.[62] Plummer would have claimed no deep familiarity with continental history—even that of the Franks, England's closest neighbour—and did not move easily in continental sources. Therefore he did not see Anglo-Saxon history as part of a whole, a close-knit history of the western Germanic kingdoms. One may instance his treatment of law, of feud, of kingship, of war, of monasticism, and of cultural matters generally. An example of how much more clearly Bede might be understood when one places his *History* in a wider continental context is in the matter of the burial of kings and queens. Bede's Christian rulers were laid to rest in a number of very different churches, of which St. Augustine's Canterbury, York minster and Whitby are only the most famous; different in their foundations, dedications, relics, organization and wealth. What caused royal kindreds to lay their dead in one kind of church rather than another? Were they dynastic or 'national' mausoleums? Was it important to be buried near bishops? Of how many saints would a king seek the patronage, and why is he sometimes apparently deliberately not buried near their relics? What significance have architectural differences between basilicas? These and related questions, all raised by Bede's text, can only be answered when we take a wider view, that embraces the royal sanctuaries and burial-places at Paris, Tours, Soissons, Orleans, Pavia, Monza, Ravenna and ultimately Constantinople (to mention, again, only the most famous).[63] Ecclesiastical history is bad at observing national frontiers. Plummer's Anglo-Saxons were thus more isolated from their brethren than they needed to be, or in fact were.

Plummer's commentary was nobly conceived and beautifully executed. It should not surprise us that he relates Bede to William of Malmesbury and Dean Liddon, rather than to Gregory of Tours and Eusebius; that he looks to the continent to explain this or that event in the Anglo-Saxon kingdoms, but without any real awareness that they live one life; that he sees the miraculous in terms of beguiling stories, not in terms of the most dramatic example of God's patronage through the saints of a troubled society; that he sees paganism as immoral barbarism, not as an elaborate propitiation of the spiritual world, and that he sees ecclesiastical history as an account of an institution, not as an arrangement of past events in terms of Providence. Such an approach was natural to an English scholar of his generation; it dates his work in some respects but does not vitiate it. Ecclesiastical history was a very special craft. To evaluate it, to be sure of the rules and to appreciate its objectives, we shall continue to need all the help that Plummer and scholars of his calibre can give us.[64]

NOTES

1 *Proceedings of the British Academy* xxii (1936), pp. 29–30.
2 Ibid., xv (1929), pp. 463–76.
3 *Baedae Historia Ecclesiastica gentis Anglorum: Venerabilis Baedae opera historica*, 2 vols. (Oxford, 1896).
4 *HE*, I, p. iii.
5 Ibid., p. v.
6 *Studies in Chronology and History* (Oxford, 1934).
7 *England and the Continent in the Eighth Century* (Oxford, 1946).
8 *Bedae Opera de Temporibus* (Cambridge, Mass. 1943).
9 E.g. Kenneth Harrison, 'The *Annus Domini* in some early charters', *Journal of the Society of Archivists* IV (1973): 'Early Wessex Annals in the Anglo-Saxon Chronicle', *English Historical Review*, lxxxvi (1971), pp. 527–533.
10 *HE*, II, 98 (Bk. ii, c. 12).
11 Ibid., p. 82 (ii. 4).
12 Ibid., p. 124 (iii. 2).
13 Ibid., p. 219 (iv. 9).
14 Ibid., p. 218 (iv. 7–10).
15 E.g. ibid., pp. 169–70 (iii. 19).
16 *E.H.R.* xii (1897), p. 339.
17 *HE*, II, 190 (iii. 25).
18 Ibid., pp. 103–4. See now R. Forsberg, 'On OE *ād* in English Placenames', *Namn och Bygd* lviii (1971), pp. 20–82.

19 *HE* I, p. lxxix.

20 *HE* v. 16.

21 'Bede as Historian' in *Bede. His Life, Times and Writings*, ed. A. Hamilton Thompson (Oxford, 1935), p. 143; repr. *Aus Rheinischer und Fränkischer Frühzeit* (Düsseldorf, 1948), p. 375.

22 See R. W. Hanning, *The Vision of History in Early Britain* (Columbia, 1966), ch. 3.

23 *HE* I, 6.

24 See J. N. L. Myres, 'Pelagius and the end of Roman Rule in Britain', *Journal of Roman Studies*, l (1960), pp. 21–36; and Peter Brown, 'Pelagius and his Supporters', *Journal of Theological Studies*, N.S. xix (1968), pp. 93–114.

25 This has been thoroughly investigated by D. H. Green, *The Carolingian Lord* (Cambridge, 1965), esp. chapter ix. However, I do not share the view, held by many, that paganism had no ethical content. Paganism is our word for a range of religious experience among the Germanic peoples that reached from Woden-worship at one extreme to that of sticks and stones at the other. How can one divorce paganism from the ethic of the warband, or how deny ethical content to the religious beliefs of peasants?

26 *HE* ii, 13.

27 Cf. Ep. 22. 5. Also R. A. Markus, *Saeculum: History and Society in the Theology of St Augustine* (Cambridge, 1970), p. 140.

28 *Die Briefen des Heiligen Bonifatius und Lullus*, ed. M. Tangl (Berlin, 1955), no. 23.

29 Plummer, I, pp. xl, xli.

30 'Bede as Historian' (see n. 21 above).

31 *Beda der Ehrwürdige und seine Zeit* (Vienna, 1881), p. 104.

32 *The World of Bede* (London, 1970), p. 303.

33 See his comment on St Cuthbert, *HE* II, 271; and I, pp. lxiv-v.

34 Plummer, I, 277.

35 *HE* iv. 32.

36 *Bedas metrische Vita sancti Cuthberti*, ed. Werner Jaager (Leipzig, 1935), p. 57.

37 *HE* v. 12.

38 Ibid., iv. 22.

39 Acts 12. 7. See also Gregory of Tours, *H.F.*, X, 6, ed. Krusch and Levison, *MGH Scr. Rer. Mero.* (p. 488), and elsewhere.

40 See H. Fuhrmann, *Einfluss und Verbreitung der pseudoisidorischen Fälschungen*, vol. 1 (Stuttgart 1972), ch. 1.

41 *HE* v. 4.

42 Matt. 8. 14–15.

43 E.g. 'signa miraculorum usque hodie narrari' (*HE* iii 8) and 'in hoc etenim monasterio plura virtutum sunt signa patrata' (iv. 7).

44 *HE* I, p. lxv.

45 *Saeculum*, ch. 7, esp. p. 185.

46 *HE* iv. 19.

47 Ibid., c. 20. Plummer provides some biblical analogies, II, 241.

48 Despite his long note on St. Aldhelm, II, 308, Plummer was not interested

in the content of his thought but, like others, was obsessed with his style—
which Bede accepted, however.

49 *HE* iv. 20, l. 25 of poem; Venantius, *Vita Martini* II, 376 (*MGH, Auct. Ant.*,
   IV, 1, p. 326).
50 Bede, ibid., 12 lines from end; Venantius, *Carmina* viii. 3. 330 (*Auct. Ant.*,
   IV, 1, p. 190).
51 See P. Riché, 'La Magie à l'époque carolingienne', *Académie des Inscriptions et Belles-Lettres, comptes rendus* (Paris 1973), pp. 127–38.
52 *HE* iii. 11.
53 *H.F.*, VII, 44, ed. Krusch and Levison, p. 364.
54 Luke 8:30. Ed. Hurst, *CCSL* cxx, 184.
55 Bede to Albinus, *HE* I, p. 3.
56 *HE* v. 19.
57 *Two Lives of St Cuthbert* (Cambridge, 1940), pp. 11–12.
58 It should be noted that Bede also used Paulinus of Périgueux on St. Martin.
59 As Levison pointed out, 'Bede as Historian', *BLTW*, p. 142; *Aus Rhein
   u. Fränk. Früh.*, p. 375.
60 'Northumbria and the Book of Kells', *ASE* i (1972), pp. 219–46.
61 H. Moonen, *Eddius Stephanus, Het Leven van Sint Wilfrid* (1946), pp. 12–
   16.
62 I agree with James Campbell, 'The first century of Christianity in England', *Ampleforth Journal*, lxxvi (1971), pp. 16 ff., that this is one of the
   respects in which Bede's reticence is misleading.
63 A basic instrument for this work is now K. H. Krüger, *Königsgrabkirchen
   der Franken, Angelsachsen und Langobarden bis zur Mitte des 8. Jahrhun-
   derts*, Münstersche Mittelalter-Schriften 4 (Munich 1971).
64 In preparing this paper I have been conscious of the debt I owe to my
   research pupils for discussion of this or related matters, in particular to Mr.
   Patrick Wormald, Mr. Alfred Smyth, Miss Clare Stancliffe and Mr. Alan
   Thacker; and I thank them.

VI

Gregory of Tours and Bede: their views on the personal qualities of kings[1][*]

What follows is not an investigation of the textual relationship of Bede and Gregory of Tours, though whether Bede used Gregory, and at what stage, is worth some thought. Wilhelm Levison drew attention[2] to certain common features in their histories, and in particular noted that in Bede's *Liber Retractationis in Actus Apostolorum* (chap. 28, 8) we have a clear use of Gregory, but then once only: *meminit huius morbi et Gregorius in libro historiarum suarum quinto*, which passage he then cites.[3] But the fact of the matter is that the substance of Gregory's history would have been largely irrelevant to Bede at whatever stage he had met it.

Gregory and Bede, different as they are in many respects, belong to the historiographical genre of Cassiodorus and Jordanes, Isidore, Fredegar and Paul the Deacon. They tell some part of the story of the taking-over of the western Roman provinces by Germanic tribes, and of the settling-down of those tribes in a Christian, romanizing milieu. For all their idiosyncrasies, they have that in common which separates them from the last pagan, classical historians (notably Ammianus Marcellinus) and, but less distinctively, from the first great ecclesiastical historian, Eusebius, and his immediate followers. We cannot call them ancient historians, and only in a particular sense are they ecclesiastical historians. What they really are is medieval historians, the first of their kind. To borrow a convenient legal term, they write Vulgar history, post-classical history: Latin, Catholic, apologetic, provincial. They at once witness to and, in a way, help to create, the early Middle Ages. They write history for a new society. We use them so often, because we must, as storehouses

* References for this chapter start on p. 111.

of information that we forget that they are historians; they controlled the information available to them, put it in a way that suited them, and left us a picture of their past that is an artefact. This could be shown over a wide field, but here I shall consider one question only in relation to Gregory and Bede—namely, their approach as historians to the personal qualifications of kings, as these emerge in their writings; for kings, however real, are also artefacts, and very important artefacts, by the time their deeds and characteristics have been winnowed and sorted and committed to a few lines of writing.

Gregory's history is chiefly concerned with quite recent events. Book I goes from the Creation to the year 397 (the death of St. Martin) and Book II to 511 (the death of Clovis). Gregory's Clovis is thus depicted by one who could have talked with those who remembered the great barbarian in his heyday; in fact, Clovis died not more than twenty-eight years before Gregory's own birth. Of the remaining eight Books, Book III falls partly within Gregory's lifetime, and the other seven entirely so. Books V to X span a mere fifteen years, all told. Predominantly, then, he is dealing with recent events and is writing contemporary history.[4] Is it skill or chance that imparts perspective and distance to happenings that crowd so close upon each other? Does Clovis speak to us from a remote past in Gregory's pages because only his heroic outline had survived or because that was all that the historian required of him?

In respect of kings, however, Gregory's history begins much earlier than Clovis, with the rulers of Israel and Pilate, Herod and Nero. Essentially they are copy-book stuff, yet also they serve as prototypes of a kind of king that Gregory had had dealings with and desired to categorize. None of them was like Solomon who, Gregory reminds us, asked for wisdom. Such are the creatures of his first Book. In Book II he bends his mind to more modern kings. In its prologue we are told that Eusebius, Severus and Jerome in their chronicles, and also Orosius, had woven together the wars of kings with the wonderful tales of martyrs; and he proposes to go on in the same way.[5] It is far from certain how much of these writers was known to Gregory at first hand. Sometimes one has the impression that he is using a historical compendium, though on the other hand it seems not improbable that Tours or Clermont would have had a manuscript of Orosius at least.[6] Through Orosius or directly, he has imbibed something significant from Eusebius and allows it to

affect his historical thinking. To Eusebius in the last resort we must
surely attribute his grip on the idea of a universal history reduced to
a synchronistic history of empires and kingdoms as instruments of
providence and points of historical convergence.[7] St. Augustine's
approach had been rather different. *Bella regum*, within this
framework, struck Gregory as a distinct strand of history, an activity
characteristic of kings. Such wars were neither good nor bad in
themselves, however; they could be either, depending on their
objectives. Gregory liked peace within the kin but was less certain
than Bede that absence of war was sometimes a good in itself that
should cost a king no loss of dignity. Gregory's kings do not often
stop fighting, though the reality may have been rather different:
they were, after all, heirs in a small way to the Vicars and Governors
of Roman Gaul. The point understandably escaped Einhard in his
famous description[8] of the last Merovingians trundling round their
estates in their ox-waggons, for he could not see behind them to
the Gallo-Roman Governors doing their rounds in the *angariae* of
the *cursus clabularis*, the imperial slow-post; but it also, less excus-
ably, escaped Gregory. The fighting and feuding of his kings was
the side of their activity that he most often found himself describing,
and in this they diverged furthest from the standards he had set
himself for kings. In his long passage[9] on the origins of Frankish
kingship, based on the now-lost texts of Frigeridus and Sulpicius
Alexander, he takes us into his workshop; we can watch him weighing up the sources as he gropes for firm ground: *cum autem eos
regales vocet, nescimus utrum reges fuerint an in vices tenuerunt
regnum . . . Iterum, hic, relictis tam ducibus quam regalibus, aperte
Francos regem habere designat, huiusque nomen praetermissum.*
He wanted to know what the earliest kings were like for an excellent reason: they were associated in his mind with the kings that he
himself knew. Between the two, ancient and modern, he placed his
starkly majestic portrait of Clovis. It is a portrait that cannot quite
be explained as the tradition of Merovingian court-saga, or as that
of the people. Gregory's Clovis stems from the Church. He is the
protégé of St. Remigius, the conqueror under St. Martin's banner,
the Merovingian who captured for his dynasty the great Gallic cultus
initiated in the pages of Sulpicius Severus, the ruler whose success
was a function of his dependence upon bishops. He is the Novus
Constantinus,[10] the convert-king *par excellence*; he is neither admin-
istrator nor lawgiver, and his characteristics, insofar as Gregory

bothers with them at all, owe as much to literature as to reality. To take an example, the king's cunning, his *dolus*, is to some extent influenced by Gregory's biblical reading; and Louis Halphen[11] was right to draw attention to the effect on Gregory of such a story as that of Ehud in the Book of Judges,[12] with its circumstantial account of how the left-hander slew the Moabite king in his summer-parlour with a two-edged dagger. Gregory does more than collect scattered records of Clovis' progress against dynastic and heretical opposition; he gives these records proportion and perspective within a narrative, and does so because of the potential significance of Clovis to the sixth century. Clovis had made war upon the Arians at uncertain dates and for mixed reasons; this much is certain; but we do not know that anyone before Gregory, in the prologue to his third Book, had directly associated the conquest of the heretics with the extension of Frankish power to southern Gaul. At best, Gregory's picture was an over-simplification; but without it his subsequent development of Merovingian kingship would be hard indeed to understand.

Much scholarship has been devoted to Gregory: to his text, his language, his sources, his reliability.[13] It is another matter when one comes to consider his position as historian, which still remains largely unexplored. One recent scholar, indeed, Signor Gustavo Vinay, has given thought to it.[14] His conclusion is that Gregory wrote to please himself, without didactic purpose, and was content to let his reasons for writing history develop while he wrote; how they developed may be seen, according to Vinay, in the revision of the first six Books, when he discarded much hagiographical and autobiographical detail in favour of more of the story of the Frankish kings. When Gregory remarks, after a diversion, that he will return to history,[15] this is the history he means. Vinay further claims that what fascinates Gregory is the frankishness of the Franks—the *feretas gentium*, with its special aspect, *furor regum*. That ferocity, yoked to Catholicism, could become a saving political force in Gaul; the Arians, because they were Arians, were to be seen as weak, vacillating, unmartial; the Franks were different, and so also their kings. Only in the Eastern emperors does Gregory allow regal quality comparable to that of the Merovingians at their best.[16] Without condoning Frankish standards of violence, Gregory could see some use for them. What had to be done was to harness the new kings to the purposes of a God who was the defender of priests, the judge of persecutors, the guardian of shrines and the avenger of blood. Gregory's God acts as a national God in particular and contingent cases; he is not the vigilant Providence of the true Middle Ages.

Signor Vinay's interpretation of Gregory's historical outlook is perhaps too neat, and cannot always be sustained in detail; but it goes some way towards explaining why the *bella civilia* of his own day shocked Gregory so much: they diverted *strenuitas*, energy, into fruitless channels. He had no objection in principle to kings shedding blood, so long as it was the right blood. If it was the wrong blood, then kings were activated by whim; they were behaving as if they were ordinary people, whose offices had never been explained to them by bishops.

This is exemplified in the case of King Chilperic and Fredegundis, his queen. The couple had certain personal advantages—one would hesitate to call them virtues: her loyalty as a wife was passionate and she was a devoted mother when she chose to be; he was clearly intelligent, sometimes capable of restraint, not without judgement and not without excuse, for he was a man of sorrows.[17] Gregory, however, was not concerned with the totality of their characters but with their worthlessness as exemplars, and this quite apart from his strong private reasons for disliking them. Summing up Chilperic, he forgets his good points and reverts to his own picture of Nero and Herod.[18] Wrathful and greedy, Chilperic showed that he was worthless first by engaging in feuds that destroyed the peace of his family, just as a lesser man might have done.[19] Worse than this, he turned on the bishops, accusing them of robbing him of his power and his honour. The famous passage in Book VI, chapter 46, reads as follows:

Sacerdotes Domini assiduae blasphemabat, nec aliunde magis, dum secricius esset, exercebat ridicola vel iocos quam de ecclesiarum episcopis. Illum ferebat levem, alium superbum, illum habundantem, istum luxoriosum; illum adserebat elatum, hunc tumidum, nullum plus odio quam eclesias habens. Aiebat enim plerumque: 'Ecce pauper remansit fiscus noster, ecce divitiae nostrae ad eclesias sunt translatae; nulli penitus nisi soli episcopi regnant; periet honor noster et translatus est ad episcopus civitatum.' Haec agens, adsiduae testamenta, quae in eclesias conscripta erant, plerumque disrupit ipsasque patris sui praeceptiones, potans, quod non remanerit qui voluntatem servaret, saepe calcavit. Iam de libidine atque luxoria non potest repperire in cogitatione, quod non perpetrasset in opere, novaquae semper ad ledendum populum ingenia perquaerebat . . . Nullum umquam pure dilexit, a nullo dilectus est, . . .

One observes the writer's main point: Chilperic hated bishops; but there is also a subsidiary point: personal cruelty should have no part in a kingly disposition. Gregory has assimilated something of the Church's teaching on the need for gentleness towards subjects. He is going somewhat beyond the usual range of royal qualities, as he ascribes them, for example, to King Theudebert: *magnum se atque in omni bonitate praecipuum reddidit. Erat enim regnum cum iustitia regens, sacerdotes venerans, pauperes relevans et multa multis beneficia pia ac dulcissima accomodans voluntate.*[20] The historian has moved nearer the position of Pope Gregory the Great, so clearly stated in the papal correspondence. We may instance the pope's letter to King Reccared:[21] a king's personal life should be an example to his subjects, he must be well-disposed towards them and conceal his naked power when he can. As so often with Pope Gregory, he is really developing a biblical theme and applying it to a new political situation. Others of his generation thought in something of the same way, if with less intensity. For his part, Gregory of Tours saw in Chilperic a king whose private life was unkingly, a king who did not bend heroic virtues to the service of a *regnum christianum* as the Church understood it. His career, then, must read as a terrible warning; and what were venial shortcomings in other men could not be overlooked in him.

A king at least as well known to Gregory was Guntram, the uncle-figure of the Merovingians; a shrewd man motivated by a strong sense of family-tradition. The last of Gregory's many pictures of Guntram is at the baptism of his nephew, Chlotar II, when he recalls the greatness of that Novus David, the first Chlotar,[22] who had died proclaiming God the greater king.[23] For Gregory this baptism was significant because kingship and kinship were still closely linked. Gregory's Guntram is an improvement on Chilperic, so much so that he was acknowledged to have a magic about him that made common folk believe in his thaumaturgical power.[24] Gregory believed in it, too. In an emergency, says Gregory, Guntram could behave almost like a bishop: *ut iam tunc non rex tantum sed etiam sacerdus Domini putaretur*.[25] Even so, he did not always listen to his bishops, and his authority was not always at their disposal for the asking. The historian strongly approved his dedication to his family and noted his generosity to the Church; he did not sell bishoprics;[26] he was kind and merciful,[27] tolerant[28] and affable[29] and charitable.[30] All in all, Gregory depicts Guntram as he knew him, his good personal qualities being also good kingly qualities. Certainly he lacked the Catholic heroism of Clovis, but on the other hand Gregory endowed him with character. Guntram was no hero, but he comes as near as any of Gregory's kings to his idea of a good king in action. He is no more a simple Germanic chieftain than was his brother Chilperic or any other of the early Merovingians. Gregory looks at them from what was special to the politics of his own day: a permanent royal relationship with a Catholic hierarchy in a territorialized society that was no longer Roman or German. He gives shape to what he sees in the form of history. Moreover, it is a kind of history specially adapted to his purpose. It is nearly, but not quite, 'history of salvation',[31] in the tradition of Eusebius and Orosius; in many respects its models are biblical. The numerous anecdotes, for example, seem to be directly biblical in inspiration. It was in the Bible rather than in Eusebius that Gregory found his models for discursive anecdotes like that of the feud of Sichar and Chramnesind,[32] to which Erich Auerbach devoted some valuable pages.[33] Yet Auerbach was unable to account at all satisfactorily for the dominant role of anecdote in Gregory's history. Nor is it quite enough to say, as does a recent American writer, that he felt an urge 'to record graphically the human, passionate lives of the barbarian Franks',[34] for ever at each other's throats. It is a bishop who writes. He comes within measurable distance, whether consciously I cannot be sure, of the teaching tradition of Caesarius of Arles. Like Gregory the Great,[35] if in a humbler way, he has a direct pastoral care; his concern is with what actually happens because of this. He writes as a man who means to be heard and understood. His style, like his material, reflects his purpose. He is at one with St. Augustine: Christian literary style must match its subject.[36] An anecdote like that of Sichar and Chramnesind, vivid and confused, must be explained within this framework. Auerbach comments: 'from his activity in the pursuit of his duties [Gregory] acquires his ability to observe and the desire to write down what he observes'.[37] But observation and desire may not be thus connected; there may be more to it than that: Gregory has designed a history-book that places his people in a direct biblical succession. In something of the same way, Gregory the Great's *Dialogues* picture the holy men of contemporary Italy as modern heirs of the saints of the Bible and of the Early Church, heirs protected by the same God and in the same way. Gregory of Tours' anecdotes, considered as a whole, place the Franks in a present-day equivalent of the milieu of the Chosen People. They make it easier to picture the field in which God actually works, and do not signify the historian's innocent love of human drama nor any obsession with a brutalized society. His plan was to set his account of royal salvation through God against a background of ordinary men's actions and motives as they really are without God. This was a pastoral aim. In a world of plague and portent and greed, everyday perfidy and duplicity meet their own punishment at God's hands or at man's. Kings are not exempt from the temptations of their subjects. Indeed, their capacity for evil, as also for good, is often greater. King Guntram was still alive at the time of Gregory's death.

Bede was a better-equipped historian than Gregory, and an abler man. This will make some difference. But his intentions were not quite the same as Gregory's. These are reflected in the proportions of their histories. Bede gives more space to the distant past, less to contemporary events; more to explaining how the present came about, and none at all to self-justification (an important motive in Gregory's writing). Something of the difference may be revealed in their titles, whether or not they chose them for themselves: Bede's is an ecclesiastical history of the English people in the true Eusebian sense, whereas Gregory's is simply *libri historiarum*. What is more, Bede's intellectual preparation as historian differed from Gregory's in at least three important respects. In the first place, he was deeply influenced by the Celtic missionaries he had known and read about; by their personal saintliness but also by their relationship with the kings under whom they worked and the view this relationship implied of the role of kings in a Christian society. Secondly, he was a connoisseur of Gildas' *Historia Brittonum*.[38] From Gildas he derived not only the source-material he acknowledges but also a clearer conception of a nation's destiny under God than from any source other than the Bible. Gildas had correlated national prosperity with salvation and national disaster with sin: it was for the historian to

set this forth. Gildas' national heroes have an educative role as well
as a saving one; and so do Bede's. Work has still to be done on the
indebtedness of Bede to Gildas; the debt is certainly there. Meanwhile, there is a third respect in which Bede differs from Gregory
of Tours: Bede knew the teaching of Gregory the Great, and among
much else had read the *Liber Regulae Pastoralis*[39]—that most sensitive investigation of the nature of rule, specifically of a bishop but
in fact of rule of any kind. In consequence, Bede has a view of the
moral basis of rule and the equipment necessary for its exercise that
affected the way he looked at kings. Their aims could no longer be
as simple as those of the kings Gregory of Tours had described;
they could not be content with fighting the right enemies and
endowing the right churches, though they could not neglect these,
either. The truth was, kings were not always fighting or endowing,
and the historian could not pretend that they were.

Whereas Gregory placed his material about kings in a large
number of disorderly vignettes, stories of action from which we must
infer what we can about his ideas of kingship, Bede's king-stories
are fewer and their role in his history clearer and more consistent.
It does not follow from this that Gregory in his volubility poured
out all that he knew about his kings whereas Bede's masterly terse-
ness hides much that he might have said. Both writers withheld
dangerous material. Bede did not find his material easy to come by.
He explains carefully the main sources of his regional information:
Bishop Daniel of Winchester for the West and South Saxons, the
monks of Lastingham for the Mercians and East Saxons, Abbot Esi
in part for the East Angles, Cunebert for Lindsey. His Northumbrian sources he could not particularize.[40] His debt to Canterbury,
however, is the one he chooses to emphasize. It is a debt so dominant
that it might be profitable to inquire how far his picture of the
English heptarchy as a whole is affected by it. To some extent, even
his own country, Northumbria, and perhaps its great bishop,
Wilfrid, are seen in Canterbury's perspective.[41] Bede's history owes
most of all to a Canterbury monk, Albinus, *ad quam me scribendam
iamdudum instigaveras.* The inducement to write about the emer-
gence of Anglo-Saxon kingship under the guidance of the Church
of Rome, as well as the furnishing of much material to that end, was
provided by Canterbury. Some allowance should therefore be made
for the possibility that the structure of Bede's history may be affected
by Canterbury's wish to bring history to the service of present needs.

Bede's history has what Gregory's never had: royal approval. In his prefatory letter addressed to King Ceolwulf of Northumbria, Bede says that the king had already seen and approved a draft of the history; he now sends it to him again to be transcribed and read at leisure. He does not thank the king for any information or help received. On the contrary, he hopes that the king will profit from what he will learn here, and will see that his subjects also profit from the deeds and words of former men of renown.[42] Perhaps Bede was hoping that his history would serve the royal court as a Christian counterpart to the traditional barbarian songs. His hymn in honour of Queen Aethelthryth—Book IV, 20—suggests a modest challenge to Virgil: *Bella Maro resonet, nos pacis dona canamus.* Gregory also had had some awareness of epic: he did not, he said, withhold permission for his history to be put into verse: *te scribere versu non abnuo.*[43] We thus have this assurance about Bede's kings: that King Ceolwulf found them acceptable and that the Church of Canterbury had some notion of how Bede would treat them. Canterbury could trust Bede: he was the soul of discretion. This makes these kings and their setting 'official' in a sense that Gregory's never were.

There is no Clovis in Bede's history, or in England's; but there are two among his Anglo-Saxon kings who are something like founding fathers: Aethelberht of Kent and Edwin of Northumbria. Both were remoter than Clovis was from the time of the migration of their kindred, and, unlike Clovis, neither, so far as we know, had inherited anything significant of Roman provincial tradition in government. A similarity with Clovis comes, however, with their conversion; and it was because of their conversion that they bulked at all large in the historical tradition transmitted by the Church through Bede. While still a pagan, Aethelberht had made himself overlord of the southern English kings at least. He must, then, have been a warrior; but Bede does not dwell on this, not because Aethelberht's conquests were pagan—he was rather proud of the pagan Aethelfrith's victories over the British[44]—but because they were irrelevant. It was not through conquest that Aethelberht achieved a new kind of kingship. Nor was it through marriage into the house of Clovis.[45] It was by and through the Church of Rome. Augustine, landing in Kent, tells Aethelberht that he comes from Rome with a joyful message of a kingdom that would never end;[46] Pope Gregory writes to assure the new convert that a king's gifts are from God, who will render his fame more glorious to posterity; and he

H

cites the example of Constantine.[47] Help Augustine, he exhorts, and Augustine will help you with God: *quaeque vos ammonet, libenter audite, devote peragite, studiose in memoria reservate; quia, si vos eum in eo quod pro omnipotente Deo loquitur, auditis, isdem omnipotens Deus hunc pro vobis exorantem celerius exaudit.*[48] Do not, he urges, be apprehensive when you think you see the approaching signs of Domesday: they are not for you. Two other elements in Bede's picture are related to this Roman takeover. Aethelberht is the first lawgiver of his people, *iuxta exempla Romanorum*, albeit in the vernacular.[49] These laws happen to survive in reasonable shape in the *Textus Roffensis*.[50] But for this happy accident, however, we should only know from Bede that they had existed and that they had settled the compensation due to the Church for robbery: this was all that in his judgement, and perhaps in Canterbury's, was worth knowing about them in an historical setting. The other element is the burial of Aethelberht and his successors in the Church of St. Peter and St. Paul at Canterbury—his own foundation—near the archbishops.[51] Royal families should lie inside churches, and no longer in windswept burial-mounds. Here, then, is Bede's Aethelberht: a warrior of a well-established dynasty whose special distinction it was to have brought stability to his house, fame to his *gens* and salvation to himself by throwing in his lot with the Church.[52] The kingdom of Kent becomes a microcosm of the kingdom of heaven, at least for sixteen years. The apostasy of his successors brings with it God's inevitable punishment—loss of earthly rule.[53]

Much of this pattern is discernible in the career of Bede's King Edwin of Northumbria: again the warrior, first pagan, then Christian; again, the promise of increase of power in return for conversion and as an earnest of the kingdom of heaven.[54] Indeed, Edwin only promises to accept Christianity if God grants him victory over his enemy, King Cwichelm of Wessex: *si vitam sibi et victoriam donaret pugnanti adversus regem.*[55] 'Such examples', it has been said, 'possess more than just an objective, historical importance as evidence of the progress of [conversion], for they also have a subjective value in telling us something of Bede's own attitudes to the events which he is reporting'.[56] It is not too fanciful to contrast the attitude, in the fourth century, of Bishop Wulfila, who according to Philostorgius,[57] had declined to translate the Books of Kings because 'the Gothic tribes were especially fond of war and were in more need of restraints to check their military passions than of spurs

to urge them on to deeds of war'.[58] We have come a long way from
Wulfila to Bede, who showed no reluctance to comment on the
same Books.[59] Bede gives us—from Canterbury—Pope Boniface IV's
letter to Edwin, advising him that God is the disposer of kingdoms,
and God alone the rewarder of kings;[60] St. Peter will intervene on
behalf of the king and his queen.[61] Edwin's counsellors are won over
to Christianity because they see no material gain from paganism;
that is the point of Bede's story of the conversion of Coifi, the high-
priest.[62] On the other hand, they do see a chance of something for
the future in Christianity: this is the point of the story of the spar-
row.[63] God, then, saves Edwin from his enemies and gives him his
kingdom, and Bede is content to be rather loose with chronology in
the manner in which he associates the conquest with the conversion.
God does even more: he shows the way to material prosperity and
national prestige, almost as if we were back with the children of
Israel in the Books of Kings, when *ecclesia* and *gens* were one.
Edwin's reign—and this is a consequence to Bede—is peaceful and
dignified:[64]

> *Tanta autem eo tempore pax in Brittania, quaquaversum im-*
> *perium regis Aeduini pervenerat, fuisse perhibetur, ut, sicut usque*
> *hodie in proverbio dicitur, etiam si mulier una cum recens nato*
> *parvulo vellet totam perambulare insulam a mari ad mare, nullo*
> *se ledente valeret . . . Tantum vero in regno excellentiae habuit, ut*
> *non solum in pugna ante illum vexilla gestarentur, sed et tempore*
> *pacis equitantem inter civitates sive villas aut provincias suas cum*
> *ministris, semper antecedere signifer consuesset.*

Though Edwin's reign ends in blood, the king's head is taken to
York and later deposited in St. Peter's Church there.[65] It was a
genuine royal English relic. As Bede saw it, Edwin had gone some
way towards acting on Pope Honorius' letter to him (again transmitted from Canterbury): 'your conduct as king', the pope had
written, 'is based on the knowledge you have obtained of God';
and he proceeds to recommend a study of the writings of Pope
Gregory the Great, *praedicatoris igitur vestri . . . frequenter lectione*
occupati.[66] King Alfred was later to authorize the translation of
Bede's History, and perhaps because of Bede's words there he also
translated Gregory's *Cura pastoralis*. Edwin and Aethelberht were
sketches of what Bede understood as successful kings; and as such,

it may be, they were understood by Bede's royal students among the Anglo-Saxons.

But what, for Bede, were the consequences of a more thorough-going submission to the Church? We have them in two of his kings: Oswald and Oswini, both of Northumbria. Lawgiving, like Aethel-berht's, and ordered prosperity, like Edwin's, play no part in his account of these later careers. What has come to matter now is simply their sense of being God's agents as this is exhibited in their personal saintliness. Oswald is the beloved of God, affable and generous,[67] pious and humble.[68] Piety and humility are virtues common to all Christians and not peculiar to kings; but to Bede they seemed specifically royal, after Oswald. Piety and humility make a king more kingly; Bede requires us to accept that Oswald's piety brought with it an increase in rule,[69] and he sees no contra-diction in the king's violent end at the battle of Maserfelth, *pro patria dimicans*;[70] and the real causes of the spasmodic warfare be-tween Northumbria, Mercia and the northern Welsh, in which Maserfelth was an incident, remain obscure in the *Historia Eccles-iastica*. Miracles, then and later, were performed at the spot where Oswald set up his cross before his last battle.[71] The monks of Hex-ham commemorated him;[72] his body lay in the church at Bardney, his gold and purple banner erect above his tomb;[73] his hand and arm lay unwithered in their reliquary at Bamburgh. There must have been more than Bede records to account for Oswald's success as king, but the historian is content with his saintly warrior who falls in battle against the enemy of his people and his religion, at whose shrines miracles are reported frequently to be performed. The king even stoops down from heaven on the anniversary of his own death to summon an oblate-boy, stricken with plague, to join him in bliss.[74] The power of a saintly king does not cease with his death; he continues to interest himself in his people.

The same quality of humility characterizes King Oswini; humility coupled with a traditional royal virtue with a fresh emphasis— bounty. In Bede's extraordinary tale[75] of Oswini's gift of a horse to Bishop Aidan, which Aidan then gave to a beggar, the king's swift anger is followed by capitulation: *numquam, inquit, deinceps aliquid loquar de hoc aut iudicabo quid vel quantum de pecunia nostra filiis Dei tribuas*; and by Aidan's sorrowful reflection, *num-quam enim ante haec vidi humilem regem. Undé animadverto illum citius ex hac vita rapiendum; non enim digna est haec gens talem habere rectorem.* Soon, in fact, the king did die. But the point had been made: the gifts of a good king will be lavished as his bishop chooses and not otherwise; he will owe to his bishop neither more nor less than obedience. The political consequences could have been startling.[76]

Bede's sketches of other kings and queens reinforce, if incidentally, the substance of these ideas: kings punished for apostasy or weakness; kings rewarded for founding churches and religious houses; kings who won great Christian victories; kings who earned their place in the kingdom of heaven. When King Oswiu presided at the synod of Whitby,[77] what in Bede's account settled the disciplinary issue between Roman and Celtic usages on that occasion was not the exact presentation of a case nor any rational argument but the realization by Oswiu himself of the role of St Peter. His words as Bede gives them are: *et ego vobis dico, quia hic est ostiarius ille, cui ego contradicere nolo; sed, in quanto novi vel valeo, huius cupio in omnibus oboedire statutis; ne forte, me adveniente ad fores regni caelorum, non sit qui reseret, averso illo, qui claves tenere probatur.* Oswiu was seeing a literal kingdom of heaven, and so was Bede. (St. Peter armed with a formidable key appears on the coffin of St. Cuthbert, which is contemporary Northumbrian work).[78] Through St. Peter Rome was mistress of kings, because by her alone could they gain access to the kingdom of heaven, at once their exemplar and reward. It is not, then, surprising to find that the kings for whom Bede has a special word of approval were those who resigned, or planned to resign, their temporal power to end their days as pilgrims or monks. We may instance Sigeberht of the East Anglians,[79] the Northumbrian Oswiu,[80] Sebbi of the East Saxons,[81] Cadwalla and Ine of the West Saxons,[82] Cenred of the Mercians,[83] Offa of the East Saxons[84] and Ethelred of the Mercians.[85] Some, though not all, of these kings resigned after long reigns; but however long they reigned it can hardly be supposed that such resignations made in general for political stability. Bede, for his part, sees the matter from another angle. He reports that the young king Offa of Essex was missed by his people when he retired to Rome—*iuvenis amantissimae aetatis et venustatis, totaeque suae genti ad tenenda servandaque regni sceptra exoptatissimus.*[86] It seemed a pity that he should have gone, but he had only done his kingly duty, as had others before him. Thus, Bede presents to King Ceolwulf a picture of kingship in England that lays some stress on royal pilgrimages to Rome; it can hardly be accidental. As he looked about him, Bede found little comfort in the present: his pilgrim-kings do not contribute to the discomfort but rather show a way out of it. The England of his last days was no longer the happy land of Archbishop Theodore and Abbot Hadrian, when

> *fortissimos Christianosque habentes reges cunctis barbaris nationibus essent terrori, et omnium vota ad nuper audita caelestis regni gaudia penderent, et quicumque lectionibus sacris cuperent erudiri, haberent in promtu magistros, qui docerent.*[87]

In sum, the descriptions of kings we meet in Gregory and Bede, though based on authentic information, were never meant to constitute a careful synthesis of all that was knowable about them; they are literary creations, one effect of which would be to make readers and hearers consider the problems of kingship as they met it in the light of the past. The two historians approach their kings in a different spirit; and this difference may have less to do with the contrast between the turbulent Merovingian world of about 600 and the quieter times of Bede's England about 700—which in any case has been over-emphasized—than with the literary background of the two, and more especially with the influence upon Bede of the pastoral teaching of Gregory the Great and of the Celtic missionaries. If the famous letter of Abbot Ceolfrith to King Naitan is indeed from Bede's pen,[88] then we possess explicit approval by the historian of the Lactantian statement of the role of the Catholic king; but in any case, it is not likely that Bede would have thought differently:

> *Nam et vere omnino dixit quidam saecularium scriptorum, quia felicissimo mundus statu ageretur, si vel reges philosopharentur, vel regnarent philosophi. Quod si de philosophia huius mundi vere intellegere, de statu huius mundi merito deligere potuit homo huius mundi; quanto magis civibus patriae caelestis in hoc mundo peregrinantibus optandum est, et totis animi viribus supplicandum, ut, quo plus in mundo quique valent, eo amplius eius, qui super omnia est, Iudicis mandatis auscultare contendant, atque ad haec observanda secum eos quoque, qui sibi commissi sunt, exemplis simul et auctoritate instituant?*

Pope Gregory's conception of earthly rule as a professional occupation, to which training and anxious thought should be given, are reflected in Bede. He seems to want his kings to rule their subjects in the spirit in which the pope meant his bishops to rule their flocks. It can go even deeper than this, for a ruler may achieve that degree of spiritual success that would justify him in laying down his heavy responsibilities and fulfilling his own salvation alone, as a pilgrim or monk. Gregory of Tours was content with less, though his general disposition was not unlike. Both, certainly, had some awareness that what they wrote about kings, and how they wrote it, could influence the important folk who pondered their words.

NOTES

1 *Frühmittelalterliche Studien*, vol. 2 (1968), 31–44. This paper, originally composed for an Anglo-French conference at Dijon in 1965, was recast for delivery to the historical seminars of several German universities in the course of a tour undertaken for the British Council in the summer of 1967. I am grateful to my French and German colleagues for much helpful comment.

2 W. Levison, 'Bede as Historian' (*Aus Rheinischer und Fränkischer Frühzeit*, 1948), 366.

3 *Expositio Actuum Apostolorum et Retractatio* (ed. M. L. W. Laistner, 1939) 145–6. The same chapter (V, 24) of Gregory's History—I cite the Monumenta text of Krusch and Levison (*SS rer. Merov.* I²), hereafter abbreviated as 'Hist.'—with its *haec prodigia gravissima lues est subsecuta*, may account for Bede's famous *gravissima Saracenorum lues* in *Historia Ecclesiastica Gentis Anglorum* (hereafter 'H. E.') which I cite from the edition of Charles Plummer (1896), that of Colgrave and Mynors having appeared subsequently. On this *lues* see D. H. Wright's important review of P. Hunter Blair's edition of the Moore Manuscript of H. E. (*Anglia* 82, 1964, 114).

4 Isidore would have agreed that this was the proper business of the historian. See his definitions *de historia*, *de primis auctoribus historiarum*, *de utilitate historiae* and *de generibus historiae* in *Etymologiae* I, 41–4, ed. W. M. Lindsay (1911). These would have been known to Bede, to whom the *Etymologiae* were available (see M. L. W. Laistner, *The Intellectual Heritage of the Early Middle Ages* (1957), 117–49) though not of course to Gregory.

5 Hist. II, prol.

6 Unless my count is wrong, ten manuscripts or fragments of the *Historiae adversum Paganos* appear in E. A. Lowe's *Codices Latini Antiquiores*, and all these are ascribed to the eighth or ninth centuries with the exception of no. 298 in C. L. A. II, which is a sixth-century manuscript, perhaps Ravennese (now Florence, Laurenziana LXV. I). No. 1072 in C. L. A. VIII, excerpts of the late eighth century (now Breslau, Stadtbibl. Rehd. 107) was 'written probably at Tours', but there is no way of telling whether they were taken from a manuscript that had long been at Tours.

7 For this, and other interesting matter which I have used for this paper, see Robert W. Hanning, *The Vision of History in Early Britain* (1966), 68 ff.

8 *Vita Karoli Magni*, chap. 1 (ed. O. Holder-Egger, 1911).

9 Hist. II, 9.

10 See the valuable study of E. Ewig, 'Das Bild Constantins d. Gr. im frühen Mittelalter' (*Hist. Jahrb.* 75, 1956).

11 L. Halphen, 'Grégoire de Tours, historien de Clovis' (*Mélanges ... Ferdinand Lot*, 1925), 242.

12 Judges III: 15–26.

13 See the bibliography in Wattenbach-Levison, *Deutschlands Geschichtsquellen im Mittelalter* 1, 99–108.

14 G. Vinay, *San Gregorio di Tours* (1940).

15 Hist. IV, 38.

16 For example, the Emperor Tiberius (Hist. IV, 40; V. 19; VI, 30).

17 Hist. VI, 34.

18 Hist. VI, 46.

19 Compare Bede's picture of King Sigbert of Essex, who died because of his penchant for forgiving feuds (H. E. III, 22).

20 Hist. III, 25.

21 *Gregorii I Papae Registrum Epistolarum*, ed. Ewald and Hartmann (1891), IX, 228.

22 Hist. X, 28 and IV, 20.

23 Hist. IV, 21.

24 Hist. IX, 21.

25 Hist. IX, 21.

26 Hist. VI, 39.

27 Hist. VI, 36.

28 Hist. VII, 15.

29 Hist. VIII, 1.

30 Hist. IX, 21.

31 See Hanning (cf. n. 7) 69.

32 Hist. VII, 47 and IX, 19.

33 E. Auerbach, *Mimesis* (1946) chap. 4.

34 Hanning, 97.

35 E. Auerbach, *Literary Language and its Public* (English trans. 1965) 87 ff. draws attention to the literary similarities of the three writers.

36 *Et tamen cum doctor iste debeat rerum dictor esse magnarum, non semper eas debet granditer dicere, sed submisse, cum aliquid docetur*, and what follows (*De Doctrina Christiana*, IV, 19).

37 Auerbach, *Mimesis* (English trans.) 80.

38 Hanning draws attention to this point.

39 *Alium quoque librum conposuit egregium, qui vocatur Pastoralis, in quo manifesta luce patefecit, quales ad ecclesiae regimen adsumi, qualiter ipsi rectores vivere, qua discretione singulas quasque audientium instruere personas, et quanta consideratione propriam cotidie debeant fragilitatem pensare* (H. E. II, 1).

40 H. E., pref.

41 This point is developed by Miss Marion Gibbs in an unpublished article which she has permitted me to read.

42 There is no good reason for associating any extant manuscript of the Historia Ecclesiastica with the royal Northumbrian court, but there can be no doubt that history, like law, was not slow to find patrons in royal courts. Professor Bernard Bischoff informs me that he has the impression that some manuscripts of historical writings could be directly associated with the interests of Germanic kings.

43 Hist. X, 18.

44 H. E. I, 34.

45 There are, however, similarities between the conversion of Clovis and that of Aethelberht that point to the possibility that the Church of Canterbury might have composed its record of the latter's conversion with the former's in mind: a copy of Gregory's history at Canterbury in the seventh century is at least as likely as one at Jarrow.

46 H. E. I, 25.

47 H. E. I, 32. Papal letters to English rulers were an additional channel through which Bede absorbed Gregorian ideas about Christian rule.

48 H. E. I, 32.

49 H. E. II, 5.

50 Ed. Peter Sawyer, *Early English Manuscripts in Facsimile*, vols. VII and XI.

51 H. E. I, 33.

52 H. E. II, 5.

53 H. E. II, 5.

54 H. E. II, 9.

55 H. E. II, 9. Edwin's words call to mind the words of Clovis at Tolbiac: *tuae opis gloriam devotus efflagito, ut, si mihi victuriam super hos hostes indulseris et expertus fuero illam virtutem, quam de te populus tuo nomine dicatus probasse se praedicat, credam tibi et in nomine tuo baptizer* (Hist. II, 30).

56 D. H. Green, *The Carolingian Lord* (1965), 297.

57 *Historia Ecclesiastica* II, 5, ed. J. Bidez, 18.

58 Walford's translation, as used by J. Stevenson, *Creeds, Councils and Controversies* (1966), 85.

59 Ed. D. Hurst, *Corpus Christianorum, Series Latina*, CXIX, *Bedae Opera, pars* II, 2 (1962). From this commentary, too, something can be inferred of Bede's ideas about kingship.

60 H. E. II, 10.

61 H. E. II, 11.

62 H. E. II, 13.

63 H. E. II, 13.

64 H. E. II, 16.

65 H. E. II, 20.

66 H. E. II, 17.

67 H. E. III, 6.

68 H. E. III, 2.

69 H. E. III, 6.

70 H. E. III, 9.
71 H. E. III, 9.
72 H. E. III, 2.
73 H. E. III, 11.
74 H. E. III, 12.
75 H. E. III, 14.
76 Compare the fate of Bishop Praetextatus of Rouen, when accused before King Chilperic *contra utilitatem suam populis munera daret* (Hist. V, 18).
77 H. E. III, 25.
78 See *The Relics of Saint Cuthbert*, ed. C. F. Battiscombe (1956), plate V.
79 H. E. III, 18.
80 H. E. IV, 5.
81 H. E. IV, 11.
82 H. E. V, 7.
83 H. E. V, 19.
84 H. E. V, 19.
85 H. E. V, 19.
86 H. E. V, 19.
87 H. E. IV, 2.
88 H. E. V, 21. In Plummer's opinion 'there can be little doubt that it is the composition of Bede himself', but C. W. Jones, *Bedae Opera de Temporibus* (1943), 104, thinks otherwise. Levison leaves the matter open (*Aus Rheinischer und Fränkischer Frühzeit*, 372).

VII

Rome and the early English Church: some questions of transmission[1]*

In England we are taught, and we teach, that the popes had a special affection for the Church of the Anglo-Saxons; and that this affection was warmly returned, to the extent that Englishmen were happy in due course to repay what they saw as their debt to Rome by sending St. Boniface and others to convert some of the Germans, to reform some of the Franks and to bring a little learning to the court of Charlemagne. I would not put this view among what Dr. Kenneth Sisam has called 'those simplifying assumptions and generalisations which, in a historical subject, are convenient for teaching but unfavourable to research',[2] for in substance it is true. Nonetheless, it can stand more qualification than it usually gets; and what I have principally in mind to do is to consider afresh first, how Pope Gregory I and his immediate successors thought of their obligations to the English; secondly, what part others than the popes played in the wonderful turn in the fortunes of the English Church that came with the pontificate of Archbishop Theodore and the careers of St. Wilfrid and Benedict Biscop; and thirdly, why Bede, *verax historicus*, came to form the picture that he transmits of England's debt to Rome—to the exclusion, it might seem, of her debt to some other places. I wish that time allowed me to go on to consider how far the missionary work of Willibrord, Boniface and their friends accorded with the plans of the papacy in her western provinces and the needs of the Church in England; for that is the conclusion of the matter.

The English felt drawn to Rome; that much is clear; but they reserved their love for the pope who first helped them. It was of

* References for this chapter start on p. 133.

Gregory the heir of St. Peter, not of Rome impersonally, that the English liked first to think; and here Bede accurately reflected and did not create a tradition. To the synod of Clovesho, meeting in 747, Gregory was *patre nostro*,[3] and with his name was coupled that of his servant, Augustine of Canterbury; to the compiler of one version of the Anglo-Saxon Chronicle, Gregory was the sender of baptism: 'on his dagum sende Gregorius us fulluht';[4] in the verse preface to King Alfred's translation of the 'Pastoral Care', Augustine is reported to have brought that book 'from the South across the salt sea to (us) island-dwellers as God's champion, the pope of Rome, had previously written it. The learned Gregory, in the wisdom of his heart, had considered many good doctrines, the treasure of his mind. So he who was the best of Romans, wisest of men, highest renowned for glorious deeds, won the greatest number of mankind for the Lord in Heaven.'[5] Aldhelm and Alcuin both speak of 'our Gregory'. The same tradition finds a foreign witness in the ninth century, who can speak of the *gente Anglorum, qui maxime familiariores apostolicae sedi semper existunt*.[6] This consensus of opinion needs no labouring.

To return to the popes, however, is to encounter reactions less simple. In the first place, even if we accept the story that the conversion of the English had been long in Pope Gregory's mind before the year 596, there is no evidence that that year presented special or urgent reasons for launching a mission, nor that he had given much attention to its planning. Professor Schieffer has already written of the improbability of the dispatch of such a mission at such a time.[7] Should we not bear this in mind when we read the pope's jubilant letter to the patriarch Eulogius of Alexandria? He had sent, he says, a monk to preach to a people *in mundi angulo posita*.[8] With the help of German bishops—he did not differentiate Franks and Germans— the mission had reached the English, of whom ten thousand were now believed to have been baptized, and among whom many miracles were wrought. (In parenthesis, I cannot believe that their king was not baptized with them.) It is the letter of one surprised by success. The writer is enjoying a personal triumph, as he had every right to do. His little mission had saved 'ten thousand' English souls and I should be inclined to doubt whether the administrative consequences of such conversion bothered him much. It is easy to see that first mission as a papal attempt to recapture a lost Roman province, for Christ if not for the Empire; but it is a people, not a province, that seems to have been in the pope's mind, at least to begin with. He had done, or believed he had done, what the Frankish and British churches had not done.[9] Not that he knew much about the English. How could he? It was Byzantium that loomed large, if indefinite, over the life of barbarian Europe, and Gregory knew Byzantium by experience; England, by hearsay. At any time in his pontificate the re-establishment of imperial power in the west was a possibility. I would not go as far as Père Goubert, when he argues that only the death of the Emperor Maurice and the disaster of Phocas prevented the successful completion of Justinian's work in the west;[10] but nobody could deny that imperial interests in the west did remain alive from the time of Justinian to the unhappy expedition of Constans II, and no doubt later. Was not Pope Martin I to die in exile on the Black Sea coast fifty years after Gregory's death? The great pope's apocalyptic zeal was for saving northern souls; his view embraced all barbarian Europe. But what took up far more of his time and energy was the life of the churches of the Mediterranean world, and not least the life of the bishopric of Rome. The conversion of the English, in short, while it was no mere diversion, was not a matter on which much time could be, or was, spent. The Franks themselves, in Gregory's view, needed almost as much attention as the English. We may wonder at the muddled start of Augustine's mission, at the pope's slowness in answering the questions of his missionaries,[11] at his ignorance of English affairs of any sort and at the absence of any further legatine visitation of the English after 597—indeed until 786; yet during this time Gregory and his successors were fighting for the very existence of the Church in Rome. Of the so-called papal 'expansionist policy' not everyone can see signs in the eighth century. How much less in the sixth!

I should like to pause for a moment to consider how the picture is affected by the *Responsa* sent from Pope Gregory to Augustine in Kent. The authenticity of these *Responsa* has often been called in question, as by implication it was by St. Boniface; and it has been as often defended.[12] The most recent attack, and the most damaging, has been that of Dom Suso Brechter in *Die Quellen zur Angelsachsenmission Gregors des Grossen*, a book published during the war and too little known in consequence. Dom Brechter contends that the *libellus* or collection of *Responsa* (XI 56a) attributed to the pope in modern editions of his Register cannot as it stands be authentic. He therefore condemns the *libellus* as spurious *in toto*.[13] This is a pity: if a small portion of the *libellus* is open to grave question, the greater part can equally clearly stand as authentic. It might be wiser to judge each letter of the *libellus* independently, on its own merits; and this indeed has been done by Père Grosjean and Professor Margaret Deanesly in a forthcoming article to which I am allowed to refer.[14] These scholars hold that the *libellus* was put together for Canterbury by Nothelm, later Archbishop, in the main from genuine Gregorian materials though in *Responsio* V an addition has been made to bring it into line with canonical decisions on marriage taken since Gregory's death. *Responsio* VIII and *Responsio* IX read rather like moral discourses delivered at Canterbury that have been made to fit into the *collectio*, which Nothelm reshaped and composed a preface for. The difficulty that Bede had access to some of the material of the *libellus* before 721, since he cites it in his prose *Life* of St. Cuthbert, is got over by supposing that Canterbury provided him with two versions of the *libellus*, the second of which is inserted in the *Historia Ecclesiastica* (1, 27). Certainly Bede and Nothelm were in touch with each other before 721. We are, then, to look upon Nothelm as an editor rather than as a forger; and the *libellus*, though largely Gregorian in content, as not a Gregorian *libellus*. I say merely this: that if deliberate deception were claimed to have been practised by Nothelm upon Bede, and Bede were, in consequence, deceived, I should look again at the evidence. Bede was not easily deceived. But this may not be the claim. I allow Nothelm to have edited the Canterbury material at some stage, in the sense that I think he made at least one insertion and rearranged the format. But I also see no reason to doubt that the greater part of the *libellus* reached Canterbury as one letter in the year 601. If it was not registered by the papal *scrinium*, neither was the letter of 23 July 596 (VI 50*a*) addressed to Augustine's companions; yet that is undoubtedly genuine. How much in any case, even after the work of Bresslau, Steinacker and others, do we know about the method of entering letters in Gregory's original register? What sort of a letter was the *libellus*? For myself, the stimulating criticism of Dom Brechter, Père Grosjean and Professor Deanesly leaves this piece of Gregory's correspondence with England more or less intact; and in particular it leaves intact his recommendations as to how Augustine should make use of the Gaulish Church; and to that I shall refer again. But first we should look at the country to which Augustine was sent.

The Franks are sometimes charged with what amounts to neglect of duty in having failed, or not having tried, to bring Christianity to the English of Kent with whom, we are told, their links were many and strong. Leaving aside the Franks' ability to do any such thing, I wish to consider these links. In the first place, it has been urged that the Kentish Jutes were of Frankish blood. In 1933, Mr J. E. A. Jolliffe pointed out resemblances between Frankish and English forms of conveyance, between Frankish and Kentish customary law and between Frankish and Kentish practices in estate-inheritance (gavelkind) that struck him as associating the Kentish Jutes with the civilization of the little area lying between Düsseldorf, Mainz and Trier.[15] He thought, too, that archaeological evidence supported this conclusion. But in truth these resemblances by no means tie us to the area of the Middle Rhine, from which he happened to take his evidence; nor, on quite different grounds, should I have expected the Jutes to have originated there. More recently, Professor Hawkes has moved the home of the Jutes from the Middle to the Lower Rhine and the time of maximum migration from the fifth to the sixth centuries; and he has done lip-service to Bede's view that the men of Kent came from what we call Jutland by suggesting that the leaders at least of the Frankish migrants were Jutes.[16] It has been shown, however, by Professor Arbman that Hawkes' method of building up a fresh chronology on a typological basis is insecure.[17] The case for the strongest Frankish influence on Kentish culture rests on jewellery allegedly brought to Kent as bride-gifts by Frankish women, though one can think of other ways of accounting for the presence of such jewellery in Kent.[18] Origins and archaeology are not the business of this paper, but it has been necessary to say this much to remove any misapprehension that Frankish-Kentish contacts have been established on a wide front—which is not to deny that there were any Franks in Jutish Kent, or that ships ever crossed the Channel. Linguists, furthermore, assure us that the affinities of the earliest English were rather with Frisian than with Frankish. These peoples, like the tongues they spoke, are better not confused.

But what of the royal houses? Bertha, wife of Aethelberht of Kent, was daughter of the Frankish King Charibert, who died in 567. The reality of the family link is revealed years later when Aethelburh, Aethelberht's daughter, sent her two sons for safe keeping to the court of her kinsman King Dagobert.[19] Whether this marriage implied some kind of Frankish overlordship in Kent may be doubted. Sir Frank Stenton is cautious here,[20] and I would be more so. Pope Gregory's letter to the Frankish Kings Theuderic and Theudebert, commending his mission to their care, can be taken to mean that the English were subject to them.[21] It can also be taken to mean that the pope was largely ignorant of the political allegiances of the Germanic world, but willing to flatter. His further statement, that the English were anxious to be converted, fits oddly with Bede's evidence that the Kentish royal house was suspicious of the missionaries, and with place-name evidence that Kentish paganism was exceptionally active and tenacious.[22] The Christian Franks in Kent seem not to have over-busied themselves in thirty years in preparing the king for St. Augustine.

In practice, then, the marriage of Bertha with Aethelberht established *amicitia* between two royal dynasties not necessarily on a basis of equality. But to what extent did it francify the life of the Kentish court? Bertha brought with her a chaplain, the Frank Liudhard. He was a bishop but we do not know his see. What we do know, from the evidence of the St. Martin's hoard of Frankish and Anglo-Saxon coin-ornaments, and notably from Liudhard's medalet that belongs to it, is that Jutish Kent had connections with the Garonne region. Mr. Philip Grierson emphasizes the Visigothic nature of the hoard,[23] and this need not surprise us when we recall that Queen Bertha's father ruled over western Gaul down to the Pyrenees. Bishop Liudhard may well have come from southern Gaul, though we do not, of course, depend solely on this coin-evidence to inform us of Kent's trade with the Loire-Garonne region. The point here is that a solid piece of evidence of early Kentish-Gaulish connections points to the south of Gaul, not to the north. Paris indeed was important in Merovingian politics, and round it was a settlement-area vital to the Merovingians; it belonged to Charibert, Bertha's father; but the full extent of his power lay further south, in a host of fine cities stretching from Tours and Nantes to Poitiers, Bordeaux and beyond. This should caution us, even without the witness of diplomatic, against seeing documents from Marculf's Formulary behind the non-existent charters of King Aethelberht.[24] Perhaps he had charters; we do not know, since the Anglo-Saxon series begins only in the mid-seventh century; but if he did, they were less likely to have been modelled on charters of the Paris region than on Roman charters—a term, however, that I should not care to define too narrowly. I suspect, furthermore, that we ought to be cautious about the direct influence of *Lex Salica* on King Aethelberht's laws, the earliest extant verna-

cular laws of any Germanic people. Sir Frank Stenton rightly says
that the affinities of these laws, at least in subject-matter, are rather
with *Lex Salica* than with any law book of the western empire;[25]
and doubtless he had the derivatives of the *Codex Theodosianus* in
mind. But their affinities with other barbarian laws should not be
overlooked. I am thinking particularly of the *Lex Gundobada*.[26]
Bede makes a curious but definite reference to the composition of the
laws (which he accurately calls *decreta iudiciorum*). He remarks that
they were put together '*iuxta exempla Romanorum*' (*H.E.*, 11, 5).
If we translate this in a general way, as 'after the Roman manner',
he makes little sense, the more so when we consider that between
Aethelberht and Bede a genuine tradition of Roman law-teaching
had been established at Canterbury, of which Bede cannot have been
unaware. Does he not mean something more technical, such as 'following exemplars of', or 'supplied by the Romans'? If the exemplars
were 'of the Romans', I should understand Burgundian or perhaps
Visigothic exemplars brought by Augustine and his companions or
by subsequent missionaries passing through southern Gaul on their
way to Kent. Lyon with its great tradition of legal texts would be
an obvious possibility, though there are others. At all events
'Romani' would not be understood by Bede as having reference only
to the citizens of Rome or even to the Roman clergy. It was a word
commonly used to denote the inhabitants of southern Gaul. My
interpretation may be at fault here, but it has the merit of drawing
attention once again to Kent's links with that Roman world which
the missionaries left only when they proceeded north of the Loire.
With Tours the court of Aethelberht may indeed have had connections.[27] Unfortunately the one firm pre-Augustinian link between
the churches of Canterbury and Tours—a common dedication to St.
Martin—was not due to the influence of Queen Bertha.[28] Canterbury's associations with St. Martin long ante-dated her marriage, as
Bede knew (*H.E.*, 1, 26).[29] After 597, such links as they may have
found between Tours and Kent would certainly have been strengthened by the missionaries. I expect they established contact with
other churches, north of the Loire. But my point is this: though I do
not doubt they had their contacts, Kent and northern Francia have
not yet been shown to have had any deep-reaching association with
each other as a result either of their subjects' common blood or of a
dynastic marriage. But the missions of 597 and 601 are likely to
have developed these contacts. They needed them.

I

Whatever hopes were entertained in Rome, the Franks were of little assistance to the first generation of Roman missionaries in Kent. The few who did help received the warm thanks of Rome, notably Bishop Syagrius of Autun. The eclipse of the Kentish church in the first half of the seventh century brought no help from Rome, and none from Francia. The pity is that we know so little, beyond what Bede tells us, of the beginnings of the churches in East Anglia, Wessex and Northumbria. The East-Anglian church was founded, through the initiative of Canterbury, by a Burgundian bishop, Felix. Its Gaulish affinities need no emphasis; they lead one to Faremoutier, Chelles, Lagny, Péronne and quite possibly to Luxeuil. The case of Wessex is no clearer. We do not know the country of origin of the missionary Birinus, sent direct by Honorius I from Italy, nor in what sense the church that he founded in Dorchester was Roman. But his successors were a Frank, Agilbert, later to be Bishop of Paris,[30] and, after a pause, Agilbert's nephew Hlothere, sent by his uncle from Gaul at the express wish of the West Saxon king and with the approval of Canterbury. The only early Anglo-Saxon charter that shows unquestionable Gallic influence is a West Saxon charter witnessed by Hlothere.[31] But the Frankish church that helped in this considerable way was no longer the church that had failed Gregory the Great. It was a church in the reforming grip of Irish monks. The same church supported the Northumbrians in the second phase of their conversion, only here Gallic influence betrays itself also in church-building.

What holds together these first English churches, so distinct in the manner of their founding, is not Canterbury; nor, in any disciplinary sense, is it Rome. It is more the emotional link with the cultus of St. Peter, and thus with St. Peter's successors. Something of this lies in the mind of the anonymous author of the Whitby *Life* of Gregory the Great, as transmitted in the ninth-century St. Gallen MS. 567. Plainly it betrays how little was known of the Gregorian mission in Northumbria before Bede's researches.[32] It betrays also that the author's interest was centred on Gregory himself, not on Augustine; on Rome, not on Canterbury. Here for the first time we find the story of the pope meeting the English youths in Rome and deciding on the conversion of their countrymen. But they are Deiran youths—Northumbrians, not men of Kent.[33] We must wait until nearly the end of Bede's life before Jarrow sees fit to portray Augustine of Canterbury in an initial of folio 26 verso of what is now the

Leningrad manuscript of the *Historia Ecclesiastica*.[34] If we except Bede's own writing, this portrait is, so far as we know, Northumbria's earliest acknowledgement of the man from whom Paulinus of York first learned to know England.[35] I note in passing that certain features of this manuscript suggest Gaulish influence in the scriptorium of Bede. But to return to the seventh century: Northumbria honours Gregory, not Augustine. The emotional link that held her and her sister-churches to St. Peter was, I think, insufficiently brought out by Levison in his Ford Lectures at Oxford; nor from that distinguished book would one guess that the same emotion was felt by the continental churches. Yet Rome knew that it was.[36]

It is worth digressing to consider why the Frankish church of the sixth century proved unable to help the Gregorian mission with more than a few interpreters. We know the approximate route of the missionaries through Gaul: from Lérins to Tours they passed, as their successors were to pass, through cities of a certain culture—cities of schools of a kind, and thus of books. We may accept the conclusion, most recently stated by M. Riché, that the public schools of Gaul were dead before this time;[37] but that a tradition of Christian letters survived and flourished we may assure ourselves by considering the distinction of Arles in the fifth and sixth centuries[38] and the teaching of law in Clermont as late as the seventh century,[39] or simply by glancing through the volumes of the *Codices Latini Antiquiores*, whose great editor is not apt to err in favour of Merovingian Gaul. These cities and their bishops were not dead; and a principal duty of every bishop was to teach. The countrymen of Caesarius of Arles and of Avitus of Vienne needed to be reminded of this, but not as often as, nor in the way that, we sometimes think. Perhaps historians concern themselves overmuch with the best. They know that already in Sidonius' time Gauls were being attracted to the schools of Italy, to Milan, Pavia and Rome,[40] and that the fifth and sixth centuries witnessed a decline in Gaulish calligraphy.[41] But this is not to prove that there was no teaching and no writing in Gaul. In the matter of books, therefore, and of instruction there can be no doubt that the Gregorian mission to the English could conveniently have acquired much that it needed in Gaul. The books that we know without a shadow of doubt to have been brought direct from Rome to England in the first fifty years of the life of the English church are inevitably rare indeed. The most famous of them, the Gospels of St. Augustine that are now MS. 286 in Corpus Christi

College, Cambridge (*C.L.A.*, II, no. 126), is without much doubt a sixth-century uncial Italian manuscript from Rome. Professor Francis Wormald, who has most recently studied it, observes that 'palaeographers seem to agree' about its country and date of composition, and so reasonably places the onus upon his great predecessors.[42] There is indeed a tradition associating this book with St. Augustine himself, though no compelling reason assigns the miniatures in the text to Italy. In 'some provincial Italian centre' they may indeed have been made, as Dr Wormald suggests; but there are odd stylistic features about them that hint at parallels elsewhere in Western Europe. Too little is still known of book-production in this period to allow of many assertions about this great book. But we may surely accept it as Italian even while we bear in mind that this cannot be demonstrated with the unique assurance that permits us to assign the *Codex Amiatinus* to its rightful scriptorium. Plainly the Gregorian missionaries brought Italian books with them, and received more; Bede says they did; but they knew that they were to pass through southern Gaulish centres of the standing of Marseille, Lyons and Tours (where Bishop Gregory had only just died). Their sources of supply were various and near. Rome for all her riches was not near. I shall say more of this matter when I come to consider Bede. Now, I merely content myself with a question: why, if Gaul was able to do this much, did she not do more? The answer is two-fold. In the first place, Frankish Gaul north of the Loire was itself an area of missionary enterprise in the sixth century, and in this field Aquitaine did what she could till the Irish missionaries of the early seventh century transformed the situation.[43] St. Rémi's conversion of Clovis and his retainers was a dramatic moment, and one that may have been in Pope Gregory's mind when he referred to Constantine in a letter to Bertha (*Ep.*, XI, 29); but the conversion of the Franks was not the work of a moment: it was still in progress in the seventh century. Francia proper, therefore, was too much in the condition of England herself to afford any assistance. Meanwhile, the missionary energies of Gaul south of the Loire were directed towards the northern Rhineland. To its many bishops England must have seemed a remote appendix of *Germania*, not at all the obvious field of missionary work. If they looked outside *Romania* it would have been to Ireland, where indeed they had their contacts. Gregory's letters of recommendation addressed to the Gaulish bishops assume that they will know nothing of his missionaries' destination. He had his own anxieties for the 'Landeskirche' of Gaul, but these were not on account of its past failure to proselytize nor of any lack of learning, but were directed much more towards its inability to organize itself to deal with simony. He had some reason to hope, and his successors still more, that the Gaulish church would take the English under its wing. This is implicit in his directions to Augustine about future relations with the Metropolitan of Arles, whom he did not wish Augustine to try to patronize; in his encouragement to the missionaries—in which, unlike Dom Brechter, I see nothing out of character—to adapt to their own, Roman, uses whatever of Gallican liturgy pleased them; in his assumption that Gaulish bishops would find themselves in England and English bishops in Gaul. In a word, however strong the bond of affection holding the Christian communities in England to Rome, they were too far away to hope for guidance on everyday matters from the popes. There the Gauls could help; and I think that to some extent they did, and that this seemed natural and pleasing to Rome. Some historians still believe, what is demonstrably false, that papal control over the Gaulish church of the sixth century was limited in practice to control of certain patrimonial estates in the Midi. Pope Gregory's view of the matter would have coincided with that of Pope Pelagius II, whose sharp reminder in 586 to Bishop Aunacharius of Auxerre of the Roman origins of the Gaulish church should be better known than it is.[44] In disciplinary matters, and in affection also, Gauls and Franks not infrequently turned to Rome. What more natural, then, than that the popes should hope to see the northern churches mutually supporting one another? Would it have surprised them, and is it exceptional, that the Abbot Peter of Canterbury witnesses the canons of the great council of Paris in 614? We lack any evidence of seventh-century links between individual Gaulish and English communities; but some may be supposed: as between Tours and Canterbury, and perhaps also between Arles, Auxerre and Canterbury.[45] One might also expect Poitiers, Autun and Paris to form quite early links with the numerous pilgrims and travellers from England, who would join the Frankish contingents in the journey to Rome; for the *peregrinatio* was attractive to Franks as well as to others, and Roman relics were not an import reserved for England.

From the middle of the seventh century, the church in England moves into a new life, a life that has none of the legendary flavour

of what went before. I would like to suggest that this new life owed
more than is sometimes allowed to a shift in emphasis in the intellectual life of western Europe itself. I am thinking of what the seventh
century meant to the Christian culture of Visigothic Spain and thus
inevitably of southern Gaul. It is a century that sees the Visigothic
Church, for all that it was 'national', drawing closer to Rome and
giving repeated proof of its vigour in the long series of councils
held at Toledo. Its concern to deal effectively with heresy would
have won the whole-hearted approval of Bede. All this has been
abundantly demonstrated by Z. Garcia-Villada in his great book.[46]
But the special kind of life I have in mind, the life that gave Spain
the intellectual leadership of seventh-century Europe, was the life of
learning and labour of the schools of Seville, Toledo and Saragossa;
a life that depended upon libraries such as even Bede might have
envied. I share the view of C. H. Beeson that Spain was the country
best equipped to furnish manuscripts to the rest of Europe, certainly
better equipped than Italy in the later seventh century; and, further
that the immediate influence of Isidore—'that great inheritor and
representative of the older learning', Edmund Bishop called him—
was, in its way, as significant as that of Cassiodorus in educating the
West in the liberal arts.[47] The rapid diffusion of Isidore's writings,
especially but not exclusively the *Etymologiae*, is evidenced not
merely in the number of manuscripts still extant of the seventh and
early eighth centuries, but in the alacrity, abandon almost, with
which others cited them in writings grammatical, orthographical,
chronological and historical, to say nothing of law, medicine and
biblical commentary. Something over half the extant manuscripts
belonged to Frankish Gaul, though a few have since found homes
elsewhere (e.g. in Rome).[48] We may reasonably look upon southern
Gaul as a principal centre of distribution, while allowing that some
manuscripts went direct from Spain to other places (for example, to
southern Italy and to Ireland). In the early seventh century, Isidore's
chronicle was used in the addendum to Marius of Avenches and by
Fredegar, which proves his presence in Burgundy; and at about the
same time by Vergilius Maro in Toulouse and by Defensor in
Ligugé. This immediate, widespread Gaulish acceptance of Isidore
needs no emphasis; Gaul had a way of being a ready market for
books from Spain. Was not Martin of Braga's *De Correctione Rusti-
corum*, written in a remote corner of north-western Spain in 572,
known in Noyon and Rouen in the seventh century?[49]

In 667, Pope Vitalian chose as Archbishop of Canterbury the aged Greek monk, Theodore. He was the third person approached by the pope in his effort to bring to an end what was to be a four-year vacancy. 'This remarkable nomination', as Sir Frank Stenton calls it, could be interpreted as a sign of the pope's indifference to the English Church, since he was hardly to guess at its triumphant outcome. It is true that his thoughts were much taken up with Byzantine affairs at the time; yet I doubt if indifference can really be laid at his door. He did not want, as Dom Brechter thinks, to keep Canterbury clear of Englishmen. He wanted a good man for a rather unattractive job. The man he chose was a scholar: Christian learning and law were what he considered the English church to stand in need of. It was precisely this that was brought to Canterbury in the persons of the Abbot Hadrian and of Theodore himself. To the school they founded Aldhelm directly, and indirectly Bede, owed a debt; from Aldhelm we learn that its studies included Latin metres, calendar-computation, astronomy and Roman Law. By Roman Law he did not, as it happened, mean the Law of the Church, as he might well have done if he had followed the practice of, say, the compilers of *Lex Ribvaria*.[50] Happily we know exactly what he did mean. An Oxford manuscript (MS. Selden B. 16 of the twelfth century) is a transcription made by William of Malmesbury of a Roman Law book used by Aldhelm in the school at Canterbury.[51] Now this book is the *Breviarium Alaricianum*. William appended to it much interesting historical matter—Dares, Orosius, Eutropius, Paul, Jordanes and his own summary of later imperial history; and parts of this may have been in the Malmesbury library since Aldhelm's time. So Theodore and Hadrian, though coming from the Byzantine world that had long abandoned the *Codex Theodosianus* for the *Corpus* of Justinian—and in this we must include Rome—yet taught their Roman Law from the *Breviarium* derived from the *Codex*.[52] Where did they obtain their copy? Rome, conceivably; but the probability is that they acquired it on their journey through Gaul; perhaps at Lyons, also the likeliest home of the *Breviarium* manuscript that is now Munich 22501, and of the Paris *Codex Theodosianus* (*C.L.A.*, V, n. 591), both of the sixth century. English law in the late seventh century, of Ine in Wessex and of Wihtred in Kent, is more sophisticated than the disjointed tariffs of offences that passed for law with Aethelberht. These kings have moved nearer to real law-making. If we say, what is true, that the change must be owing to the Church, we must mean not least the law-teaching of the Canterbury school. In his small way, Ine was England's Reccesvinth or Liutprand; and he may have known this. Ine, like others of his rank, retired to Rome.

Lyon must be considered the spiritual home of the first northern English scholar we can name: Wilfrid of Ripon. No Englishman of his time was more devotedly attached to Rome; but in Lyons he had spent three formative years, there learning much, says Aeddi, *a doctoribus valde eruditis* and becoming, in Bede's view, *doctissimus*; and to Lyon he returned to collect books and very nearly to share in the extermination of the Burgundian dynasty then controlling the Lyonnais. His two loves, Rome and Gaul, were not incompatible. To his life's end Wilfrid remained a person to be reckoned with in Merovingian politics. To have effected the restoration of Dagobert II and to have turned down the bishopric of Strassburg give some idea of the stature of the man. How much that was Gallic about the Northumbrian Church was due to him? A good deal without a doubt in Church architecture, and possibly, though this is beyond proof, in the form of the charters he certainly employed:[53] one could instance charters witnessed by his protector, Bishop Aunemundus of Lyon, that he could scarcely not have known about;[54] most of all perhaps in his thoroughly Merovingian concept of episcopal might. The things that he did, the rights that he claimed and the principality that he built up in the north alarmed a succession of Northumbrian kings very different in outlook and character; and Canterbury sympathized, in some measure, with the royal objections. But nothing of his *regnum ecclesiarum* (the phrase is Aeddi's) would have surprised the Merovingians—Chlotar III, for example, at whose villa at Compiègne Wilfrid was consecrated bishop according to the Gallic rite. The bishops of Lyon enjoyed, and in that disrupted world needed to enjoy, power very similar to Wilfrid's.[55] What they did not enjoy, so far as we know, was Wilfrid's peculiar relationship with Rome. This was determined by the ascription of his two monasteries, Ripon and Hexham, to the Holy See. In other words Pope Agatho had bound them to himself with a papal privilege of exemption resembling that granted to Bobbio.[56] This is what seems to lie behind the mounting embarrassment of the popes in dealing with Wilfrid when he quarrelled with Canterbury and the Northumbrian kings: Wilfrid had a special right to the protection of Rome. His contemporary, Benedict Biscop, obtained what may have been a similar privilege from Rome, perhaps in the same year, 679. But it would be hazardous to look upon these privileges as exclusively English, for in the same decade (672–6) Pope Adeodatus granted a privilege to St. Martin's of Tours, which is also referred to in a privilege from Bishop Ibbo of Tours to the monastery, dated 720; and there are no grounds for doubting its authenticity.[57] I merely note the coincidence; there may have been others. Wilfrid's intimate connections with the Franks and with Lyon embarrassed neither the popes nor his fellow-countrymen (we may recall that Archbishop Berhtwald was sent to Lyon for consecration in 693 and I see no evidence for the view that the English suspected the primatial pretensions of Lyon). It was not this that cost him the see of Canterbury. I should suppose that the English and Frankish Churches were more intimately linked in the late seventh century than they had ever been before. Benedict Biscop himself, founder of Wearmouth and Jarrow, would have preferred, if we follow Bede, to have settled in Wessex, where there were special Frankish influences.[58] West Saxon, not Northumbrian, libraries might have benefited from his book-collecting activities in Rome and elswhere. The books he collected in Vienne might have delighted Aldhelm instead of Bede.

Bede says many things of Rome. One thing, however, that he does not say is that the libraries available to him at Jarrow and Wearmouth, indirectly at Canterbury and Hexham, and possibly elsewhere, were only stocked from Rome. He says that Benedict Biscop brought back many books from his visits to Rome, some of which could not *even* be found in Gaul. The historical material used in the introductory part of the *Historia Ecclesiastica* was collected, he says, from various quarters; and when we look, with Professor Laistner's help, at the contents of Bede's library, we quickly see why this is likely to be true, and true not only of historical materials.[59] We have to take into account not merely what was at Bede's elbow in Jarrow and Wearmouth—where we are in some danger of overestimating his resources—but the total resources of English libraries anywhere. One source of continental books must surely have been Ireland. If the Irish computus was available in Jarrow, so was other Irish and Irish-continental material. The Welsh presumably contributed nothing, though Gildas, on whom Bede drew rather heavily, had made use of Orosius, Rufinus (or Rufinus through Jerome), quite possibly the rare historian Sulpicius

Alexander, and a version of the *Life* of St. Alban that was not Bede's version.[60] Now, we may surely accept the Gallic authors as mostly direct imports by the English libraries: I mean Ausonius, Prosper, Fortunatus, Constantius' *Life* of Germanus of Auxerre, Gregory of Tours, Victor of Aquitaine, Marius of Avenches, Lupus of Troyes and (Gallo-Irish) the *Life* of St. Fursy; quite possibly Peter of Périgueux, Cassian, Vincent of Lérins, Marcellus of Bordeaux and Eucherius of Lyon, and, most curious, the extremely rare Salonius of Geneva. The list covers many subjects, exegetical, historical, poetical and other; and it is only a selection. I wish I knew why Bede did not use Caesarius of Arles or Sulpicius Severus. The latter, at least, one of the great biographers, was accessible to Aeddi in Ripon,[61] and to the anonymous author of the *Life* of St. Cuthbert.[62] The list would suggest to me, if nothing else did, that English purchasers of books knew their way to the Rhône valley and to the Midi. If there were books that could only be had in Rome, these were not among them. But what about the texts that were not Gallic in origin? What of the Fathers? Unless I am misinformed, one place specially associated with the exposition of Augustinian texts in the late seventh century, was Spain. Bede knew plenty such texts. I suspect it could be shown that they were all available for copying in southern Gaul. Lyon was particularly rich in the Fathers. However, where Bede is among the Fathers, it is as well to walk delicately. We can be less delicate, as Bede was, with Isidore. Bede's normal practice was to acknowledge his debts to other writers, and sometimes he was rather elaborate about this; consequently, we may overlook the writers whom he used but did not acknowledge. Isidore was one of these. He could be censorious about Isidore, more so, perhaps, than his large indebtedness to the Spaniard entitled him to be.[63] It has been suggested that he looked upon Isidore as a 'Petit Larousse' whom it would have been redundant to acknowledge. Yet consider the debt: the *Chronicon*, *De Natura Rerum*, the *Etymologiae*, perhaps the *Quaestiones in Vetus Testamentum* and the *Versus Titulis Bibiothecae*. Traube conjectured that the *Historia Gothorum* should be added to the list.[64] As he lay dying, Bede was translating part of St. John's Gospel into English; but he was also translating *de libris rotarum Isidori excerptiones*[65]—extracts, that is, from the *De Natura Rerum*.[66] We cannot know the extent of Bede's indebtedness to his predecessors till all his writings are critically edited:[67] his debt to Spain is likely to prove great.[68] He did not need the Spaniards to remind him of his hero, Gregory the Great; yet Spain, more than any other country but England, had early learned to venerate him and to treasure his writings. One final point: Bede's *Historia* is dedicated to King Ceolwulf of Northumbria. He needed no precedent for so doing. However, if we were to seek one of which Bede certainly had knowledge we should not need to look beyond Isidore, whose *De Natura Rerum* is dedicated to King Sisebut.

The *Historia* is a cry to Northumbrians, and to all Englishmen, to weigh the moral lessons of their past in the light of the works of Rome. As I interpret it, the preface to King Ceolwulf reflects something of the mood that finds its clearest expression in Bede's letter to Bishop Egbert of York. It has been pointed out with some justice that the condition of the English Church was not so parlous as Bede thought: the early eighth century saw the growth of the parish, the setting out of English missions to the continent, the founding of monasteries and notable achievements in scholarship and the arts.[69] For all this, however, Bede saw danger threatening. He insists in his letter to Egbert that his strictures are limited to a narrow range of shortcomings, in fact to the consequences of *avaritia*; there were many more.[70] The end of the *Historia Ecclesiastica* echoes his deep disquiet for the political future of Northumbria. We may call him an idealist if we wish; but let us not hide from ourselves the truth that his ideals are not always what we think they should have been. We find his preoccupation with heresy a little difficult to account for. We also expect him to be more interested in learning for itself than a disciple of Gregory the Great could ever have been. 'It is an illusion', wrote Mabillon, 'that the monasteries were founded primarily to serve as schools and colleges in which the teaching of the humane sciences became a profession.'[71] Bede would not have regarded the Lindisfarne Gospels as indisputable proof that the Northumbrian Church was blossoming, nor would he have singled out calligraphy as Rome's best gift to the Christian West. I repeat that he was deeply disturbed for the future. If he feared that the right kind of help was no longer to come from Rome, he feared with good reason. Historian as he was, he grasped the import of the Saracen invasions of the West that engulfed Spain, threatened Gaul and presented a fresh menace to the papacy: *gravissima Sarracenorum lues Gallias misera caede vastabat et ipsi non multo post in eadem provincia dignas suae perfidiae poenas luebant.*[72] How could Gaul help?

No doubt she was still good for some books; Aldhelm was half serious when he asked Cellanus of Péronne what help he could be expected to afford to the Franks, *famoso et florigero Francorum rure*;[73] but the great days of Frankish Gaul were over. Lyon and Vienne had been devastated and their episcopal lists ceased to be kept,[74] so ending one more Roman tradition. Small wonder that Bede evinced only a passing interest in the doings of the Franks of his own time. He seems not to have known, and Wilfrid did not know, that the relics of St. Benedict had been translated to Fleury. Perhaps they had not.[75] He must have known, but did not care to say, how the Irish missionaries had been transforming the church of the Franks even within his own lifetime. The present held no such promise for the Franks or for the English. If Bede has any prejudice against Gaul, and I am not sure that he has, it may have had its origins in his dislike of Wilfrid, the Anglo-Gaul *par excellence*, the man who had defied Canterbury, and who, moreover, had once failed, as diocesan, to defend Bede himself against a charge of heresy that was very much resented.[76] Yet, on the other hand, the debt to Gaul of Bede's master, Benedict Biscop, was not much less than Wilfrid's; and Bede loved Benedict.

I must leave the matter there. All I have done has been to hazard the suggestion that the devotion of the early English Church to Rome and to the name of Gregory the Great can a little blind us, even now, to the true nature of Rome's obligations towards England, some of which could only be fulfilled with the help of churches lying nearer to England than Rome herself lay. In England, at least, we need to be better informed about the state of the Frankish and the Visigothic churches, their teaching and learning and their ability to supply England with some of the books she needed. We need to learn not to be blinded by the highlights of insular calligraphy to the study of debased texts in humbler scripts and in barbarized Latin; and the completion of Lowe's *Codices Latini* makes a systematic appraisal of western manuscript resources in the sixth and seventh centuries a possibility at last. England is a part of this picture. We have too long regarded her, as perhaps she liked to regard herself, as Rome's only peculiar child. In truth, do her difficulties, and the help she obtained from Rome in their solution, notably distinguish her from her sister-churches in the west? Everywhere we meet the same problems: of simony, of lay-seizure of church lands, of the foundation of false monasteries, of royal incursions on ecclesiastical privileges; and many more. These are the common problems of barbarian Christendom, as St. Boniface must only too well have known. What now needs investigation is not England's debt to Rome but Rome's activity in England as an integral part of her activity in Western Europe as a whole.

NOTES

1 *Settimane di Studio del Centro Italiano di Studi sull' Alto Medioevo*, vol. 7 (2) (Spoleto, 1960), 519–48. I am indebted, for much friendly criticism, to Professor Paul Lehmann and Professor F. L. Ganshof, who heard the paper delivered and subsequently discussed it with me; and to Dr. F. E. Harmer and Dr. Kenneth Sisam, who read it at a later stage, to my very great advantage.

2 *Studies in the History of Old English Literature* (1953), p. v.

3 Haddan and Stubbs, *Councils and Ecclesiastical Documents*, III, p. 368.

4 Earle and Plummer, *Two Saxon Chronicles Parallel*, I, p. 19, s.a., 565 (E).

5 Translation from Sisam, op. cit., pp. 144–5.

6 *Gesta abbatum Fontanellensium*, ed. Lohier and Laporte, p. 75.

7 Th. Schieffer, *Winfrid-Bonifatius und die christliche Grundlegung Europas* (1954), p. 65.

8 *M.G.H., Epist.*, II, pp. 30 ff.

9 I cannot concur with S. J. Crawford, *Anglo-Saxon Influence on Western Christendom* (1933), pp. 20 ff., that Gregory may have wished to anticipate a mission to the English from the energetic Celtic Church.

10 P. Goubert, *Byzance avant l'Islam*, II (*Byzance et les Francs*) (1956).

11 Bad health is not by itself the explanation: it seldom interfered with Gregory's activity for more than weeks at a stretch, if so much.

12 Recently by W. Levison, *Bede as Historian*, cited from *Aus Rheinischer und Fränkischer Frühzeit* (1948), p. 362; and by L. Bréhier and R. Aigrain, *Grégoire le Grand, les états barbares et la conquéte arabe* (1947), p. 286.

13 Dekkers and Gaar, *Clavis Patrum Latinorum* (1951), n. 1327, accept this judgement.

14 'The Canterbury Edition of the Answers of Pope Gregory I to St. Augustine', *Journal of Ecclesiastical History*, vol. X (1959). Attention should be drawn to their use of a text of the *libellus* in Copenhagen Royal Ny. Kgl., S. 58, an uncial manuscript of the early eighth century, perhaps Frankish. It was known to Levison but not evaluated by him. To this should be added more recent work by R. A. Markus, *Journ. Eccl. Hist.* xiv (1963) and P. Meyvaert, *Rev. Bén.* lxxx (1970) which largely undermines Brechter's position.

15 *Pre-Feudal England, the Jutes.*

16 C. F. C. Hawkes, 'The Jutes of Kent', in *Dark-Age Britain, Studies presented to E. T. Leeds* (1956). Hawkes does not seem to me to have removed the sting from Myres' review of Jolliffe's book in the *Archaeological Journal* XC (1933).

17 *Medieval Archaeology*, 1 (1957), p. 173.

18 Cf. Philip Grierson, 'Commerce in the Dark Ages; a critique of the evidence', *Trans. Royal Hist. Soc.*, 5th series, IX (1959), pp. 123–40.

19 Bede, *Hist. Eccl.*, 11, 20. Bede does not record, as do the genealogies attached to Florence of Worcester, and also William of Malmesbury, that Eadbald, Aethelberht's son and successor, married Emma, daughter of a Frankish king.

20 *Anglo-Saxon England* (1943), p. 59.

21 *M.G.H., Epist.*, 1, 423 ff. (*Ep.* VI, 58).

22 See F. M. Stenton, 'The Historical Bearing of Place-Name Studies: Anglo-Saxon Heathenism', *Trans. Royal Hist. Soc.*, 4th series XXIII (1941), pp. 1–24, and map.

23 *British Numismatic Journal*, XXVII (1953), pp. 39–51.

24 See W. Levison, *England and the Continent in the Eighth Century* (1946), appendix 1; and F. M. Stenton, *Latin Charters of the Anglo-Saxon Period* (1955). If barbarians like Aethelberht did not at once grasp the utility of charters they would at least have appreciated the magical properties of the written word (cf. H. Fichtenau, *Mensch und Schrift im Mittelalter* (1946), pp. 106 ff.). For a slightly later period Dr. F. E. Harmer has shown a caution equal to Levison's, and equally justified, over the possible influence of the Frankish *indiculus* on the English writ (*Anglo-Saxon Writs* (1952), pp. 28 ff.).

25 *Anglo-Saxon England*, p. 60.

26 Is it a coincidence that the Burgundian laws, unlike the Frankish, contain a royal genealogy and that Bede, the first Englishman to record a royal genealogy, bethought himself of giving that of Aethelberht immediately after discussing his laws (*Hist. Eccl.*, 11, 5)? Cf. K. Sisam, 'Anglo-Saxon Royal Genealogies', *Proceedings, British Academy*, vol. XXXIX (1953), p. 323.

27 See M. Deanesly, 'Early English and Gallic Minsters', *Trans, Royal Hist. Soc.*, 4th series, XXIII (1941), p. 42.

28 As Mrs. N. K. Chadwick thinks (*Studies in Early British History* (1954), pp. 181, 200).

29 See the pertinent criticism of J. N. L. Myres, *Engl. Hist. Rev.*, 70 (1955), p. 93. However, Ingoberga, Bertha's mother, had an interest in St Martin when she made her will in 589, and would have reminded Gregory of Tours in that last meeting that her only daughter had married a Kentish king's son (*Lib. Hist.* IX, 26). Bertha's grandfather was Chlotar I: a king of the same name (Hlothere) ruled in Kent, 673–85.

30 This same Agilbert, Wilfrid's companion at Whitby, was connected with the noble Frank Authar, whose family founded Rebais and Jouarre (see A. Bergengruen, *Adel und Grundherrschaft im Merowingerreich* (1958), p. 77). Do such links help to explain the exodus of Anglo-Saxon ladies to Frankish religious houses?

31 Levison, *England and the Continent*, pp. 226–8.

32 As is pointed out by Professor Dorothy Whitelock, *English Historical Documents* (1955), p. 687.

33 See the observations of Brechter, op. cit., pp. 118 ff., who argues that the punning story in its developed form must be Northumbrian. It is worth

noting here that Dom Brechter's book discusses much more than the Gregorian *Responsa*.

34 See M. Schapiro, 'The Decoration of the Leningrad MS. of Bede', *Scriporium*, 12 (1958), pp. 191–207; E. A. Lowe, 'Some observations on the Leningrad Manuscript of the Historia Ecclesiastica Gentis Anglorum, a key to Bede's Scriporium', ibid., pp. 182–90. The portrait is now held to be of Gregory.

35 However, the council of Clovesho of 747 orders the observation of the feasts both of Gregory and of Augustine. Haddan and Stubbs, *Councils*, iii, p. 368.

36 General reference may be made to the article of Dom Kassius Hallinger in *Sankt Bonifatius Gedenkgabe* (1954), pp. 320–61.

37 P. Riché, La survivance des écoles publiques en Gaule au Vᵉ siècle', *Le Moyen Age*, LXIII (1957), pp. 421–36.

38 Cf. S. Cavallin, 'S. Genès le Notaire', *Eranos* (1945), 'Les clausules des hagiographes arlesiens', ibid. (1948).

39 *Vita Boniti*, M.G.H., Script. Rer. Merov., VI, p. 120

40 Cf. A. Momigliano, 'Cassiodorus and Italian Culture of his Time', *Proceedings, British Academy*, XLI (1955).

41 E. A. Lowe, *Cod. Lat. Ant.*, VI, p. xiii.

42 *The Miniatures in the Gospel of St. Augustine* (1954), p. 1. See also E. A. Lowe, *English Uncial* (1960), plate II and comment.

43 Cf. E. Ewig, 'L'Aquitaine et les pays rhénans au haut moyen âge', *Cahiers de civilisation médiévale*, Poitiers.

44 M. G. H., *Epist.*, III, p. 449–50. See also Gregory of Tours, *Hist. Lib.*, I, chap. 30.

45 Cf. E. Griffe, La Gaule chrétienne à l'époque romaine, II (1957), pp. 231 ff. Also F. Benoit, 'L'Hilarianum d'Arles', *Saint Germain d'Auxerre et son temps* (1950), pp. 181–9.

46 *Historia eclesiastica de España* (1929–36), esp. vol. II, chs. 5 and 6. The view of the matter current in England today is probably that expressed by S. J. Crawford, *Anglo-Saxon Influence on Western Christendom* (1933), an essay on which it is possible to lean too heavily. An altogether juster and better-founded appraisal is that of Edmund Bishop, 'Spanish Symptoms', *Liturgica Historica* (1918), pp. 165 ff., though I would not accept all his strictures on the Gaulish Church.

47 *Miscellanea Fr. Ehrle*, I, 50. This is not, however, to overlook the early presence of manuscripts of Cassiodorus in England.

48 Cf. C. H. Beeson, *Isidor-studien* (1913), the fine summary of R. Menéndez Pidal, *Historia de España*, III (1940), esp. pp. 381–431, and Manuel C. Diaz y Diaz, 'La cultura de la España visigotica del siglo VII', *Settimane di studio del Centro italiano di studi sull'alto medioevo*, V (Spoleto, 1953). A good idea of the diffusion of manuscripts can be had from E. Lesne, *Histoire de la propriété ecclésiastique en France*, IV, pp. 28–42. See also J. Fontaine, *Isidore de Seville et la culture classique dans l'Espagne wisigothique*, 2 vols (Paris, 1959), an epoch-making book.

49 See C. W. Barlow, *Martini Episcopi Bracarensis opera omnia* (1950), pp. 7, 165. For links between Tours and Galicia, as well as between Rome and

Galicia, Pierre David, *Études historiques sur la Galicie et le Portugal* (1947).

50 '*secundum legem Romanam quam ecclesia vivit*' (*Lex. Rib.*, 61, ed. Beyerle and Buchner, p. 109).

51 As pointed out by M. R. James, *Two Ancient English Scholars* (1931), p. 14. James does not identify the Selden MS. with Aldhelm's book, as Sir Frank Stenton states, clearly by oversight (*Anglo-Saxon England*, p. 181, note 1).

52 Bodleian Library Hatton MS. 42, inscribed on the back *Liber Sancti Dunstani*, is principally a collection of canons but contains passages from Roman and Frankish Law. This is one of several indications of a continuing interest in written law.

53 Cf. Aeddi's *Vita*, ch. 17 (ed. Colgrave, p. 36; ed. Levison. *M.G.H.*, *S.R.M.*, VI, 211 ff.; ed. Moonen, 96) on which Stenton comments that it is 'the earliest passage by an English author which points to the practice of making charters' (*Latin Charters*, p. 32). As to architecture, very interesting parallels between some southern English churches of the seventh century and one Italian church near Milan have been drawn by G. P. Bognetti, *S. Maria di Castelseprio* (1948).

54 Cf. A. Coville, *Recherches sur l'histoire de Lyon* (1928), pp. 366–9.

55 E. Ewig has written wisely of the reasons for the growth in power of the later Merovingian bishops of south-central Gaul, *Sankt Bonifatius Gedenkgabe*, pp. 424–40.

56 Aeddi, ch. 51. See also Levison, *England and the Continent*, p. 24.

57 *M.G.H.*, *Formulae*, pp. 496–8, 501–3; Pardessus, *Diplom.*, II, no. 512.

58 Bede, *Hist. Abb.*, ch. 4 (ed. Plummer, I, p. 367).

59 M. L. W. Laistner, 'Bede as a classical and as a patristic scholar', *Trans. Royal Hist. Soc.*, 4th series, XVI (1933); 'The Library of the Venerable Bede', in *Bede: His Life, Times and Writings* (1935). (Both reprinted in *The Intellectual Heritage of the Middle Ages* (1957).

60 Cf. C. E. Stevens, 'Gildas Sapiens', *Engl. Hist. Rev.*, 56 (1941), pp. 353–73.

61 I agree with H. Moonen, *Eddius Stephanus, Het Leven van Sint Wilfrid* (1946), pp. 12 ff.

62 W. Levison, *M. G. H.*, *Script. Rer. Merov.*, VI, pp. 181 ff.

63 Following Laistner, C. W. Jones sees in Bede little reverence for his great forerunner (*Bedae Opera de Temporibus* (1943), p. 131). I think this is limited to his chronological studies.

64 *Einleitung in die lateinische Philologie des Mittelalters* (1911) (vol. 2 of *Vorlesungen und Abhandlungen*), p. 176.

65 *De Obitu Baedae*, ed. Plummer, I, p. clxii.

66 Cf. Levison, *England and the Continent*, p. 42.

67 M. L. W. Laistner, *Thought and Letters in Western Europe* (2nd ed. 1957), p. 162.

68 Edmund Bishop noted (*Liturgica Historica*, 169) Aldhelm's debt to Spanish authors. It was his contention that Spanish liturgical texts reached England by way of Ireland, not Gaul.

69 D. Whitelock, *English Historical Documents*, pp. 87–8.

70 Some of these are considered by E. John, 'The imposition of the common burdens on the lands of the English Church', *Bulletin of the Institute of Historical Research*, XXXI, No. 84 (1958).

71 *Traité des études monastiques* (1691), p. 7, trans. of S. J. Crawford, op. cit., pp. 79–80.
72 *H.E.*, V, ch. 23 (ed. Plummer, I, p. 349).
73 *M.G.H.*, *Auct. Antiq.*, XV, p. 499.
74 Coville, op. cit., p. 431.
75 Cf. P. Visenin, 'La posizione di s. Beda e del suo ambiente riguardo alla traslazione del corpo di s. Benewetto in Francia', *Rev. ben.*, 167 (1957), pp. 34–48.
76 Jones, *Bedue Op. de Temp.*, p. 132 interprets the letter to Plegwin in this sense.

K

VIII

A background to St. Boniface's mission*†

An English scholar in search of a continental background to St. Boniface's mission will naturally turn to Wilhelm Levison's Ford Lectures, delivered in Oxford in 1943 and published in 1946.[1] Yet the quarter-century that has since passed has seen much activity in Levison's field, notably among his own pupils; and thus his picture can be modified in some important respects[2] and filled out in others. Generally one may say that it has become more complex, and that the Frankish scene in which Boniface lived out the second half of his long life can no longer be regarded as one of degraded isolation, politically or religiously. The time may be opportune to attempt to reassess some aspects at least of the picture.

The English never forgot their connection with the continental Saxons. For different reasons, the Franks never forgot theirs with the Germans east of the Rhine. It is a thread that runs right through the history of Frankish Gaul. We must take it up—if we wish to understand St. Boniface's situation—in the early seventh century, during the reigns of two powerful Merovingian kings, Chlotar II and his son Dagobert I, and the regency of Balthildis. The one tenaciously pursued ambition of the early Merovingians, Robert Latouche has written, 'a été de reconquérir la Germanie dans toute sa profondeur pour l'annexer à leur royaume'.[3] This is to claim rather too much, though Merovingian campaigns against Saxons, Alamans and Thuringians lend some colour to it. What is clear is that Austrasian Francia could never be secure while German tribes

---

* References for this chapter start on p. 150.
† *England before the Conquest: studies in primary sources presented to Dorothy Whitelock*, ed. P. Clemoes and K. Hughes (C.U.P., 1971), 35–48.

over the Rhine were aggressive and some of their neighbours west of the Rhine unsettled and independent. A stage in this uneasy relationship was reached in the early seventh century. One indication is that Chlotar and Dagobert provided those tribes they distrusted, but wished to conciliate, with written national laws of their own, firmly based on the Merovingian *Lex Salica* and subordinating them politically to Frankish overlordship: *Lex Ribvaria* for the tribes round Cologne, the *Pactus Alamannorum* for the Alamans, and *Lex Baiuvariorum* for the Bavarians.[4] It is no coincidence that manuscripts of the *Volksrechte* were soon to be found in the libraries of those monasteries most closely associated with Carolingian plans for Germany. Moreover, there is evidence of Frankish colonizing activity at about the same time, notably in the Main–Neckar region. It was spasmodic and unplanned and altogether more modest than what the Arnulfings were later to attempt;[5] yet there is reason to think that it had Merovingian support or approval.[6] It had a religious aspect too. The new Frankish families encouraged by the Merovingians were also monastic founders, both in western Francia and in the Rhineland. Luxeuil and her dependent houses owed their prosperity to this. There is a strong link between the Irish missionaries on the one hand and the Merovingians with their Frankish and Burgundian aristocratic supporters on the other. From these last a new generation of bishops was coming to maturity by the middle of the seventh century: no longer Gallo-Romans of the type to which Gregory of Tours had belonged, but aristocratic and often learned Franks associated with and brought up in the Irish–Frankish monastic tradition.[7] Even after the collapse of Merovingian political authority members of the dynasty can still be found interested in monastic foundations: examples are Chlotar III and his brother, Theuderic III. The last known Merovingian foundation was that of St. Peter's at Erfurt by Dagobert III (711–16). In practice, however, Merovingian monastic foundations, or encouragement of such foundations by their supporters, often wilted before local opposition. For example, not much progress was made east of the Vosges, where they came up against the family of the Etichonen, dukes of Alsace and themselves monastic founders.[8] This is about as much as should be said of late Merovingian encouragement of monasticism; for the point is soon reached (long, indeed, before the foundation of St. Peter's, Erfurt) where it is hard to know what was being done by others in their name and under their authority; in brief, the Arnulfings and other families advanced to landed power, and so emerged as monastic founders, under Merovingian aegis. Should one ascribe the advancement of the bishopric of Cologne to the Merovingians or to the Arnulfings? The first important bishop was Kunibert, successor to Arnulf of Metz as chief adviser to Dagobert I and Sigebert III, and thus colleague of the first Pippin. Kunibert was a great Merovingian servant, and quite possibly the begetter of *Lex Ribvaria*. Under him the bishopric began to penetrate its pagan surroundings, even as far away as Utrecht and Soest. The effort was premature, but Cologne was from then on a vital point in Frankish control of the north-east. Above all, it was to be an Arnulfing stronghold. From it Bishop Hildegar set out to meet his death on Pippin III's Saxon expedition of 753.[9] The Merovingians made Cologne an outpost of Frankish power: the Arnulfings were to reap the benefit.[10]

It was not the opinion of Levison that Merovingian connections with Rome had much significance. He may have been right in the sense that the connections we know of were informal for the most part and occasional; certainly they were not marked by conciliar activity such as characterized Carolingian–Roman relations. But the evidence, poor as it is, reveals that in important ways the Merovingian church was alive to Roman developments and attached importance to the link.[11] This is clearest in the field of liturgy. A form of the Roman Gelasian sacramentary reached Francia in the first half of the seventh century: there survives a copy of it in MS Vat. Reg. 316, made in Francia about 750.[12] Nor was this the only sacramentary to influence Frankish liturgical practice in the same century; other types were used. So far as is known, they owed their presence in Francia, as well as their dissemination, to private initiative; not until the time of Pippin III do we find unquestionable royal interest in such matters. Nevertheless, the liturgical link was already there. It was supported, moreover, by the circulation of the closely associated *Ordines Romani*; these, too, were in Francia well before the middle of the eighth century. Another symptom of Frankish interest in Rome was the growth of the cult of St. Peter, as evidenced in church dedications. In part at least this will have been due to the influence of St. Columbanus and his disciples, Irish and Frankish; in part, to the indigenous tradition of the Gallo-Roman church. Some thirty foundations of the seventh century were dedicated to St. Peter, whereas dedications to St. Martin, hitherto the favoured Frankish patron, dropped off.[13] If any doubt still existed as to the specifically Roman significance attached to St. Peter by the Merovingian church, one need only refer to the *Vitae Patrum Jurensium*.[14] A missionary from Aquitaine, St. Amand, who died *c.* 674, dedicated all the northern monasteries of his foundation to St. Peter; and his example was followed by others (e.g. Geretrudis of Nivelles). Already in the Merovingian *Formulae* of Bourges St. Peter appears as the protector of the Franks.[15] In short, Frankish interest in St. Peter long antedated any Anglo-Saxon influence. It may also be noted that the leader of the Petrine party at Whitby, for whom St. Wilfrid acted as spokesman, was a Frank.[16] Such interest should not prove surprising when we recall that the Franks were as involved as the English in the Roman pilgrimage; and, unlike the English, had good Roman precedent for being so. In Marculf's Formulary (and others) is plentiful evidence of Frankish pilgrimage to Rome as a normal occurrence of the seventh century;[17] and in the Merovingian *Vitae Sanctorum* there is more.[18] It was not St. Boniface who brought the Roman pilgrimage, any more than the Rule of St. Benedict with its strongly Roman links, to Francia; they were already part of Frankish life.[19] A diploma of Theuderic IV for St. Denis in 724[20] betrays so strong a sense of *missio Romana* that we should also reckon with official Merovingian recognition of Francia's special ties with the papacy. Furthermore, a privilege of Pope Adeodatus (672–6) for Tours[21] (which there is no reason to consider exceptional) makes it clear that the popes were equally conscious of those ties. The background, then, to the Roman missions of St. Willibrord and St. Boniface is not only English but also Frankish.

The Carolingian family, both in its Arnulfing and its Pippinid branches,[22] was one of several dynasties of Austrasian magnates that owed its early impetus to Merovingian backing, and whose first steps in territorial aggrandizement, on both sides of the Rhine, were associated with control of churches and monasteries. With Charles Martel, however, a change is discernible; his trans-rhenan activities have more the complexion of planned military conquest than do any of the Merovingian campaigns.[23] Carolingian historiography depicts his conquests rather more as a continuation of what had gone before than they really were. From Charles's time onwards, Carolingian expeditions against the Germans were aimed at Frankish absorption of Germany: Pippin II had shown the way with four campaigns against the Alamans (in 709, 710, 711 and 712); Charles Martel began his series of Saxon expeditions in 718; in 725 he attacked the Alamans and the Bavarians; in 730 he again attacked the Alamans and in 742–3 his son Carloman followed his example; in 745 Pippin III was active in Alamannia while Carloman went for the Saxons; and in 746 Carloman secured a resounding victory over the Alamans at Cannstadt. These were only the more notable campaigns; there were others, and there would have been still more but for Carolingian preoccupation with Aquitaine and the Arabs. They were associated with political reorganization (as with Charles Martel's in Thuringia[24]) and equally with settlements of Frankish families, especially in the Main–Neckar region. A witness to them is the mass of aristocratic *Reihengräber* of the seventh century; warrior-graves, some in hitherto vacant lands, others the result of violent dispossession.[25]

But always these activities had a religious aspect, evident in a modest way long before. Rhineland bishoprics specially involved in missionary or colonizing work (and sometimes both) in the seventh and early eighth centuries were: Cologne (Westphalia and parts of Frisia); Mainz (the Mainland, notably in the direction of Würzburg); Worms (the Neckar valley); Speyer (northern Alamannia and Alsace); and Strassburg (southern Alamannia, i.e. the Black Forest area). With all of these the early Carolingians were associated, sometimes intimately. To start with the most northerly—Cologne: it was the stronghold of Pippin II and, after his death in 714, of his widow, Plectrudis,[26] guardian of their grandson, Theudoald. Pippin's illegitimate son, Charles Martel, found Cologne a centre of legitimist Carolingian resistance to his power, and it did not soon die down. Nevertheless, Cologne became the headquarters of his campaigns against the Westphalian Saxons, who had bitten deep into the Frankish *Gaue* round Cologne between 694 and 714. Charles's counter-offensive was short-lived in its effects, but the hopes that were entertained of it may be gauged from Boniface's anxiety to have the see of Cologne as a centre for missionary work among the Saxons. It is one of several indications that Charles and Boniface had a strong common interest in expansion from the northern Middle Rhine.[27] But Cologne has a further interest. In the person of Plectrudis it became linked with Carolingian power further south, in and round Trier. North and east of Trier, between the Mosel and the Maas, lay the nucleus of the family's estates and some of their earliest ecclesiastical endowments. Plectrudis's parents were the Frankish seneschal Hugobert, bishop of Maastricht, and

Irmina, probably daughter of Theotar, a duke in western Germany,[28] whose descendants were connected with the Frankish Heteno dynasty of Thuringia. Children of the same pair were Adula of Pfalzel,[29] Chrodelind, Regentrud and Bertrada (to be distinguished from her granddaughter of the same name, who married Pippin III). In the course of a few years this clan founded, or participated in founding, monasteries at Pfalzel, Echternach (which they gave to Willibrord), and Prüm. When we add to these certain nearby foundations, and foundations by neighbouring families (e.g. Mettlach, Hornbach, St. Maria ad Martyres at Trier, and the revival of St. Eucher and St. Paulin, also at Trier), we shall be justified in considering the late seventh and early eighth centuries the first serious revival of religious life in the district of the Middle Rhine–Mosel since the barbarian invasions.[30] Moreover, with the exception of Mettlach, we can claim that these new aristocratic monasteries marked some weakening of episcopal authority; the territory was showing signs of emancipation from the city, at least for a time. What of the bishops of Trier? The period is covered by the rule of Basin, his nephew Liutwin and Liutwin's son Milo. The family were Franks from the Upper Saar.[31] Basin, who died in 705, was on friendly terms with St. Willibrord, who put his name in his calendar, perhaps because Basin had played some part in the foundation of Echternach. Not only Basin but also Liutwin were honoured as saints in Trier; both were benefactors of monasteries. Yet Liutwin was also *dux* in Trier; he was trusted by those in power further west, and may indeed have had his own ties with Neustria; he dedicated his monastery of Mettlach to St. Denis and not to any saint specially honoured by the Irish or Anglo-Saxons. It is another matter to infer that he was more cautious about supporting foreigners than his uncle had been. Milo, then, was heir not merely to large family possessions and official power in the Rhineland and beyond (Charles Martel put Reims and Laon in Liutwin's hands, and afterwards Milo's, as a result of the opposition of Bishop Rigobert) but also to a tradition of generosity to monasteries. Milo stood close to Charles Martel. He was probably not in bishop's orders and very likely secularized some ecclesiastical property; but he was not deprived of office by any reforming council and left a good name behind him locally, in his monastery of Mettlach. It was his hunting that annoyed Boniface; and I know of no evidence that he and the English missionaries were normally hostile to one another. The most one can infer is coldness, and even this will depend on how one interprets a possible friendliness between Milo and St. Pirmin. Charles Martel was certainly not hostile to the English in the Mosel–Rhine region: he was himself a benefactor of Echternach; nor was he hostile to St. Willibrord, to whom he gave the castle of Utrecht as a base for his resumed operations in Frisia.

A further centre of Arnulfing power (this time well west of the Rhine) was Metz, the see of their ancestor, St. Arnulf. The earliest evidence of their awareness of the value to them of St. Arnulf's patronage is the gift by Pippin II and Plectrudis, in 691, of a villa at Norroy to the church of Metz, *ubi domnus et avus noster Arnulphus in corpore requiescit.*[32] The church was known as St. Arnulf's by about the year 700, and closer Carolingian interest in it is evident. Charles Martel's nine-year-old son, Jerome, wrote a Life of St. Arnulf.[33] The more important members of the family were buried in the great Merovingian monastery of St. Denis; and it was here that Charles put his sons, Carloman and Pippin III, to be educated. But Metz was still vital to the family. The see was entrusted by them to no less a man than Chrodegang in 742, when he was aged thirty. Chrodegang was a Frank of aristocratic birth from the Maasland, a relation of Chancor (founder of Lorsch) and brother of its first abbot.[34] He was brought up at Charles Martel's court, where he was *referendarius.* He witnessed Charles's last extant deed on 17 September 741.[35] He was, then, very much the man of Charles Martel, though it was to Pippin III that he owed Metz. We know nothing of his education or of the influences that made him the first great Frankish church-reformer; something must have been due to the court circle itself, and something also perhaps to the monastery of St. Trond, where Charles was later alleged to have found him.[36] Chrodegang was to become, in the 740s, the new representative of Francia's traditional ties with Rome. But it is not by any means certain that he stood for a Frankish tradition of hostility to St. Boniface, nor that his master Pippin III was glad to take advantage of it. There was collaboration between him and the Bonifacian bishops of Mainz, Würzburg and Cambrai. He certainly had a link with St. Pirmin, whose missionary activity reached at least as far north as Metz. In brief, Chrodegang linked much: not only the Frankish court circle with the followers of Boniface and Pirmin but also with Frankish episcopal interests wider afield, where Boniface was powerless. The reform of the Frankish church outside the Austrasian area of synodal activity owed most to him, and there is evidence that he had something there to build on. Ewig has shown that in the seventh and early eighth centuries there were interesting liturgical developments in Neustria and Burgundy largely independent of Austrasian influence, and has illustrated this from the Soissons Litany.[37] Nor should it be overlooked that both Corbinian of Freising and Emmeram of Regensburg were West Franks.

Mainz had long been the Frankish advance-post for penetration of the Mainland and central Germany generally. How far it was ever an active mission centre is more debatable; in the mid and later seventh century there seems to have been more missionary activity from Trier-Echternach, Speyer-Weissenburg and Worms (the home of the Frankish Bishop Rupert of Salzburg).[38] Not surprisingly, this middle area of the Rhine was a centre of opposition to St. Boniface: Gewilib of Mainz was one of the two Frankish bishops who were criticized by name by Boniface.[39] In due course he was deposed for the specific sin of having taken blood-vengeance for the killing of his father (and predecessor as bishop), Gerold. We do not know that any other charge was laid against him; his succession to the see of Mainz was regular, and he may well have been in bishop's orders.[40] What interest he took in the extension of his diocese east of the Rhine is not known; but his opposition to Boniface's activity in Hesse and Thuringia, which may reasonably be inferred, suggests that he took some. His colleague of Worms may well have sympathized with him; but Bishop David of Speyer (also abbot of Weissenburg) seems to have been readier to collaborate with the English. From these centres, not so long before, Irish missionaries must have set out with Frankish support for Würzburg,[41] where St. Kilian met his death in about 689. There were at least fourteen monasteries in Würzburg diocese alone, founded on the properties of substantial families, some Frankish, some Thuringian. One of them, Kitzingen, was founded by Hadeloga, allegedly a daughter of Charles Martel and in fact very probably connected with him. But the interesting point about St. Kilian is not so much his mission as his subsequent career as a saint.[42] In 752, Bishop Burchard of Würzburg translated his relics with much publicity, proclaiming him in effect the symbol and patron of Carolingian *Ostpolitik*.[43] This open championing of an Irish saint in territory peculiarly Bonifacian (Fulda was not far away), and by an English disciple and confidant of Boniface, is indicative of how some English missionaries thought it natural and profitable to work closely with the Carolingians in Germany, as St. Willibrord had done. The translation had the full approval of Pippin III. I do not, however, see that it can be represented as a betrayal of Boniface, since the translation took place *mediante Bonifatio archiepiscopo*; it had his approval, too.

Further south, it is possible to argue that Boniface did in practice find himself excluded by Carolingian encouragement of others. In Alamannia and Alsace, for example, from which he was not excluded by his papal brief, there were others at work with Carolingian support. Pre-eminently it was the mission field of St. Pirmin,[44] who knew how to make the best of Burgundian-Alsatian family connections and cast his net far afield.[45] Nowhere else can we see so clearly the importance to Charles Martel of church support than in the reorganization of Alamannia; the gifts of land to the missionary centres of Reichenau and St. Gallen lay far to their north, in Alamannic territory.[46] From these monasteries, rather than from bishoprics, the early Carolingians planned their control of the approaches to Bavaria. It may well be that in the Christian princess's grave at Wittislingen in eastern Alamannia we have evidence of the seventh- and eighth-century eastward expansion of Frankish Rhineland families into an area already rich in *Reihengräber*.[47] Perhaps Boniface excused himself from participation through pique or hostility to Pirmin: this might seem the more plausible if Pirmin were an Irishman and not a Spaniard, as he is generally held to have been. But it is just as likely that he felt he had enough to do elsewhere. Pirmin showed no hostility to the English and their known supporters, and none ought to be inferred from his collaboration with Chrodegang of Metz. The only Englishman who certainly had reservations about Chrodegang was Lul,[48] his unsuccessful rival for the succession to Boniface as archbishop. Plainly we cannot infer hostility to Boniface from Chrodegang's reforming colleague at St. Denis, Fulrad (a Frankish aristocrat from the Mosel-Saar area),[49] since it was to him that Boniface addressed his plea for official protection of his disciples.[50]

Where, then, did hostility lie? One possible direction that may indicate others is the Irishman, Virgil of Salzburg. He was Pippin III's man in a real sense. He not only owed his see to Pippin's influence with the Bavarian duke, Odilo, but first spent two years at the Carolingian court; his Latin style bears strong traces of Frankish influence.[51] It is mostly in their learning that one sees the wide gulf between him and Boniface. From the so-called Cosmography of Aethicus Ister,[52] now recognized as Virgil's, emerges the proud and prickly mind of a master of the quadrivium, a lover of Greek thought and a geometrician, a despiser moreover of the narrower and more old-fashioned masters of the trivium, of whom the grammarian Boniface was a good example. The book is, among other things, a *reductio ad absurdum* of the traditionalist approach to antique literature that contented itself with Donatus and little else. However, the missionary aims of the two men were not incompatible; for Virgil, too, was a missionary (in Carinthia), and his work had papal approval. Moreover, the Bavarian church, for all its independence and despite its historical ties with the Franks, owed much to Boniface. The Cosmography is rather a cry of despair than of triumph, addressed to friends in Bavaria who thought too highly of the Englishman. There were other than intellectual reasons for mutual antipathy; they differed for example in their conception of the bishop's office. Belonging to the Irish tradition, Virgil preferred to operate as an abbot and left his episcopal functions for as long as he could to his Irish colleague Dobdagrecus.[53] Yet it would be wrong to represent him as an insurance policy taken out by Pippin III against Boniface and the English. The hostility did not stem from the Franks but from Virgil's Irish background; and to the Irish rather than to the Franks I should be inclined to attribute opposition to the English.

When it comes to evidence, there is nothing to show that the Carolingians ever withdrew the special protection accorded to Boniface by Charles Martel in a remarkable document;[54] a *peregrinus* acquires a *patronus*, a protector at law for his life and goods against those who could otherwise enslave or even kill him as a lordless man. Moreover, the Frankish *mundeburdium* implies not merely protection but authority over the protected.[55] It was probably accorded to other missionaries, English and Irish, in the same way. In the political sense, then, Boniface ceased to be a *peregrinus*; in the religious sense, he insisted to the end on the reality of his *peregrinatio*. In this, indeed, may lie something of his basic difficulty in relation to his Frankish masters: he desired always to stand apart. The cries of despair in his correspondence are caused less by specific grievances, though these do occur, than by constant self-reminders that he is an exile in the world, an old man among young men, not by choice a missionary who must make the best of what he finds but a pilgrim whose role is and must be to suffer. His idea of himself may well, as Eugen Ewig has suggested,[56] be derived from St. Paul, whose apostleship was equally set in a world of pagans, *ignorami* and *falsi fratres*.[57] Boniface's authority was derived from Rome; his interpretation of it came from St. Paul. It cannot be shown that his episcopal ordination in 726, which certainly alienated some of the bishops with jurisdiction east of the Rhine, ever alienated Charles Martel. Nor is it clear that Boniface's establishment of sees at Würzburg, Buraburg and Erfurt was possible only after Charles's death in October 741. Much turns on the dating of the *Concilium Germanicum* which Schieffer[58] and others would place in 743 instead of 742; for if the traditional date (supported by the texts) of 742 be correct, then the foundation of the bishoprics will almost certainly have been in the last months of Charles's life. 742 continues to find supporters.[59] Charles had much to gain by helping Boniface east of the Rhine. They had a common interest in the Saxons, and it may be that Charles's failure in 738 to subdue them, and thus to open up to Boniface the mission field he really sought, caused both to think more seriously of holding-operations on Saxony's southern frontier in Hesse and Thuringia. Would it be going too far to connect this shift of effort with Boniface's disappointment over the see of Cologne?[60] The assumption is made that, at the last minute, Cologne was denied him through the machinations of the Frankish aristocrat-bishops; but an assumption it remains. Mainz, which in fact he obtained, had more to be said for it as a place from which to control the central German sees and to plan future advances into Saxon territory from Thuringia. Mainz was at least as important to Carloman and Pippin as it had been to Charles Martel; and they may in the end have placed Boniface where he could be of most use to them. Perhaps Boniface, too, could see the practical advantages of attempting the conversion of the Saxons from the direction of Thuringia. This also corresponded with the ultimate intentions of the papacy; and if Echternach was originally intended as a mission centre rather than as a retreat, Willibrord too had had some such idea. This, rather than personal animosity or unwillingness to work close with the Franks, is the likeliest reason why Boniface declined to succeed Willibrord in his Frisian mission: there was more to be said for a base in the Middle Rhine area.

In the last resort, the case against Charles Martel as an opponent of Boniface rests on his general reputation as a despoiler of church property. That he was such on a massive scale cannot be disputed. But this is to put the matter too baldly. It may be significant that Boniface himself, who did not hesitate to castigate King Æthelbald of Mercia for the same sin,[61] brought no such charge against Charles.[62] Nor indeed could it easily have been brought so far as the German territories known to Boniface were concerned, since the spoliations were confined to traditional Frankish-controlled territory: Burgundy, Provence, Aquitaine, and the regions of the Meuse, Seine, Loire, and the Austrasian Rhineland. Within these areas, as Lesne has shown,[63] the spoliation was haphazard, affecting both rich and poor communities. It was, in Lesne's words, *sans doute le produit spontané du désordre*,[64] and as such was resorted to not only by Charles but by many of his contemporaries, to say nothing of Franks of an earlier time. Like them, he was a benefactor as well as a despoiler: many churches and monasteries could have borne witness to this. His problem was that of a conqueror of a land long prone to disorder and self-help. He had not merely to reward his faithful followers[65] but to dispose of close-knit nuclei of secular and church lands held by former opponents. The situation he faced but did not create in Neustria and Burgundy was at every turn bound up with church property: with the collapse of secular local authority, bishops had assumed control of large areas which they ruled in effect as ecclesiastical republics. Just such a situation greeted St. Wilfrid when he stayed with the bishop of Lyon.[66] A notable case of a bishop who took every opportunity to feather his own nest was that of Savaric of Auxerre.[67] Other prince-bishops enjoyed a better reputation; for example, Charles Martel's own nephew, Hugo of Rouen, was remembered at St. Wandrille as a great benefactor.[68] His successors, Grimo and Ragenfrid, left less savoury local reputations, yet were known elsewhere as friends to reform. As and when Charles Martel overcame huge ecclesiastical communities that were hostile to him, it followed that the conglomerations of secular and church estates that formed them would lose much—and most in the areas where secular power had collapsed longest.[69] He cannot be blamed for seeing the situation politically; indeed, without his ruthless restoration of secular power, the ecclesiastical reforms of his sons could never have taken place. Their very half-heartedness is proof of the difficulty of reversing the slow decline of generations. Carloman himself acknowledged as much when he admitted that he could not carry out the full restitutions anticipated by Boniface.[70] Francia was still on a war-footing, and to have deprived his father's followers of their offices and lands would have been madness—and in many cases unnecessary.[71] In fact, however, Boniface seems to have been less concerned about questions of property than about vacant sees and unworthy holders of church offices.[72] As a firm upholder of the principle of a national church protected by its ruler, he expected the Carolingians to exercise more, not less, authority in the choice of suitable bishops and abbots; and so, in due course, they did. Thus, reform of the kind Boniface championed was not in principle distasteful to any of the Carolingian princes he knew; but it was impossible as an immediate objective. Its reverberations echoed down the entire ninth century.

Research since the days of Levison has done nothing to dim the splendour of Boniface's achievement; it was greater than that of any other missionary of his time. What research has done is to reveal the complexity of the situation he faced, the varieties of Christian experience already available in the lands of his mission, and the difficulties of the men who supported him. These, and not hostility, were the forces to which he was a martyr.[73]

NOTES

1 Levison, ch. 4 and app. 7. The shorter study of S. J. Crawford, *Anglo-Saxon Influence on Western Christendom, 600–800* (Oxford, 1933), though clear and good in some ways, is marred by factual error (for some, see M. L. W. Laistner's review in *History* XVIII (1934), as well as outmoded in interpretation. G. W. Greenaway's *Saint Boniface* (London, 1955) is an excellent introductory sketch, written in the wake of Levison's book. The penetrating résumés of Sir Frank Stenton, *Anglo-Saxon England*, pp. 167–73, and of Professor Dorothy Whitelock, *EHD* I, 88, should not be overlooked. The outstanding recent study of St. Boniface is Th. Schieffer's *Winfrid-Bonifatius und die Christliche Grundlegung Europas* (Freiburg, 1954; reprinted Darmstadt 1972, with an additional note), based on his own researches in *Angelsachsen und Franken* (Akad. d. Wiss. und d. Lit., Mainz, 1950). Also essential is the *Sankt Bonifatius Gedenkgabe* (Fulda, 1954), to which reference is frequently made in this essay; its very full bibliographies should be referred to for well-known studies not cited explicitly here.

2 I am not here referring to matters of detail on which more recent scholars have taken a different view (e.g. the establishment of sees at Erfurt and Eichstätt) but to problems of interpretation.

3 *Les Origines de l'Économie Occidentale* (Paris, 1956), p. 155.

4 I summarize this in *The Long-Haired Kings* (London, 1962), pp. 213–14.

See also R. Buchner, Wattenbach-Levison's *Deutschlands Geschichtsquellen im Mittelalter: die Rechtsquellen* (Weimar, 1953), pp. 15-33.
5 On this distinction see R. Sprandel, *Der Merovingische Adel und die Gebiete östlich des Rheins*, Forschungen zur Oberrheinischen Landesgeschichte 5 (Freiburg, 1957), esp. pp. 96-116.
6 See A. Bergengruen, *Adel und Grundherrschaft im Merowingerreich* (Wiesbaden, 1958), p. 124, and Th. Mayer, *Mittelalterliche Studien* (Konstanz, 1959), p. 297.
7 The situation is well described by F. Prinz, *Frühes Mönchtum im Frankenreich* (Munich-Vienna, 1965), pp. 488-9.
8 See Mayer, 'St. Trudpert und der Breisgau', op. cit., pp. 273-88.
9 *Geschichte des Erzbistums Köln* i, ed. W. Neuss (Cologne, 1964), 146.
10 This has been demonstrated by E. Ewig, 'Die Civitas Ubiorum, die Francia Rinensis und das Land Ribuarien', *Rheinische Vierteljahrs-Blätter* XIX (1954), 1-29.
11 The important work in this field is K. Hallinger, 'Römische Voraussetzungen der bonifatianischen Wirksamkeit im Frankenreich', *Bon. Gedenkgabe*, pp. 320-61, the main conclusions of which are accepted by M. Coens, 'S. Boniface et sa Mission Historique d'après Quelques Auteurs Récents', *Analecta Bollandiana* LXXIII (1955), 462-95.
12 Cf. C. Vogel, 'Les Relations en Matière Liturgique entre l'Église Franque et l'Église Romaine', Settimane di Spoleto 7 (1960), esp. 209 ff.; and H. Frank, 'Die Briefe des hl. Bonifatius und das von ihm benutzte Sakramentar', *Bon. Gedenkgabe*, pp. 58-88.
13 See esp. Th. Zwölfer, *St Peter, Apostelfürst und Himmelspförtner* (Stuttgart, 1929), pp. 74 ff.
14 *MGH, Script. Rer. Merov.* III, 151 ff. Also *Vie des Pères du Jura*, ed. F. Martine (Sources Chrétiennes, 142, 1968), 350 ff.
15 *MGH, Formulae*, p. 181.
16 Bede, *HE* III, 25; Eddius, ch. 10.
17 *MGH, Formulae*, pp. 104, 181, 217 and 278.
18 E.g. *Vitae Columbani* (*MGH, Script. Rer. Merov.* IV, 145); *Fursei* ibid., p. 441; *Audoini* (*Script. Rer. Merov.* V, 559 ff.); *Geretrudis* 2 (*Script. Rer. Merov.* II, 455); *Amandi* 1 and 2 (*Script. Rer. Merov.* V, 434 ff. and 452 ff.).
19 On which see Hallinger's comments on the Frankish use of the word *romensis* in relation to the Rule (*Bon. Gedenkgabe*, pp. 343-6).
20 *MGH, Diplomata* I, no. 93. Schieffer, *Angelsachsen und Franken*, p. 1441, draws attention to its significance.
21 *MGH, Formulae*, pp. 496-8.
22 I usually follow normal usage in employing 'Arnulfing' to describe the family before the accession of Pippin III, and 'Carolingian' thereafter.
23 The point is made, perhaps too forcibly, by Sprandel, op. cit., pp. 115-16.
24 Cf. Mayer, op. cit., pp. 128, 133, 303, 320 and 325, for instances of early Carolingian reorganization after conquest.
25 Sprandel, op. cit., p. 98; Bergengruen, op. cit., pp. 154-61.
26 Cf. Ewig., loc. cit., p. 26.
27 It should be noted that the continuator of Fredegar's Chronicle does not

confine his association of Charles Martel with the divine purpose to Charles' campaigns against the Arabs. In recording Charles's birth his mind turns to Luke 1: 80, and perhaps also to Hebrews 11: 23 (ch. 6: ed. Krusch, *MGH, Script. Rer. Merow.* II, 172; ed. Wallace-Hadrill, *Fredegarius* [London, 1960], p. 86); it was with God's help that he escaped from Plectrudis's clutches (ch. 8: ed. Krusch, p. 173; ed. Wallace-Hadrill, p. 88); in 738 he was victorius against the Saxons *opitulante Domino* (ch. 19: ed. Krusch, p. 177; ed. Wallace-Hadrill, p. 93).

28 A good family-tree, showing the connections of the Arnulfings with other houses, is provided by E. Hlawitschka in *Karl der Grosse* (1, 73).

29 It has been pointed out more than once that Boniface in his early days found no difficulty in associating with this great Frankish lady's household, where he found one of his disciples, her grandson, Gregory, the future bishop of Utrecht. There is no evidence that his feelings towards the family ever changed.

30 Such is the conclusion of Ewig, *Trier im Merowingerreich* (Trier, 1954), pp. 139 ff.

31 On it see Ewig, *Trier*, pp. 133–5, and 'Milo et Eiusmodi Similes', *Bon. Gedenkgabe*, pp. 415 ff.

32 *MGH, Diplomata* I, 92, no. 2; and see the important study of O. G. Oexle, 'Die Karolinger und die Stadt des heiligen Arnulf', *Frühmittelalterliche Studien* I (1967), 250–364.

33 *MGH, Script. Rer. Merov.* II, 429.

34 See the fundamental work of Ewig, 'Beobachtungen zur Entwicklung der fränkischen Reichskirche unter Chrodegang von Metz', *Frühmitt. Studien* II (1968), 67–77.

35 *MGH, Diplomata* I, 101 ff., no. 14.

36 Early Carolingian relations with St. Trond are interesting. Cf. Prinz, op. cit., p. 204.

37 'Beobachtungen', loc. cit., pp. 74–7.

38 See E. Zöllner, 'Woher stammt der hl. Rupert?', *Mitt. d. Inst für Österr. Geschichte* LVII (1949), 1–22.

39 *Die Briefe des heiligen Bonifatius und Lullus*, ed. M. Tangl, *MGH, Epistolae Selectae* I, 124, Ep. 60 (of 745), where Pope Zacharius refers to Gewilib as having been mentioned in a letter from Boniface. It is not quite clear from Zacharius's letter of 751 (ibid., p. 198, Ep. 87) that Milo had been mentioned directly by Boniface, but it is a fair assumption.

40 So Ewig, 'Milo', op. cit., p. 422.

41 See H. Büttner, 'Mission und Kirchenorganisation des Frankenreiches bis zum Tode Karls des Grossen', *Karl der Grosse* I, 458.

42 Kilian has left no literary traces at Würzburg. Cf. B. Bischoff and J. Hofmann, *Libri Sancti Kyliani* (Würzburg, 1952), p. 5.

43 See J. Dienemann, *Der Kult des heiligen Kilian* (Würzburg, 1956); Karl Bosl, *Franken um 800* (Munich, 1959), pp. 88 and 98; 'Die Passio des heiligen Kilian und seiner Gefahrten', *Würzburger Diözesangeschichtsblätter* (1952), p. 1.

44 For a general study see G. Jecker, 'St Pirmins Erden- und Ordensheimat', *Archiv für Mittelrheinische Kirchengeschichte* V (1953), 9–41.

45 Cf. Ewig, 'Beobachtungen', loc. cit., pp. 70–1, and 'Descriptio Franciae', *Karl der Gross* I, 174–5.

46 Mayer, op. cit., pp. 303–25.

47 See J. Werner, *Das Alamannische Fürstengrab von Wittislingen* (Munich, 1950).

48 See Ewig, 'Descriptio Franciae', op. cit., p. 173.

49 So Sprandel, op. cit., p. 97.

50 *MGH, Epistolae Selectae* I, 212, Ep. 93.

51 See H. Löwe, *Ein literarischer Widersacher des Bonifatius: Virgil von Salzburg und die Kosmographie des Aethicus Ister* (Akad. d. Wiss. und d. Lit., Mainz, 1951), p. 966 and *passim*; and B. Bischoff, 'Il monachesimo irlandese nei suoi rapporti col continente', Settimane di Spoleto 4 (1957), 130. See also K. Hillkowitz, *Zur Kosmographie des Aethicus* (Frankfurt, 1973) for another view.

52 Ed. (in part) by Krusch, *MGH, Script. Rer. Merov.* VII, 517 ff.; in full, but unsatisfactorily, by H. Wuttke, *Die Kosmographie des Istriers Aithikos* (Leipzig, 1853).

53 Cf. Löwe, op. cit., p. 931.

54 *MGH, Epistolae Selectae* I, 37–8, Ep. 22. See also the comments of F. L. Ganshof, 'L'Étranger dans la Monarchie Franque', *Recueils de la Société Jean Bodin* X (1958), 5–36, and Schieffer, *Winifrid-Bonifatius*, pp. 145–6.

55 For examples see Marculf's Formulary I, 24 (p. 58) and *Additamenta*, no. 2 (p. 111).

56 'Milo', op. cit., p. 412.

57 Boniface's *falsi fratres* were of several nationalities, to judge by their names: Frankish, Irish and English (perhaps Willibrord's men?).

58 *Angelsachsen und Franken*, pp. 1463–71.

59 E.g. Löwe in *Deutsches Archiv* XI (1955), 583–4, A. Bigelmair, 'Die Gründung der mitteldeutschen Bistümer', *Bon. Gedenkgabe*, pp. 271–3, and less positively Coens, loc. cit., pp. 489–90. It was also the opinion of Levison, pp. 80 ff.

60 *MGH, Epistolae Selectae* I, 235–6, Ep. 109 might suggest that Boniface's interest in Cologne was bound up with the problem of Utrecht. Zacharius's letter to Boniface of 31 October 745 does not state that this was why he had done as the Franks asked in the first place and appointed him to Cologne (ibid., p. 124, Ep. 60). On the matter generally see *Geschichte . . . Köln* I, 144, and Büttner, *Karl der Grosse* I, 465.

61 *MGH, Epistolae Selectae* I, 152, Ep. 73: 'multa privilegia ecclesiarum et monasteriorum fregisses et abstulisses inde quasdam facultates.' See also ibid., p. 169, Ep. 78.

62 An addition to Boniface's letter (ibid., Ep. 73) adds the name of Charles Martel as an example of a spoliator, and this is the earliest known charge against him. The author of the first detailed charge is Hincmar of Reims (*MGH, Script. Rer, Merov.* III, 252).

63 *La Propriété Ecclésiastique en France* II (2), 263. Lesne's extended treatment of Charles Martel's policy towards church property is ibid., II, (1).

64 Ibid., II, (1), 2.

L

65 There is no evidence for the oft-repeated statement that Charles needed lands to enfeoff cavalry to meet the Arab threat.

66 Eddius, chs. 4 and 6.

67 For which see Ewig, 'Milo', op. cit., p. 427.

68 *Gesta Sanctorum Patrum Fontanellensium*, ed. Lohier and Laporte (Rouen–Paris, 1936), ch. 8.

69 Cf. Ewig, 'Milo', op. cit., pp. 434–8.

70 *MGH, Epistolae Selectae* I, 123, Ep. 60.

71 W. Goffart, *The Le Mans Forgeries* (Harvard, 1966), pp. 6–22, has argued that Charles Martel's successors pursued a policy of *divisio* based on the actual needs of the churches and monasteries that had suffered deprivation. This may well be true; but it needs further investigation.

72 The point was made by Lesne, op. cit., II (1), 34–5.

73 This article was completed before the publication of D. A. Bullough's *'Europae Pater:* Charlemagne and his Achievement in the Light of Recent Scholarship', *EHR* LXXXV (1970), 59-105, where valuable observations on the Rhineland families will be found. A valuable work of reference is Horst Ebling, *Prosopographic der Amtsträger des Merowingerreiches von Chlothar II (613) bis Karl Martell (741)* (Munich, 1974).

IX

Charlemagne and England*†

The death of Carloman and the beginning of the sole rule of Charlemagne, in 771, were recorded, not long after, by a Northumbrian annalist. These are his words: *Eodem quoque anno Karlmon famosissimus rex Francorum subita praeventus infirmitate defunctus est. Sed et frater ejus Karl, cum dimidium prius patris obtinuit principatum, totius regni monarchiam et Francorum fastigium populorum dehinc est indeptus invicta fortitudine.*[1] It is a record of great happenings far away; but it is not the only one of its kind. Northumbrian monks heard about the Carolingian kings from various sources, including compatriots in Carolingian lands. Such news, when it could be had, took equal place in the Northumbrian annal with news of the Mercians. Especially interesting to the Northumbrians was the Carolingian drive to establish Frankish arms and religion throughout the Saxon world and thus complete what had been begun by St. Willibrord and Pippin II, St. Boniface and Charles Martel. There was Willibald's Life of St. Boniface, the ink scarce dry, to remind Englishmen of that astounding career. It had been written in response to requests from Englishmen among others.[2] Clear proof of English interest in Charlemagne's Saxon campaigns of 772/73 is a letter from the Northumbrian king Alhred and his queen to Lul, asking him to act as intermediary between their messengers and Charlemagne.[3] There are other signs that the Northumbrians felt that they were concerned as a people in the conversion, imminent as it seemed to them, of the Old Saxons. It had been the same king Alhred whose synod had dispatched Willehad on a

---

* References for this chapter start on p. 173.
† *Karl der Grosse, Persönlichkeit und Geschichte*, ed. H. Beumann (Düsseldorf, Schwann, 1965), 683–98.

mission to the Frisians, from which he was later to be called by Charlemagne to higher responsibility among the Saxons. Lul seems never to have had the ear of his Frankish masters in quite the same way as had Boniface, though even he had seldom felt secure; but Charlemagne's Saxon campaigns were based on Mainz, Lul's own see, and the two men were clearly in touch, as the above letter testifies. Only with Charlemagne's active concurrence can Lul have been promoted to archbishop in 780 or soon after.[4] Charlemagne's Saxon campaigns, at least in their early stages, must have seemed to promise the realization of a Northumbrian dream that had begun long ago with the mission of St. Willibrord.

Meanwhile, King Offa of Mercia showed no interest in the prospects that excited the Northumbrians, or none that we know of. His time was taken up in campaigns of his own, that widened his authority beyond what any previous English king had known. Some of them seem to have been against the Northumbrians.[5] This campaigning corresponds in time with a comparable widening of Carolingian authority by Pippin III and Charlemagne, and, like theirs, is reflected in the titles of royal charters. Offa is *rex Merciorum, rex Anglorum*, and once, in 774, *rex totius Anglorum patriae*.[6] Sir Frank Stenton has taught us to treat these words with care.[7] It was also in 774 that Charlemagne enlarged his title to *rex Francorum et Langobardorum* to correspond with realities.[8] They were following paths not dissimilar. We may here notice another feature of the titles of Offa. He is *rex a rege regum constitutus*.[9] Unconsecrated like his ancestors and very conscious of his lineage, he also follows good English tradition in proclaiming that his kingship owes something to God's approval. He does not choose to define the debt. As early as 764 he is styled, in a grant of land on the Medway to the Bishop of Rochester, *rex Merciorum, regali prosapia Merciorum oriundus atque omnipotentis Dei dispensatione ejusdem constitutus in regem*,[10] where the claim of blood and the protection of God are neatly brought together. He reigns *gratia Dei*.[11]

There were several Englishmen resident wholly or partially in Francia from whom Charlemagne could at any time have learnt about England; but the one with whom he was most often in touch, between 781 and 804, was Alcuin.[12] Considering the relationship from Charlemagne's viewpoint we may note, first, that Alcuin fully shared the opinion of several, perhaps many, of his contemporaries, including King Offa, that there existed an English *patria*. It distinguished all Englishmen from the Celtic and continental peoples, though not from the Old Saxons. Alcuin could sense the historic roots of this *patria* from his reading of Bede. In a letter to Archbishop Æthelheard, he inserts a history-lesson to point the moral that what had been won by their ancestors might be lost by their own shortcomings. It is a *patria* that is at stake: *fiat haec patria ab illo nobis nostrisque nepotibus conservata in benedictione sempiterna;*[13] a *patria* with inseparable religious overtones. Beyond this, however, we must recognize in Alcuin a narrower patriotism. He was a Northumbrian. Charlemagne, himself alive to the implications of *patria*, learnt most about English affairs from a man whose sympathies were first Northumbrian, who cannot always have applauded Mercian intervention north of the Humber, and who was capable of shrewd analysis of Offa's local difficulties.

Victories rather than difficulties marked the two or three years following Alcuin's arrival at Charlemagne's court; and the effect of these cannot have been lost on England. The Anglo-Saxon chronicler notes, under 782, that 'in this year the Old Saxons and the Franks fought'.[14] The Frankish annals mark the consequence: the Saxon leader, Widukind, fled for refuge to the Danes.[15] It would also not have escaped notice in England that in 781 Charlemagne's sons, Pippin and Louis, had been anointed kings in Rome by Pope Hadrian.[16] Offa, meanwhile, had much strengthened his position. The process brought him in touch with the big men of Europe. There exists an extraordinary letter from Pope Hadrian to his friend Charlemagne that shows the kind of way in which this happened. It seems to belong to the year 784 or 785.[17] In it, the pope writes that he has learned from Charlemagne of a rumour which Offa himself wishes to discredit. It is to the effect that Offa had approached Charlemagne with a proposal that the pope should be deposed and replaced by a Frankish candidate. The whole story, concludes the pope, is *incredibilis*. Nonetheless, the tone of his letter, and the mere fact of the consideration he gives it, suggests that there may have been something behind it. The pope was frightened. For his part, Charlemagne cannot have relished the implication that an English king was ready to interest himself in the person of the pope. It meant that Offa had discovered that a pope, like a king, was an office-holder, and as such might be deprived of office if found unworthy to exercise it. This was the price of the new emphasis upon worthiness for public office.

But why might Offa have been so dissatisfied with Hadrian as to have approached Charlemagne in this way? A solution may lie in the relations of Offa with Jaenberht, his archbishop of Canterbury. If Jaenberht had identified himself with Kentish resistance to the Mercians—and it is likely enough that he did—this alone would hardly be reason for an open rupture in 784 or 785. The immediate trouble may have lain in Offa's plan to anoint[18] his only son, Ecgfrith. What more likely than that the hostile Jaenberht had declined to anoint Ecgfrith, that Offa had appealed to the pope to depose him and substitute a compliant archbishop, and that the pope had refused? Whether for this or some other reason, the pope was alerted to the danger of neglecting the English Church.

We can only concern ourselves with the subsequent papal mission and legatine synods in England in so far as they touch Charlemagne. Of the two legates, one was in a sense Charlemagne's man. George of Ostia, bishop of Amiens, had many connections with the Frankish court. These have been summarized by Wilhelm Levison.[19] Of particular interest is his known familiarity with the synodal procedures of the Frankish Church; for there can be no doubt of a parallelism of English and Frankish interests in church reform at this time, as exemplified in synodal decrees and measures of ecclesiastical administration. What is more, the two legates were accompanied by an official observer of Charlemagne's, the abbot Wigbod. We do not know his role; but his presence means that Charlemagne was not prepared to let the pope look after his own affairs in England, and that Offa was ready to tolerate a kind of Frankish supervisory interest at a critical moment. Moreover, the team was joined by Alcuin, a familiar figure at the Frankish court, though possibly less well known at Offa's.

Offa was serious about the reform of the English Church and willing to re-establish England's ancient link with Rome; to be masterful with churchmen was not to question the might of the heavenly hosts arrayed on the king's side through their mediation.[20] However, his immediate gain from the Roman mission was the settlement of his differences with Canterbury. This took the form of a division of the province of Canterbury and the consequent establishment of a Mercian province with its see at Lichfield. Offa must have been aware of recent Carolingian policy in the creation of archbishoprics,[21] for it had involved Englishmen. Charlemagne seems to have had some part in persuading the pope to sanction this deviation from the plan once approved by Pope Gregory the Great. He would have agreed with Offa that an archbishop hostile to his king was intolerable, and with the pope that measures of reform were reasonably bought at the price of the establishment of the province of Lichfield.[22] The administrative gain to Offa may have been appreciable; the political gain, in the anointing to kingship of his son, Ecgfrith, presumably by an acquiescent archbishop, was not less. The Anglo-Saxon chronicle records these happenings in such a way as to culminate in the consecration.[23] It only makes sense against the background of contemporary Carolingian practice of associating an anointed prince in his father's rule. Offa was playing the Carolingian to strengthen his dynasty in English eyes. In so doing he was binding himself ever more closely to the Church. This too, was the Carolingian way.

It is reasonable to associate with this consecration an admonitory letter addressed by Alcuin to King Ecgfrith:[24] reasonable because the consecration provides the best occasion, and because the writer emphasizes the virtuous example of Ecgfrith's parents, as if they were still living. The letter is a reminder, in authentic Carolingian tradition, that a king is consecrated to moral duties; his people's prosperity depends on this. He must attend to the Church's teaching: *cupiens te proficere in Deo virtutumque floribus ornari et cunctis Anglorum populis prodesse in prosperitatem*. In a world of treachery and uncertain loyalties Offa and Ecgfrith saw added security for their house in acceptance of the Church's guidance. Offa must have pondered the meaning of the eleventh canon of the legatine council, *de officio regum*, with its stress on obedience to bishops, and have weighed it against the twelfth, *de ordinatione et honore regum* on the sacred character of a *christus domini, rex totius regni* and *haeres patriae*.[25] These were no empty phrases. They were read aloud to him in the vernacular.[26]

Probably we ought also to associate with these events an important development in Offa's coinage—namely, the beginning of the issue of portrait-coins of Offa and of his queen, Cynethryth.[27] These have been interpreted as a reminder to Charlemagne and others of Offa's power in England,[28] but Charlemagne had no such coins of his own before his imperial coronation, and the point might have been lost on him. The portraits are of high quality and are the work of native artists. Contemporary manuscripts of the Canterbury School are enough to show what English artists could do in this

way.[29] But why should Offa have conceived the idea of portrait-coins
when he did? Late-classical Roman inspiration is plain enough in
a general way, but we have no particular reason to think that Roman
coins became available to Offa only about the year 787. A possibility
that might be worth consideration is that Offa found his inspiration
in some Roman gem used as a seal on a Carolingian document. The
use of gem-seals was a Carolingian introduction, and thus relatively
new. Offa's friends in Francia who would certainly have been
familiar with them would have included Alcuin and Gervold (or
Gerbod), abbot of Saint-Wandrille since about 787, and previously
bishop of Évreux. Gervold was also supervisor of customs in the
Channel ports, and it was because of this that he became friendly
with Offa. If considerations of foreign trade or prestige abroad
played any part in Offa's issue of portait-coins, the effect would
have been principally felt in the area of the Seine ports and those
near by, over which Gervold exercised control. Charlemagne used
two seals. One was an oval gem with a bust 'en face' of Antoninus
Pius (or Commodus, according to Sickel), in a metal setting
bearing the inscription † *XPE PROTEGE CAROLUM REGE
FRANCR*; the other, with no inscription, was an oval gem with a
bust 'en face' of Jupiter Serapis.[30] A glance at the Carolingian gem-
seals reproduced by Mabillon will suffice to show that Offa's artists
did not copy either of these; but the resemblance is enough to suggest that Offa may have taken Charlemagne's seals to be genuine
portraits and accordingly have ordered his skilled artists to represent
him in the same kingly fashion on his coins. They could then have
turned to Roman coins in Canterbury for models. The result would
be less a challenge to Charlemagne than an English adaptation of a
Carolingian practice. This may have happened in another instance.
A unique offering-coin of Pippin III may be the inspiration of Offa's
lost *S. Petrus* coin, which is now thought to have been part of his
offering of 365 mancuses to Rome in gratitude for St. Peter's help
in victory.[31]

Whatever we make of this (and coins are tricky), Offa was clearly
alive to what rulers outside England were doing. We may almost
think in terms of a kind of dawning professionalism among the
western kings. Another aspect of this professionalism was growing
concern with the business of law-making and learning and teaching.
Though nothing survives of Offa's legislation, unless obliquely in
Alfred's, we still know something about it that is interesting. We

know that it was grounded in *mores*. Alcuin twice refers to this, in letters written in 787.[32] The Carolingians also believed that the enforcement of moral teaching was the proper business of legislation, and none more than Charlemagne. Alcuin proffered the same moral advice to Carolingian, Mercian and Northumbrian kings. In the long run it may matter more to reflect on this than to search for diplomatic relationships. As to teaching, Alcuin sent to Offa, at the latter's request, one of his favourite pupils, to be a teacher: *praevidete ei discipulos*,[33] he adds. He is delighted that Offa has an *intentionem lectionis*: thus might the light of wisdom shine in his kingdom. *Vos estis decus Brittaniae, tuba praedicationis*. Cathwulf or Jonas would have addressed his Carolingian master in just such terms. Had Offa some intention of establishing a palace school of his own?

In this atmosphere of emulation some match-making was attempted. It may, however, be as well to recall that dynastic marriages were designed to bring an end to periods of hostility or coldness as often as they affirmed longstanding friendly relations. In 711, for example (and it is one of the rare instances of a Carolingian marrying a foreigner), Pippin II had married his son Grimoald to a Frisian princess to secure his victory over Radbod, the Frisian ruler. The initiative now came from Charlemagne, who proposed that Charles, his eldest son, should marry one of Offa's daughters.[34] The young Charles had been made a king in 788 and had taken over the duchy of Maine in the following year. Plainly he was to devote himself to western affairs. No better match, therefore, could have presented itself to the Frank. The Gesta of the abbots of Saint-Wandrille, written shortly after Charlemagne's death, are our authority for the negotiation.[35] Offa, they report, would not accede unless Bertha, Charlemagne's daughter, were betrothed to his son, Ecgfrith. Charlemagne, *aliquantulum commotus*, broke off negotiations and closed his ports to English merchants. But why should he have reacted thus? One explanation is that he thought himself demeaned: recalling his Bible, he might have reflected that 'the thistle that was in Lebanon sent to the cedar that was in Lebanon, saying, Give thy daughter to my son to wife' (2 Chron. 25, 18). His grandson, Charles the Bald, on the other hand, was to see nothing demeaning in marrying his daughter Judith to Æthelwulf in 856. Moreover, Ecgfrith was already an anointed king, whereas the young Charles seems to have had to wait till Christmas, 800, for that honour.

Another explanation is that Charlemagne had no intention of marrying any of his daughters. Einhard states that he wished never to part with them.[36] But in practice this was not quite what happened. For example, though it came to nothing, his infant daughter, Rotrudis, was betrothed to the emperor Constantine VI in 781,[37] though the initiative appears to have been taken by Constantine's mother, the Empress Eirene. On the face of it, Offa seemed to be suggesting a fair bargain. But it was a fair bargain that implied a certain lack of trust on his part. Any connoisseur of heroic tales would have known how risky dynastic marriages were. It may be that he planned to keep what amounted to a Carolingian hostage at his own court, in case Charlemagne were tempted to use the added power that the presence of the Mercian princess would give him to influence Offa's enemies in England or elsewhere. The consequent closing of Frankish ports to English merchants (always objects of suspicion) provoked Offa to reciprocal action.[38] The quarrel took some time to patch up. It may have been no coincidence that the abbot Gervold of Saint-Wandrille took some part in the marriage-negotiations and later managed to get the ports open once more. Contemporary interest in the projected marriage may find some reflection in two later tales linking Charlemagne and Offa in marriage. The tale of Drida, *consanguinea* of Charlemagne, is told in the thirteenth-century St. Albans *Vitae Duorum Offarum*.[39] According to this, Drida was banished for her crimes from Francia and took refuge with Offa. He married her, but finally built St. Albans as a thank-offering for her assassination. The second tale, reported by Asser,[40] is that when Offa's daughter Eadburh was left a widow (she married Beorhtric of Wessex during the time of the quarrel) she fled to Charlemagne, who presented her with the choice of marrying his son or himself. By making the wrong choice, she got neither. It may be that the historical Eadburh did flee to Francia: we cannot disprove it.

There could, too, be some connection between the dispute and Charlemagne's decision to admit Egbert of Wessex to Francia, when the latter was driven out by Beorhtric and Offa in 789.[41] He remained an exile in Francia for three years.[42] It was not necessarily from Francia direct that he returned to Wessex in 802, and we do not know if he resumed his throne with Frankish help. The exile was long enough, however, and the person important enough, to show the unwisdom of falling out with Charlemagne. He was too powerful and too near not to offer a natural refuge to Offa's enemies;

and there were plenty of these. It is easy to see why Offa had his doubts about Alcuin's loyalty,[43] and why he was sensitive to the presence in Francia of English exiles. Charlemagne personally interceded with Offa for one such party of exiles, when its leader, Umhringstan, had died, but his excuses for sheltering them in the first place sound rather thin.[44]

Friendly relations between the two kings were re-established some time in 791.[45] Offa took an early opportunity to up-grade the weight of his penny coinage and increase the size of the flange on which the coins were struck, so bringing his coinage into line with the recently-modified coinage of Charlemagne.[46] This may argue English economic dependence on Frankish markets, to an undetermined extent. Another explanation is that Offa simply saw a profit to himself in monetary reform, as Charlemagne also may have done. A third, that a general reform of weights and measures was taking place in Francia and England.[47]

Charlemagne was more obviously concerned to win English support in his quarrel with Byzantium on image-worship than to further Franco-English trade.[48] The defence of theological orthodoxy lay at the heart of his notion of kingship and at that of Alcuin, his mentor. The atmosphere in which they thought out their position was tense with emotion. The years 792 and 793 were critical in English and European history, and were felt to be so. In the first place, there was famine, associated with portents and, by the English, with the sack of Lindisfarne and the earliest attacks of the Norsemen.[49] For Charlemagne, this was accompanied by the revolt of the Saxons. The anxious spirit of the Anglo-Saxon chronicler is echoed by the fathers of the church assembled at Frankfurt in 794: *experimento enim didicimus in anno quo illa valida famis inrepsit, ebullire vacuas anonas a daemonibus devoratas et voces exprobationis auditas.*[50] In sacking Lindisfarne first, the Norsemen happened to have chosen a place peculiarly sacred to the English. It awakened in Alcuin's mind a whole picture of England's past, of his people's pagan beginnings, their conversion and their subsequent prosperity under Christian rule. In a letter of consolation to Bishop Higbald of Lindisfarne, he added that he would speak to Charlemagne when he returned from campaigning and see whether he would be prepared to use his influence with the Danes to succour the captured *pueri* of Lindisfarne or to help in any other way.[51] So we know that in 793 Charlemagne was able to contact the Danes and that, in the opinion of someone well placed to know, they might listen to what he had to say. Monastic *pueri* being in question, one is tempted to think that the Danish king was expected to look upon Charlemagne as the natural spokesman for the Western Church.

The spokesman, whether or not he intervened, was soon afterwards immersed in the great reforming synod of Frankfurt. The English Church may have been represented at the synod, which, though not ecumenical, was certainly more than Frankish.[52] It has been argued that English (or British) representation would have been unnecessary since the English Church was not interested in the synod's main business, the heresy of Adoptionism.[53] But other matters more interesting to the English were discussed, to judge from the capitulary: monastic discipline, for example, and the jurisdiction of metropolitans and bishops. This last would have been especially interesting to Englishmen, in view of the recent difficulties of Offa and Jaenberht. Everyone knew that disaster was the fruit of disobedience to the divine will. In face of material disaster of several kinds, English churchmen might have wished to join with their continental colleagues in an attempt to find ways to assuage God's wrath. We need not read into this the subjection of Offa to Charlemagne, which is unlikely enough on other grounds. But Offa could have gone thus far towards accepting Charlemagne's moral leadership in a crisis.

We have now reached the time when thoughts of empire were taking shape in the mind of Charlemagne, perhaps placed there and nourished by Alcuin. They were thoughts of a religious bent.[54] He uses the title *defensor sanctae dei ecclesiae* in a letter asking Offa, his *dilecto fratri et amico*, to recall a Scottish priest from the diocese of Cologne, where his flesh-eating in Lent had caused scandal and the bishop had chosen to refer the case to the priest's home-diocese for judgement.[55] His tone is not that of master to subordinate, any more than it is in the letter, already referred to, asking Archbishop Æthelheard to intercede with Offa for Umhringstan's friends in exile.[56] On the other hand, his position is not just that of the well-meaning foreign friend. We can see this when he comes to distribute the Avar treasure captured in 795,[57] for part of it went as a thank-offering in gifts to foreign churches. The English bishops received their share. We have Alcuin's letter that presumably accompanied the gift: *sciat quoque dilectio vestra, quod dominus Carolus res vestrae sanctitatis valde desiderat ad Dominum suplicationes, seu pro se ipso et sui stabilitate regni, etiam et pro dilatatione christiani nominis, seu pro anima beatissimi Adriani pape.* And later: *Vos vero gratanter deprecor suscipite quae misit, et fideliter peragite que deposcit.*[58] The *fidelitas* here required of the English bishops was perfectly consistent with loyalty to their native kings. Nevertheless, they were invited to accept gifts from the victorious leader of Chrisian Europe on the same terms as the bishops directly subject to him: they were bound to pray for him, for the durability of his rule and for the extension of Christianity under his leadership.

The gifts reached kings also. At least two English kings were to be recipients, and perhaps others not strictly English, if we do not limit to any one occasion the gifts made to the kings to whom Einhard alludes when he writes of *reges Scotorum* who had been bound to Charlemagne by the latter's *munificentia*.[59] Offa received from the Avar hoard a belt and sword, together with two silk robes. At the same time he was politely informed of the gifts distributed *per metropolitanas civitates* and was asked to pray for Charlemagne, for Charlemagne's faithful people and above all for the whole *populus christianus*.[60] Another recipient would have been King Æthelred of Northumbria, had he not been murdered in the meantime. His assassination once more roused Charlemagne to an exhibition of anger that looks disproportionate in a foreign king. Alcuin wrote to Offa on the matter.[61] After expressing Charlemagne's continued esteem for Offa and referring to the presents already sent, he goes on to give an account of Charlemagne's reaction to the news of the murder: *in tantum iratus est contra gentem— ut ait, 'illam perfidam et perversam et homicidam dominorum suorum', peiorem eam paganis estimans—ut omnino, nisi ego intercessor essem pro ea, quicquid eis boni abstrahere potuisset et mali machinare, iam fecisset.* The perfidy of faithful men to their king had provoked the protector of the *populus christianus* very nearly to the point of active intervention. To Offa no threat was intended, and he was enough a man of the world to see that Alcuin's part in the business had lost nothing in the telling; but he cannot have misunderstood this plain statement that Charlemagne would forcibly intervene in the affairs of an English kingdom afflicted by *infidelitas*. Nor would he have missed the point that Charlemagne was as warmly interested in the Northumbrian dynasty as in his own, and had intended to treat Æthelred and himself as equal and independent recipients of his largesse.

In the letter[62] in which Charlemagne announced that he was sending Avar war-gear to Offa, he tells Offa that English pilgrims might continue to pass through his territories to Rome without molestation; but he wouuld not tolerate merchants disguised as pilgrims to avoid payment of *telonea*. Charlemagne adds, in reply to Offa's inquiry, that English merchants travelling aboard *protectionem et patrocinium habeant in regno nostro legitime iuxta antiquam consuetudinem negotiandi*. In case of trouble they might refer to him or to his officers. He expects reciprocal protection for Frankish merchants in England—*ne aliqua inter nostros alicubi oboriri possit perturbatio*. The accepted position was that pilgrims were a privileged class. In 802, indeed, Charlemagne fixed a minimum scale of entertainment for all foreign pilgrims.[63] But merchants were not privileged. Like all other foreigners abroad, they were lawless and lordless, liable not merely to pay *telonea* but even to be sold into slavery unless someone took them under his protection. There are known cases, notably concerning English merchants at Saint-Denis in 710 and 753, when foreigners were protected against special hardship by a king. But such privileges were *ad hoc* and repealable.[64] Therefore, in offering his *patrocinium* to all bona fide English merchants, Charlemagne was bestowing a privilege conceived within the limits of an undefined *antiquam consuetudinem negotiandi*. But it was in response to pressure from Offa. It would be possible to interpret this initiative as evidence that Offa had felt the effects of the recent period of commercial isolation more keenly than had Charlemagne: he wished to get back to the old arrangements as they had stood before the closing of the ports and the lapsing of the privileges of those who used them.

Charlemagne's letter goes on to reveal one particular aspect of England's Frankish trade. He writes that Offa shall certainly have his assistance in obtaining certain black stones he requires[65] but since he has been explicit about their length, Charlemagne will pass on a request from his subjects (*nostri*) about the length or width (probably the latter) of English exported *saga*: *ut tales iubeatis fieri quales antiquis temporibus ad nos venire solebant*. Perhaps the *saga* had also been victims of the quarrel. Whether we understand by *sagum* a finished article such as a cloak or blanket, or a length of material, e.g. serge (and all these are possible translations), we are dealing with a woollen product and, to judge from the context, a product of quality. We can infer nothing as to quantity, and have no reason to think that these *saga* were destined for any particular (e.g. military) use.[66] Pirenne made a good case, if no more, for the view that the famous *pallia fresonica* were lengths of cloth manufactured in Flanders;[67] or at least some of them were: we cannot entirely rule out Frisia as a source of supply and should be very unwise to rule out England. Professor Carus-Wilson thinks the evidence points to a considerable sale of cloth on the open market in Western Europe in the seventh and eighth centuries, with England catering for high-grade exports. She further thinks that religious communities and great lay households would have been a steady market for commercially-produced cloth, though she is cautious about the scope of such an industry.[68] We must reckon with the possibility that commerce may have brought Offa into quite close touch with foreign communities great and small, particularly in the Seine valley and areas dependent upon it. These would include Saint-Josse, Saint-Wandrille, and Saint-Denis.[69] Making all allowances—and there is little evidence beyond Charlemagne's remark to Offa—we conclude that English cloth was known in the Frankish markets of the eighth century, and that buyers were accustomed to take some of it at a standard size. Cloth merchants must have been among the English merchants whose activities abroad are established;[70] but we cannot say that their business was either regular or large. Charlemagne could suddenly bring it to a stop without fear of repercussions among his wealthy subjects. He could also expect that an English king might intervene to regulate exported textiles.[71] The numismatic evidence will not much help us to a view of the significance of English exports, whether cloth or any other. Offa's coins have been found fairly widely scattered,[72] but they have not been found in Francia and Carolingian coins in the British Isles are few and far between. This has been interpreted as 'perhaps the strongest caveat against citing Carolingian coins and coin finds as evidence of commercial relations, or the absence of numismatic remains as evidence of no commercial relations. It is probable that such international dealings were uniformly conducted in a species of money other than coin . . . coinage and commerce are not inseparable.'[73]

The death of the great Offa in 796, and the brief reign of his only son, Ecgfrith, revealed the personal nature of his political achievement. What he had built collapsed. He had never made peace with his Kentish subjects. The last year of his life saw a further revolt against his overlordship in Kent, and this continued for two years.

We cannot connect it with Charlemagne; all the same, it is worth
remembering that his protégé, Egbert, was probably the son of
Ealhmund, once ruler of independent Kent.[74] Alcuin attributed this
collapse to moral causes; he knew of the bloody beginnings of Offa's
reign. The 'décomposition', moral as well as political, that struck
the Frankish Empire almost from the moment of its inception in
800,[75] struck England four years earlier: *tempora periculosa sunt
in Britannia, et mors regum miseriae signum est.*[76] Alcuin did not
say that God would have looked more kindly on the English people
if Offa had been a consecrated king, though he may have believed
it. Years at the Carolingian court had done nothing to dim his sense
of the value of ancient lineage. In 797 he writes to the people of
Kent, apropos the disturbed state of the country: *Et illi ipsi populi
Anglorum et regna et reges dissentiunt inter se. Et vix aliquis modo,
quod sine lacrimis non dicam, ex antiqua regum prosapia invenitur,
et tanto incertioris sunt originis, quanto minoris sunt fortitudinis.*[77]
The kings that had gone and the power they had derived from
blood were much in people's minds. This is a reason for assigning
to the critical year 796, during a few months of which King Ecgfrith
reigned alone in Mercia, the famous Mercian royal genealogy recorded in an early ninth-century Mercian manuscript.[78] Here,
certainly, no Carolingian precedent could be cited; unlike the Merovingians, they lacked any motive to draw attention to their descent.
If we were to seek a precedent anywhere it might be in the Bible,
with its recurrent concern with genealogy,[79] but even this would
leave us with a study that was an Insular speciality. Threatened
from all sides in a disintegrating realm and none too sure of the
reactions of Charlemagne, Ecgfrith turned for support to genealogy
to bolster his royal unction.

Cenwulf, Ecgfrith's successor, never stood as near to Charlemagne
as Offa had done. He too, however was an anointed king,[80] and,
about three years before Charlemagne's imperial coronation, we find
him using the title *imperator* in a way that some have thought provo-
cative and others defensive, though it may have been neither. The
evidence is a land-grant to a *dux* Oswulf, in which Cenwulf describes
himself as *Ego [?Deo conced] ente rector et imperator Merciorum
regni, anno secundo imperii nostri.*[81] The charter is authentic,
unique though it is in respect of the title. The difficulty is one of
interpretation. If we allow, with Stenton,[82] that those who drafted
English royal charters of the eighth century were precise in their

phraseology and innocent of the exuberance of later times, it follows
that the drafter of Cenwulf's charter meant something by *imperator*.
Mercian overlordship had shrunk since Offa's time, but it still embraced Kent, where lay the properties involved in Cenwulf's grant.
Imperator Merciorum might mean Mercian overlord, as seen from
the Kentish point of view; or it might have a religious overtone.[83]
A good English tradition, reaching back to Bede, sanctioned the inter-
change of *imperium* and *regnum*, though not of *imperator* and *rex*.
Alcuin's use of *imperium christianum* in his letters to Charlemagne
was a specialized development of this tradition.[84] The clerical tendency to experiment with 'imperial' words and phrases was affecting
both sides of the Channel at about the same time. It would be super-
ficial to think of one country, as such, influencing the other in
matters of this sort, and absurd to argue from the evidence that
England influenced Charlemagne's decision to become an emperor.
Exchanges between Englishmen and Franks clearly affected their
terminology of government; and we must leave it at that.

There is no hint that Charlemagne saw the Viking attacks on his
shores, which began shortly before his imperial coronation,[85] as part
of a concerted attack on the wealth of England and Francia. As his
armies approached the Danish frontiers, he felt no need to share
his problems of strategy with English rulers. His sense of religious
responsibility, however, was always alerted in the day of battle, and
he may have looked afresh at England as a potential victim of
Danish paganism. Disasters played as large a part as victories in
making him susceptible to the influence of those who wished to see
him a great Christian emperor: the plainest result of the coronation
was an enhancement of his religious responsibility. The Northumbrian annalist gives a shocked account of the attack on Pope Leo III
that led directly to Charlemagne's intervention in Roman affairs in
799,[86] and he continues with a curious note on Charlemagne's actions
in Rome in the following months. He believes that Charlemagne
accepted his new dignity *ut imperator totius orbis appellaretur et
esset*.[87] He further believes that the emperor at once acceded to the
request of envoys from Byzantium and Jerusalem for his protection:
*annuit benignissimus rex beatis precibus qui ad se confluxerant, et
non solum se paratum esse ad devincendos inimicos in terra verume-
tiam in mari si necessitas compulisset.* Alcuin's famous letter to
Charlemagne in May, 799, on the subject of the three world-powers,[88]
strongly supports the annalist's view that in a certain circle

M

Charlemagne's Christian leadership was held no longer to be confined to the lands he ruled as king. The emperor did not interefere, so far as is known, in the negotiations that led Pope Leo III to reverse his predecessor's decision on the archbishopric of Lichfield. He may have had no need to. The pope's letter to Archbishop Æthelheard of Canterbury confirming the rights of his see, is dated: *imperante domino Karolo piissimo consule, Augusto a Deo coronato, magno pacificoque imperatore, anno secundo post consulatum ejusdem domini,*[89] but this implies nothing about the loyalty or obligations of the English Church. Alcuin, also writing to the archbishop, reminds him of the difference between royal and episcopal power but does not mention imperial power.[90] Whatever his claims, Charlemagne may have had no more authority over the English Church than he had over the Asturian or the Beneventan Churches, neither of which ever admitted his claim to exercise imperial *auctoritas*.[91] But this may be too easy a solution. One awkward piece of evidence is the extraordinary incident of the restoration of King Eardwulf of Northumbria. The so-called Lindisfarne annals note (797) that Eardwulf *duxit uxorem filiam regis Karoli*.[92] This information is unconfirmed, and is unlikely enough, though it is not impossible. Levison detected here a twelfth-century confusion with Æthelwulf's marriage to Judith,[93] but did not consider the possibility that Eardwulf married a Frankish princess who, without being Charlemagne's daughter, was still a member of the extensive Carolingian family. At all events, Eardwulf was driven out in 808. He took refuge with Charlemagne, and in 809 was restored by emperor and pope acting jointly. Precisely how they did this it would be interesting to know. Eardwulf was a consecrated king.[94] Charlemagne would be sensitive on this count, quite apart from a long-standing interest in Northumbria that may have been strengthened by dynastic marriage. The Frankish annals are quite clear about Charlemagne's part in the restoration. They report that Eardwulf fled to Charlemagne at Nijmegen, then went on to the pope and finally *Romaque rediens per legatos Romani pontificis et domni imperatoris in regnum suum reducitur.*[95] Charlemagne's two *legati* are named. He was acting here by what he may have considered his overriding imperial authority in a matter of moral importance. This was the pope's opinion. He wrote to the emperor that Eardwulf *vester semper fidelis extitit* and concluded *pro qua re vestra imperialis defensio ubique multipliciter resonat.*[96] Eardwulf, doubtless heartened with a share of Carolingian *munificentia*, returned to his throne as the *fidelis* of an emperor who had exercised the power of *imperialis defensio*. We do not know what the English Church and King Cenwulf thought about the matter; English sources are perhaps significantly silent. But Archbishop Eanbald II of York had taken a leading part in the conspiracy and must have been persuaded by the pope rather than by the emperor to accept reconciliation with Eardwulf. Cenwulf had been sufficiently alarmed by Eardwulf's flight abroad to write to Charlemagne, presumably to put the case against the fugitive, since they were enemies. But he, like the archbishop, accepted the restoration, at least to the extent of not intervening. It is unsafe to conclude that no Englishman, apart from Eardwulf and his followers, shared Charlemagne's view of his right to intervene.[97]

With Eardwulf thus restored and Egbert, once a Carolingian protégé, back in Wessex, Cenwulf cannot have felt altogether happy about Charlemagne. But nothing is known of their relationship. After 804, there was no Alcuin to correspond with English friends. The Anglo-Saxon chronicle notes the year of the death of 'King Charles' and the length of his reign.[98] It does not refer to him as emperor or comment in any way on his pre-eminence. There was, however, an occasion—somewhere between 817 and 821—when Cenwulf may have revealed something of what he thought of the Carolingians. A serious quarrel had broken out between the king and Archbishop Wulfred of Canterbury. It was patched up at a council held in 821, the king insisting on the acceptance of certain prior conditions without which the archbishop should be banished *et nunquam nec verbis domni papae nec Caesaris seu alterius alicujus gradu huc in patriam iterum recipisse*.[99] Haddan and Stubbs saw in these words a probable allusion by the king to the case of Eardwulf and added, 'they may be regarded as a proof of the jealousy with which he regarded imperial interference, and suggest some inter-course between the Emperor Lewis and Wulfred'. Certainly the archbishop had had his Frankish contacts: it was he who introduced the monks of Christ Church, Canterbury, to the form of the *vita canonica* practised by Saint Boniface on the continent and set down as a rule by Chrodegang of Metz.[100] But this does not mean that he was influenced by the Emperor Louis the Pious in a way distasteful to his master. The king's angry words are at least an admission that he recognized the formidable union of the papacy with the Carolingian emperors. When all is said, King Cenwulf did not love

Caesar and was prepared to warn him that his intervention would be unwelcome. But if Cenwulf was, as Alcuin believed, a *tyrannus*,[101] it may have been as well for him that Charlemagne and Louis had less and less time for the troubles of other people than their own.

Charlemagne's relations with England lack precision. This can in part be attributed to our paucity of information. Yet when we have information, we are left to wonder. Who can say how far he was prepared to go in using exiles from English courts to divide and weaken English rulers, or what motives he might have for doing so? The cases of Egbert and Eardwulf, of Queen Eadburh, Umhringstan and even Alcuin, are suggestive in their different ways of Charlemagne's advantages. Can we be sure that Einhard's *reges Scotorum* may not have included the Welsh rulers with whom Offa and Cenwulf were often at war?[102] The increasingly close relations of the English and Frankish churches led to some degree of mutual understanding and even collaboration, but also gave Charlemagne a channel of information about English affairs, and a means of influencing them, that English kings would not have liked. These dangers were always present, and they were not diminished in the emotional atmosphere of the years immediately following the imperial coronation. On the other hand, Charlemagne had something to fear from England. The English could have been dangerous enemies when the Franks were heavily committed with Frisians, Saxons and Danes. They had, too, their own traditional ties with the papacy. In comparison with Offa's dynasty, the Carolingians were parvenus in a society where the claims of blood were still paramount. All in all, we cannot wonder that Charlemagne and Offa treated each other with wary respect and patched up their differences in good time. European historians have underestimated the power of Offa as it would have appeared to Charlemagne. English historians may not have appreciated how formidable Charlemagne was to English kings willing to experiment with the magic of unction.[103]

NOTES

1 In Symeon of Durham, *Historia Regum*, s. a. 771, ed. T. Arnold, *Symeonis monachi Dunelm. opera omnia* 2 (Rolls Series, London 1885), p. 44. On the annals, P. H. Blair, 'Some observations on the Historia Regum attributed to Symeon of Durham' (*Celt and Saxon: Studies in the Early British Border*, Cambridge 1963), pp. 93 ff.; H. Löwe, 'Von den Grenzen des Kaisergedankens in der Karolingerzeit' (DA 14, 1958), pp. 352 ff.; Wattenbach-Levison, *Deutschlands Geschichtsquellen im Mittelalter, Vorzeit und Karolinger* 2, Weimar 1953, p. 248 note 284. On the Frankish material, R. Pauli, 'Karl der Große in northumbrischen Annalen' (*Forschungen zur Deutschen Geschichte* 12, 1872), pp. 139-66. The possibility that Alcuin was Northumbria's principal informant on Frankish affairs is perhaps strengthened by this: the last entry in the original Northumbrian chronicle (the story of Eadburh and Charlemagne, *sub anno* 802) coincides, within a matter of months, with Alcuin's retirement from public activity. Bishop Stubbs noted the point, *Chronica Magistri Rogeri de Hoveden* 1 (*Rolls Series* 51, London, 1868), pp. xi and xxviii. It does not, however, appeal to R. Constantinescu, 'Mélanges d'histoire litéraire carolingienne', *Revue Roumaine d'Histoire*, 2 (1970), p. 231.

2 *Vitae s. Bonifatii*, ed. W. Levison, MG. SS. rer. Germ., 1905, p. 2.

3 *Die Briefe des heiligen Bonifatius und Lullus*, ed. M. Tangl, MG. Epp. selectae 1, 1916, 121, pp. 257 f. There is no reason why we should connect letter 120 (from abbot Eanwulf to Charlemagne) with Northumbria, though that may be its provenance. See D. Whitelock, *English Historical Documents* 1 (London, 1955), 186, p. 766. Professor Whitelock publishes translations of several of the letters discussed below and her notes on them may be consulted with profit.

4 See Th. Scheiffer, *Angelsachsen und Franken* (*Akademie der Wissenschaften und der Literatur in Mainz, Abhandlungen der geistes- und sozialwissenschaftl. Kl.* 20, 1950), pp. 1512-17, on the relations of Charlemagne with Lul.

5 On these early conquests, and the reign generally, see F. M. Stenton's fundamental article 'The Supremacy of the Mercian Kings' (*English Historical Review* 33, 1918), esp. pp. 447 ff. In a posthumously published paper, 'The Anglo-Saxon coinage and the historian', *Preparatory to Anglo-Saxon England* (Oxford, 1970), pp. 378 ff., Sir Frank Stenton considers Offa's relations with the Carolingians.

6 *Cartularium Saxonicum*, ed. W. de G. Birch (London, 1885), 1, 214, p. 302.

7 'Supremacy', p. 452.

8 The earliest example given by Mühlbacher, MG. DDKar., is dated from Pavia, 5 June 774 and is no. 80, p. 114.

9 Haddan and Stubbs, *Councils and Ecclesiastical Documents* 3 (Oxford, 1871), p. 483. English readers will find that several of the documents cited below from a (better) Monumenta edition are also printed in Haddan

and Stubbs, often with English translations in Professor Whitelock's *English Historical Documents*.

10 Birch, *Cart. Sax.* 1, 195, p. 276. I am grateful to Sir Frank Stenton for drawing my attention to this charter.

11 Dr. W. Ullmann has considered the English use of *gratia dei* titles in his *Principles of Government and Politics in the Middle Ages* (London, 1961), pp. 118–19. He rightly refuses to derive Carolingian practice from English rather than from Lombard precedents, both of which are possible sources.

12 Lul received his pallium within a year, either way, of Alcuin's arrival at Charlemagne's court (Schieffer, *Angelsachsen und Franken*, p. 1512).

13 MG. Epp. 4, letter 17, pp. 47 f.

14 D. Whitelock, *The Anglo-Saxon Chronicle* (London, 1961), s. a. 782, p. 34. This is the revised text of Professor Whitelock's translation in *English Historical Documents*. Divergent datings of the manuscripts of the chronicle are noted. The only edition to give the various versions of the chronicle is that of B. Thorpe, *The Anglo-Saxon Chronicle* 1 (Rolls Series, London, 1861).

15 *Annales regni Francorum*, s. a. 782, ed. F. Kurze, MG. SS. rer. Germ. (1895), p. 61.

16 Ibid., s. a. 781, p. 56.

17 The dating is discussed by Haddan and Stubbs 3, pp. 440–3, and by W. Gundlach, in his edition of the Codex Carolinus, MG. Epp. 3, p. 629. I accept the view of Sir Frank Stenton, *Anglo-Saxon England* (Oxford, 1943), pp. 213 f.

18 It may be that a hallowing or blessing by bishops rather than an anointing was contemplated.

19 *England and the Continent in the Eighth Century* (Oxford, 1946), pp. 127 f.

20 Sir Frank Stenton considers that 'no other Anglo-Saxon king has ever regarded the world at large with so secular a mind' (*Anglo-Saxon England*, p. 223). If E. John is right—*Land Tenure in Early England* (Leicester, 1960), p. 78—English ecclesiastical lands were first assessed to fyrd-service by Offa. Yet he was often a benefactor and protector, as several Mercian churches could have borne witness. All in all, he behaved much as Charlemagne in these matters.

21 See E. Lesne, *La Hiérarchie Épiscopale* (Lille-Paris, 1905), *passim*.

22 When in 798 King Cenwulf opened negotiations with Rome for the abolition of the Lichfield province and its reabsorption into a single southern province of London or Canterbury, he admitted that Offa had acted *propter inimicitiam cum venerabili Janberto et gente Cantuariorum acceptam* (Haddan and Stubbs, *Councils* 3, p. 522). But Rome may have known this already.

23 Whitelock, *Chronicle*, s. a. 796, p. 36.

24 MG. Epp. 4, letter 61, pp. 104 f. Dümmler dates it 786–96.

25 Ibid., letter 3, pp. 23 f. The canons are known to us by the report of the legates.

26 The word used in the legatine report is *theodiscae*, on the implications of which see Levison, *England and the Continent*, pp. 126–31.

27 On what follows see the important paper of C. E. Blunt, 'The Coinage of Offa', *Anglo-Saxon Coins*, ed. R. H. M. Dolley (London, 1961), pp. 39–62.

28 Ibid., p. 47.

29 See for example the portraits in the Stockholm Codex Aureus, of which the Canterbury provenance and the late eighth-century workmanship are accepted by E. A. Lowe, *English Uncial* (Oxford, 1960), p. 22. Plates in E. H. Zimmermann, *Vorkarolingische Miniaturen* (Berlin, 1916), Tafel 204a, 280–6.

30 Plates in Mabillon, *De re diplomatica* (ed. 1709), pp. 385–7. See Mühlbacher, MG. DDKar., p. 79, and R. L. Poole's two paper's 'Seals and Documents' and 'The Seal and Monogram of Charles the Great' reprinted in his *Studies in Chronology and History* (Oxford, 1934). An analogous procedure to that outlined above may be suggested by Poole's conclusion on the introduction of the leaden bull into English diplomatic practice in Cenwulf's reign: 'I suggest, therefore, that the idea of using a leaden bull comes from Rome, but that the engravers fell back upon a coin for a model of the lettering' (*Studies*, p. 105). See also P. E. Schramm, 'Karl der Grosse im Lichte seiner Siegel und Bullen sowie der Bild- und Wortzeugnisse über sein Aussehen', repr. in *Kaiser, Könige und Päpste*, 2 (Stuttgart, 1968), 34–44.

31 See Blunt, 'The Coinage of Offa', pp. 44 f. There is no pressing reason to associate Offa's gift (though it was probably intended to be perpetual) with the origin of Peter's Pence, or with the foundation of the English *schola* at Rome. See the discussion in W. E. Lunt, *Financial Relations of the Papacy with England to 1327*, vol. 1 (Cambridge, Mass. 1939), esp. p. 8. Mr. Grierson, however, informs me that he considers the *S. Petrus* coin very dubious.

32 MG. Epp. 4, letter 122, p. 180, and letter 123, p. 181. On *mores principum* at this time see L. Wallach, *Alcuin and Charlemagne* (Cornell, 1959), pp. 13 ff., 64 ff. Lul, writing to York, associated laws and morals thus: *moderni principes novos mores novasque leges secundum sua desideria condunt* (ed. Tangl, 125, p. 262).

33 MG. Epp. 4, letter 64, p. 107.

34 Stenton, *Anglo-Saxon England*, pp. 218 f., infers that the intended bride was probably Ælfflaed.

35 Ed. Dom Lohier and J. Laporte, *Gesta Sanctorum Patrum Fontanellensis Coenobii* 12, Gesta Gervoldi (Paris-Rouen, 1936), ch. 2, pp. 86 f.

36 *Vita Karoli Magni*, ch. 19, ed. O. Holder-Egger, MG. SS. rer. Germ. (1905), p. 21.

37 *Annals of Lorsch*, MG. SS. 1, p. 32, and SS. 16, p. 497. An earlier instance of a Byzantine proposal to heal a breach by a son–daughter and daughter–son marriage and counter-marriage is recorded by Gregory of Tours, *Hist. Lib.* V, 30.

38 Alcuin to Colcu, MG. Epp. 4, letter 7, p. 32. Note that here and in his letter to abbot Adalhard of Corbie (ibid., p. 35) Alcuin betrays no knowledge of the cause of the quarrel, and asks for information.

39 Ed. R. W. Chambers *Beowulf* (Cambridge, 1921), pp. 217–43. The tale of Drida is on pp. 238 ff. Chambers considers (pp. 31–40) the possible con-

nection between Drida and the historical queen Cynethryth, and Drida and Thryth in Beowulf. What we undoubtedly have in the story is a marriage-connection between Charlemagne and Offa.

40 *Life of King Alfred*, ed. W. H. Stevenson (Oxford, 1904), chs. 14–15, pp. 12 ff. Another version of the same story, related to Asser's but not necessarily dependent on it, is in Symeon of Durham, *Hist. Regum*, s. a. 802, pp. 66 ff. See the comments of P. H. Blair (see note 1), pp. 100 ff. Like Stevenson (pp. 206 ff.) and, by implication, K. Sisam, *Studies in the History of Old English Literature* (Oxford, 1953), p. 289, I cannot dismiss the story as legend, apart from the details of the interview between Eadburh and Charlemagne.

41 The suggestion is Stevenson's, *Asser's Life*, p. 207.

42 See Stenton, *Anglo-Saxon England*, p. 218, note 4.

43 See Alcuin's protestation to Beornwin—*vere Offa regi nec genti Anglorum numquam infidelis fui* (MG. Epp. 4. letter 82, p. 125).

44 Charlemagne wrote to Archbishop Æthelheard to intercede with Offa on their behalf and to protest their loyalty: *propter reconciliationem non propter inimicitias aliquantisper retinuimus apud nos* (MG. Epp. 4, letter 85, p. 128). But it may not have looked that way to Offa.

45 It is clear from letters of Alcuin to Joseph and to Adalhard, written at the end of 790, that the ports had not yet been opened (MG. Epp. 4, letters 8 and 9, pp. 33 ff.).

46 I here summarize C. E. Blunt, 'Coinage of Offa', p. 53. Mr Philip Grierson dates Charlemagne's new deniers, which Offa's pennies almost certainly copied in the increase in their diameter and weight, 'poco posteriore al 789. In attesa di nuove prove si propone pertanto che la data dell'introduzione del nouvo denaro sia fissata, con probabilità, non con certezza, all'anno 790' ('Cronologia delle riforme monetarie di Carlo Magno' [*Rivista italiana di numismatica* 56, 1954], p. 14). In 'La trouvaille monétaire d'Ilanz', *Gazette numismatique suisse* 4 (1953), p. 47, Mr. Grierson writes 'il est probable que cela se passa en 790 ou 791'. See also K. F. Morrison, 'Numismatics and Carolingian trade: a critique of the evidence', *Speculum* 38 (1963), pp. 412 ff.

47 This is the opinion of Mr. Grierson.

48 The Northumbrian annalist records that Charlemagne sent on to Britain the *synodalem librum* he had received from Constantinople (Symeon of Durham, *Hist. Regum*, s. a. 792, p. 53).

49 Whitelock, *Chronicle*, s. a. 793, p. 36.

50 MG. Capit. 1, no. 28, cl. 25, p. 76. Compare Charlemagne's religious and charitable measures, taken at Ratisbon in 793, to placate God and assist the starving (ibid., no. 21, p. 52). See F. L. Ganshof, 'Observations sur le synode de Francfort de 794' (*Miscellanea Historica Alberti de Meyer*, Louvain 1946), p. 310, note 5.

51 MG. Epp. 4, letter 20, p. 58.

52 The case is well put by Professor Ganshof, 'Observations sur le synode de Francfort', p. 310.

53 By Wallach, *Alcuin and Charlemagne*, p. 166. To argue, as does Dr. Wallach (p. 167), that Charlemagne's reference, in his letter to Elipand,

to the presence of learned men from Britain is merely Alcuin's rhetoric, and that in fact Alcuin himself was the only Briton present (and then in an unrepresentative capacity), is to strain the evidence rather far. Why should we doubt the accuracy of what Alcuin writes in his master's name?

54 Alcuin's *via regia* letter of 794–5 to Charlemagne well exemplifies the exalted mood (MG. Epp. 4, letter 41, pp. 84 f.) On Charlemagne's personal sense of the religious duties of *imperium* see F. L. Ganshof, 'Le programme de gouvernement impérial de Charlemagne' (*Atti della Giornata Internazionale di Studio per il Millenario* (Ravenna, 1961).

55 MG. Epp. 4, letter 87, p. 131, correctly dated 793–6 by Dümmler.

56 MG. Epp. 4, letter 85, p. 128. Yet another case of an English exile worrying Offa is that of Odberht (Eadberht), referred to by Charlemagne, ibid., letter 100, p. 145. Einhard, *Vita Karoli Magni*, ch. 21, p. 22, reports Charlemagne's personal curiosity about foreigners.

57 *Annales regni Francorum*, s. a. 795; Northumbrian annals (Symeon of Durham, *Hist. Regum*), s. a. 794, p. 57.

58 MG. Epp. 4, letter 104, pp. 150 f.

59 *Vita Karoli Magni*, ch. 16, p. 16.

60 MG. Epp. 4, letter 100, p. 146. In the opinion of L. Wallach, *Alcuin and Charlemagne*, p. 25, Alcuin wrote this letter. In the same context we may recall Charlemagne's letter to Pope Leo III on the subject of their respective duties, his own being to defend the Church *undique* (ibid., letter 93, p. 137. The date was 796.

61 Ibid., letter 101, pp. 147 ff.

62 Ibid., letter 100, p. 145.

63 MG. Capit. 1, no. 33, cl. 27, p. 96.

64 This summarizes the conclusions of F. L. Ganshof, 'L'Étranger dans la monarchie franque' (*Recueils de la Société Jean Bodin* 10, 1958). I am, however, reluctant to follow Professor Ganshof in his suggestion (p. 36) that foreigners holding appointments under the Carolingians (e.g. Boniface, Lul, Beornrad, Willehad, Alcuin) were made Frankish subjects and ceased to be rated as foreigners.

65 What were these *petras nigras*? Certainly not jet or obsidian. Tournai marble for fonts has been suggested; but why the reference to length? The same objection can be raised, as Mr. Grierson has pointed out to me, to their being basalt for mill-stones. In the context of the letter, I should like to associate the *petras* with the cloth or wool trade and see in them the raw material from which stone weights were to be cut. However, there are also difficulties here.

66 Compare the story in the *Gesta Karoli Magni* I 34, that Charlemagne forbad the importation by the Frisians of *brevissima palliola*, and his reasons for so doing (MG. SS. rer. Germ., NS. 12, ed. H. Haefele (1959), p. 47). Mr. Grierson inclines to the view that the change in the width of cloth was a result of a reform in measures.

67 'Draps de Frise ou draps de Flandre?' Reprinted in *Histoire Économique de l'Occident Médiéval* (Brussels, 1951), pp. 53–61. It is worth noting that Gregory the Great sent Eulogius of Alexandria 'sex minora Aquitanica pallia'. *Reg.* I, p. 486.

68 *Cambridge Economic History of Europe* 2 (Cambridge, 1952), pp. 363–6. Professor M. Postan, ibid., p. 239, is also cautious about the activities of English merchants abroad. R. Latouche's statement in *Les Origines de l'économie occidentale* (Paris, 1956), p. 198 (English transl., p. 171) that 'l'hypothèse du reste peu vraisemblable' that *pallia fresonica* were in reality English, is not in fact advanced in the *Cambridge Economic History* 2, p. 234, but is simply mentioned there as a theory advanced by Klumker and others.

69 Offa's charter for Saint-Denis (Birch, *Cart. Sax.* 1, 259, pp. 360 ff.) has been exposed as a forgery by W. H. Stevenson, *English Historical Review* 6 (1891), pp. 736–42, and by Sir Frank Stenton, *The Latin Charters of the Anglo-Saxon Period* (Oxford, 1955), pp. 10 f., but it may, as Stevenson said, relate to actual grants of the pre-Domesday period. There may be a kernel of historical truth in it.

70 English trade with the Seine ports and with Saint-Denis is discussed by L. Levillain in part IV of his 'Études sur l'abbaye de Saint-Denis à l'époque mérovingienne', *Bibliothèque de l'École des Chartes* 91 (1930), pp. 5–65.

71 As Stenton concludes, *Anglo-Saxon England*, pp. 219 f.

72 The one surviving gold coin issued in Offa's name in imitation of an Arabic dinar may have been struck for use in overseas trade, as Mr. Blunt suggests ('The Coinage of Offa', p. 51); but this is only one possibility, and not one that I much favour.

73 K. F. Morrison, *Numismatics and Carolingian Trade* (see note 46), p. 432.

74 See Stenton, *Anglo-Saxon England*, p. 208.

75 See F. L. Ganshof, 'La Fin du règne de Charlemagne: une décomposition', *Zeitschrift für Schweizerische Geschichte* 28 (1948), pp. 433–52; a searching analysis of the Empire's moral shortcomings is H. Fichtenau's *Das Karolingische Imperium* (Zürich, 1949, English trans., 1957).

76 Alcuin to Archbishop Eanbald II of York, MG. Epp. 4, letter 116, p. 171.

77 Ibid., letter 129, p. 192.

78 This is a British Museum Cottonian manuscript, Vespasian B. VI, foll. 108 ff. Edited by Sweet, *The Oldest English Texts*, Early English Text Society 83 (1885), pp. 169 ff. Dr. K. Sisam shows that the Vespasian collection is Mercian, probably from Lichfield, and datable to about 812 (*Anglo-Saxon Genealogies* [Proceedings of the British Academy 39, 1953], pp. 288 ff.). See also K. Jackson, 'On the Northern British Section in Nennius' (*Celt and Saxon* [see note 1]), pp. 23 ff.

79 For example, St. Matthew's gospel starts with the genealogy of Christ the King. In the Irish MacRegol Gospels (8th–9th cent.) in the Bodleian Library, Oxford (Auct. D. II 19) St. Matthew's Liber Generationis Jesu Christi and the following verses to ch. 2, verse 7 (foll. 1ᵛ–3) are framed in red, green or violet lines to enhance their importance; so, too, is the Liber Generationis in St. Chad's Gospels in Lichfield Cathedral Library. See Patrick McGurk, *Latin Gospel Books from A.D. 400 to A.D. 800*, (Paris etc.) 1961, pp. 31 and 40.

80 Birch, *Cart. Sax.* 1, 370, p. 509.

81 Ibid., 289, p. 400.

82 'Supremacy,' pp. 450 ff. R. Drögereit, 'Kaiseridee und Kaisertitel bei den Angelsachsen', *Zeitschrift der Savigny Stiftung für Rechtsgeschichte, Germ. Abt.* 69 (1952), p. 55, is surely wrong to question its authenticity.

83 As also the *imperii piissimi regis Merciorum* of Cenwulf's 811 grant to Archbishop Wulfred (Birch, *Cart. Sax.* 1,335, p. 466).

84 In a discussion of this and other possible links, Levison goes some distance towards Stengel's thesis of an Anglo-Saxon antecedent for the Carolingian *imperator (England and the Continent*, pp. 121 ff.). Cf. E. E. Stengel, 'Imperator und Imperium bei den Angelsachsen', repr. in *Abhandlungen und Untersuchungen zur Geschichte des Kaisergedankens im Mittelalter* (Cologne-Graz, 1965), 289–342.

85 See L. Halphen, *Charlemagne et l'empire carolingien* (Paris, 1947), p. 94.

86 Symeon of Durham, *Hist. Regum*, s. a. 799, pp. 62 ff.

87 H. Löwe, *Von den Grenzen des Kaisergedankens* (see note 1), p. 352, is not necessarily right to suppose that the annalist's account of the coronation reflects more the outlook of the exiled English than of the English at home. Pauli, *Karl der Große*, p. 164, infers some basis in fact for the annalist's account of the years 799–800.

88 MG. Epp. 4, letter 174, pp. 288 f.

89 Haddan and Stubbs, *Councils* 3, p. 537.

90 MG. Epp. 4, letter 255, p. 413.

91 See H. Löwe, *Von den Grenzen des Kaisergedankens*, pp. 354 ff.

92 MG. SS. 19, p. 506, and (a better edition) W. Levison, 'Die "Annales Lindisfarnenses et Dunelmenses" kritisch untersucht und neu herausgegeben' (DA 17, 1961), pp. 447–506, p. 483. Levison dates these annals late eleventh century at the earliest.

93 *England and the Continent*, p. 114.

94 Northumbrian Annals, in Symeon of Durham, *Hist. Regum*, s. a. 796, p. 58; or, if not technically consecrated, certainly hallowed.

95 *Annales regni Francorum*, s. a. 808, pp. 126 f.

96 MG. Epp. 5, p. 90, no. 2. See also no. 3, p. 92.

97 See H. Löwe, *Von den Grenzen des Kaisergedankens*, pp. 353 ff. in a rather different sense. The possible roles of pope and emperor in the restoration are considered by K. Hampe, 'Die Wiedereinsetzung des Königs Eardwulf von Northumbrien durch Karl den Großen und Papst Leo III', *Deutsche Zeitschrift für Geschichtswissenschaft* 11 (1894), pt. 2, pp. 352–9.

98 Whitelock, *Chronicle*, s. a. 814, p. 39.

99 Haddan and Stubbs, *Councils* 3, p. 587.

100 See M. Deanesly, 'The Familia at Christ Church, Canterbury', *Essays in Medieval History presented to Thomas Frederick Tout*, ed. A. G. Little and F. M. Powicke (Manchester, 1925), pp. 10–13.

101 MG. Epp. 4, letter 300, p. 458.

102 E. Bishop, *Liturgica Historica* (Oxford, 1918), p. 172, has written of contemporary English hatred of Irish clerics; and Mrs. N. K. Chadwick surmises (*Celt and Saxon* [see note 1], p. 348) that Offa had an eye to possible Irish danger through Wales.

103 I should like to thank Professor Philip Grierson for his comments on this article. Dr. D. M. Metcalf's 'Offa's Pence Reconsidered', *Cunobelin* 9 (1963) and Dr. K. Sisam's note on Thryth in his *The Structure of Beowulf* (Oxford, 1965), reached me after this article had gone to press.

X

The *Via Regia* of the Carolingian age*†

I borrow my title from the abbot Smaragdus, of St. Michael's, Verdun,[1] or rather, we both borrow it from the Book of Numbers, chapter 21, verse 22: *via regia gradiemur*—'we will go along by the king's high way'. In context, this is a real highway. But Smaragdus lived in the ninth century, and was a man of his own times; and so his *via regia* becomes the Whole Duty of a King. It was this highway, rather than that of the Book of Numbers, which the men of the ninth century made specially and passionately their own. They had not much time for the large matters of political theory, and when it came to the point were glad enough to accept what they found and could grasp in the writings of the Fathers. But in authority they were interested, and in particular the authority of the ruler. Here they had something to say. We can pick our way along their road well enough to see that their opinions about authority form at least one basis of medieval kingship. These opinions were not easily reached, nor were they dominated by any one theme—as, for example, by preoccupation with the delimitation of authority.[2] What rulers might not do or should not do were matters for discussion now and again, as they generally have been. But you cannot systematically restrict a ruler's powers before you have a clear idea of what you want a ruler for, and in consequence the Carolingian age remained hazy about any right to resist authority. The age was also hazy—perhaps hazier than we are—about its heritage of 'Germanic' kingship. Connoisseurs of the early Merovingians will know how little of kingship of any kind came over the Rhine with the Franks.

* References for this chapter start on p. 198.
† *Trends in Medieval Political Thought,* ed. Beryl Smalley (Oxford, Blackwell, 1965), 22–41.

Merovingian kingship was constructed in Gaul out of war-leadership and Roman administrative techniques; and the men who did the work were as often as not churchmen. Thus, the kingship the Carolingians inherited had almost nothing 'Germanic' about it, if by 'Germanic' we mean what Tacitus meant by his *reges a nobilitate*.[3] I speak of the kingship of the Franks, but much the same could be said of the kingship of other barbarian successor-states in the west: of the Visigoths, for example, so much exercised by kingship during their astonishing seventh-century councils at Toledo and so little aware of any 'Germanic' heritage; or Anglo-Saxon England, where Bede not merely described but defined kingship of a kind that Hengist and Horsa could not have guessed at. I doubt if we appreciate the novelty of the Christian kingship that Bede knew, or the creative skill of his picture of it, or the effect that his picture had in England and on the continent in the eighth century, when manuscripts of his biblical commentaries and of the *Ecclesiastical History* became widely diffused. There is, then, if I am right, a long incubation before we reach the *via regia* of the Carolingians. Most of what proved useful and stable in pre-Carolingian kingship was due to churchmen who knew their Bible and their law, and who found their rulers willing listeners. The immediate difference between Carolingian kingship and what preceded it was a difference in temper—and in temperature. A certain amount, then, that I shall say of Carolingian kingship could be found foreshadowed or implicit in a slightly earlier time.

The *via regia*, the king's way, was also God's way, as the ninth century saw it; and so it becomes necessary to speak of the ninth-century notion of the kingship of God. The Carolingians saw God as King of Heaven.[4] To Him they transferred the essential features, duly magnified, of royal power, and then, as it were, borrowed them back. God thus became not only the source of their power but also their model. God in His Heaven was a mighty ruler in His fortress; a fortress, moreover, realistically conceived as prototype of the Carolingian palace at Aix. From this fortress, at once seat of cosmic order and model for its earthly counterpart, God sent forth his Son to do battle for the souls of men. The Father was a great king, the Son a princely conqueror. Perhaps inevitably, the second person of the Trinity stood in some danger of losing his identity or characteristics in those of the first person: it is not the suffering servant that one sees in the Carolingian Christ but the conqueror and the creator.

The Carolingian view of the act of salvation, without denying the Cross, certainly minimized it; and this is reflected in the art of the day.[5] To some, the model and source of power of earthly kings was God the Father; to others it was the Son. On the whole, the Carolingians favoured the Father, though Smaragdus himself was an exception. Their view was theocentric, and not, like the Ottonians', christocentric.[6] Cathwulf put it thus to Charlemagne: *quod tu (rex) es in vice illius (Dei) super omnia membra eius custodire et regere, et rationem reddere in die iudicii.*[7] We should not underestimate the impact of this large, simple vision. Carolingian churchmen could boldly approach the consequences of the connection between their rulers and their God because those rulers could see God as a king. One expression of this, direct and concrete, was the liturgical acclamation of the Carolingian kings known as the *Laudes Regiae*.[8] The *Laudes* were formally a liturgical investigation of parallels between earthly and heavenly rule, pitched in a key that would have been quite foreign to pre-Carolingian ears. They invited reflection on the parallel between a conquering God with his heavenly hierarchy and the king with his earthly hierarchy, each order or member of one having a counterpart in the other; and they uniquely invoked the approval of the earthly ruler by the heavenly. There is correlation at every step, and the tone is one of triumph and conquest and command. Whether his counterpart were God the Father or Christ, the earthly king achieved something of the likeness of God in his heavenly City merely by reason of his supreme position in the corresponding hierarchy: borrowing perhaps from Byzantium, Kosmocrator faced Pantocrator. The king's character was in real truth different from other men's because his position on earth corresponded to that of God in the Kingdom of Heaven—and this altogether apart from the consequences of any king-making rite that might be employed. 'The word of my lord the king shall now be comfortable: for as an angel of God, so is my lord the king to discern good and bad.' The Book of Samuel [II, 14, 17] was familiar to the men who composed the *Laudes Regiae*. Here was no priest-king, no second Melchisedek, but a king who was seen, and who saw himself, as a triumphant warrior because that was how God appeared to him to be:

Rex regum, Christus vincit.
Rex noster, Christus vincit.

> *Gloria nostra . . .*
> *Fortitudo nostra . . .*
> *Victoria nostra . . .*
> *Arma nostra invictissima . . .*
> *Murus noster inexpugnabilis . . .*
> *Defensio et exaltatio nostra . . .*
> *Lux, via et vita nostra, Christus vincit.*

These are among the invocations of the *Laudes Regiae*.[9] They might fit in quite nicely with a barbarian king's determination to go campaigning anyway, but the imagery is specialized. It was derived from imperial Roman acclamations and from the Bible.

When a Carolingian wanted a picture of how a God-directed king should behave, his attention was directed to the Old Testament, and in particular to the two Books of Samuel and the two Books of Kings. At these he could look either directly, for himself, or indirectly, by way of the commentaries of the Fathers: which is one reason why it is so difficult to disentangle the immediate from the more distant sources of ninth-century political thought. Sooner or later, however, it would emerge that the Old Testament kings had got off to a poor start. It was not the prophet Samuel who wanted kings in Israel, but the people; and it was the people that had had to take the consequences. Bede, in his commentary on I Samuel, calls this pressing for kings the pertinacity of a disobedient people.[10] Furthermore, there was from the start the idea that a king of Israel could be good or bad, according to his ability to do the will of Jehovah and to listen to Jehovah's prophets and priests. His was not, properly speaking, a restricted power so much as a power aimed at a certain set of objectives: it existed for no other purpose, and its durability depended on keeping the objectives steadily to the fore. To this extent, the kingship of Israel was an office, a ministry, which could be forfeited like any other office. The Old Testament king could be rebuked or abased, or could abase himself. All the same, it is not clear that this abasing of biblical kings much troubled the Carolingians, who would otherwise have been less keen than they were to see themselves as biblical kings. There was another side to the picture. If the king were God-like and God-given, then conspiracy and rebellion were acts against God. Hraban Maur was very strong on the sinfulness of revolt and listed several examples of what befell those who revolted against their rightful kings;[11] and he started with the good example of David: *David unctus iam rex non ausus est levare manum suam contra Saul regem*, and this though nobody had thought Saul a particularly good king. In practice, then, the Old Testament kings could be said to have enjoyed a certain security of tenure, though their independence of spiritual authority was not nearly so marked as was that of New Testament rulers. They sounded sufficiently attractive to the Carolingians to warrant a cultus of biblical kingship in court circles. It was not to Byzantium that Charlemagne looked for an imperial model but to the Book of Kings: he preferred to see himself as a new David;[12] his son Louis was to see himself as a second Solomon; and to Pippin III, first Carolingian king, Pope Stephen II had written: *quid enim aliud quam novum te dixerim Moysen et praefulgidum asseram David regem?*[13] The mode of comparison goes back even further, to the Merovingians. Nor was it considered any weakening of the royal position when attention was drawn to the official nature of David's rule. He ruled *propter ordinem*, and on this depended his power and his honour; and so, in the *Libri Carolini*, we find the *sanctissimus rex*, David, characterized as *divinae incarnationis minister*. Moses, David, Josiah and Solomon were the great exemplars, and their professional standing and virtues were not confused. Archbishop Hincmar, the Ezekiel of the ninth century, distinguished nicely between rulers chosen direct by God (like Moses and Josiah), rulers who owed their power to God, though men played some part in their making (such as Joshua and David) and rulers who owed their power to men, though divine approval had not been withheld.[14] The idea of the personal sanctity of the ruler, to which I must return, comes straight from the Old Testament. Jonas of Orleans, in his *De Institutione Regia*, bids his king turn to Deuteronomy when he comes to consider *qualis esse vel quid cavere debeat*.[15] Hincmar, again, rebuking Louis the German for his incursion into his brother's lands, refers him to the Book of Kings if he wishes to find out the proper way to treat a brother-ruler.[16] This, then, was the biblical background to Carolingian kingship. Perhaps if we knew the Old Testament as well as the Carolingians did, we should find their royal activity less confusing.

I come next to the making of kings. It is possible to examine the *ordines* of Carolingian consecrations, to evaluate each phrase and word in them and so to arrive at a very clear notion of their total possible significance. What we cannot be sure of, however, is their

N

actual significance to particular people on particular occasions. Schramm's work on early Carolingian coronations and anointings showed that they were confused in aim and uncertain in outcome;[17] and Marc Bloch was struck by the sense of novelty that enveloped them.[18] They varied so much in form through the ninth century that one cannot feel sure what to make of them. Charlemagne was angry on Christmas Day, 800, and we do not know why. His successors were mostly eager to be crowned and anointed; but we do not know why, either. We do not know what each one thought was happening to him. We can only guess; and guessing is a bad start for political theorists.

Nevertheless, we can start from the fairly firm position that a royal consecration in the ninth century, involving unction or coronation or both, was a kind of sacrament. It had to do with the Church. The Church designed it and thought it out with Old Testament precedents very much in view. Whether consecration made a king or confirmed him or admitted him, it bore witness to a link between the king and God, as the Old Testament anointings had done. Was it a new way of making an old kind of king, or an old way of making a new one? We have to be on our guard against the assumption that the western clergy had never taken any interest or part in king-making before 751. It is not certain that 'co-operation with the Church did not become imperative before the rite of royal anointment was introduced',[19] for we have almost no evidence. Imperative or not, however, ecclesiastical participation need have been constitutive only in the sense of assent to the fact of elevation. The stages that preceded ninth-century king-making were not at all new. One way or the other, a suitable candidate had to be found, a man whose qualities were right, a man of *potestas* and, if possible, of the right blood.[20] Thus far he might almost choose himself. There had to be a presumptive right to rule. He had to know that he commanded support. He might then be raised on a shield or acclaimed in more ways than one. But what more? There followed a church ceremony, a ritual, that gave him something extra. It turned him into the ninth-century idea of a ruler in Israel, with all that this might imply about God, God's king, God's priests and God's people. Through a piece of church-magic, as he may have seen it, the Carolingian was put directly in touch with the source of his power. He found himself called son of God by adoption;[21] and I doubt if he paused to consider whether what had been done might not also be undone. What unction did was to bring the Carolingians right into the Old-Testament world of kings, and to invite reappraisal of the basis of rule.

What had the king or emperor (in this context it does not matter which) gained by becoming adoptive son of God in a sense that nobody else in his kingdom or empire could presume to claim? First, he had obtained divine protection for himself and perhaps for his family. 'Who knows', asks Bloch, 'whether rulers did not attach more meaning to this than we to-day suppose, and whether the wish to benefit from the scriptural promise may not have drawn more than one of them to seek the Church's consecration?'[22] In a word, you eliminated rivals. But we must be careful here: it could well be, for example, that the first Carolingian king, Pippin III, was anointed with his family not to protect the dynasty from rivals but because of revived interest in liturgifying biblical parallels[23] and putting them to what we should call political use. Secondly, the king had opened up a new channel to *felicitas*, to good luck and prosperity. This is where the sense of a magic comes in. Charles the Bald believed that by having his queen Irmintrud crowned and anointed in 866, she would again become fruitful and give him better children than the bad lot he had already had.[24] Thirdly, by accepting the burden that God laid upon him, the king increased his own chances of salvation. If this benefit seems imponderable it could none the less have been the greatest of all. Lastly, the king gained a job, with authority to carry it out. He gained it, and was commissioned to undertake it, at his consecration and not before. The *ordines* stress this job-aspect of kingship, and there is no reason to suppose that candidates for unction took this as a grim warning. It was what they wanted to hear: it made them grander; and it gave them a recognizable goal. Any consecrated king had a definite Christian role not less majestic in its way than that of the Byzantine emperors. He was *a Deo coronatus*. To sum this up, consecration did make a different kind of ruler, and not a weaker or more circumscribed kind. It marked no conscious victory for the Church in the sense of the bishops having captured kingship by way of unction. Unction was an experiment, the outcome of which cannot have been foreseen. Further, it was the experiment of an episcopate which, as a coherent *ordo*, was a phenomenon of the Carolingian age;[25] and so when we think of experimental unction we must remember to see it in the setting of a new episcopate and a new kingship at work upon a new relationship that strengthened both. Carolingian consecrations were surely not designed as a series of wily counter-checks on royal absolutism, nor were they based on an acknowledged principle of contract between a king and his consecrators. His contract was with God.

What, then, was an anointed king's job, and what authority had he for his actions?

Charlemagne was quite clear that he was a Christian sovereign ruling a Christian people, though, towards the end of his life, he inquired whether, in view of all that went on, he and his people really were Christians: *utrum vere Christiani sumus?*[26] It is, then, as a community of belief, in an Augustinian sense, that we have to regard the Carolingian state.[27] There was no other state. For its well-being the ruler was responsible and, because its whole purpose was the salvation of its members' souls, the ruler's responsibility could not be confined to their material well-being, any more than was that of the kings of Israel; it was spiritual, too. Charlemagne's interventions in moral and doctrinal issues are readily understandable in this light. Not so readily understandable are the religious motives underlying some of his actions in a more traditional kingly sphere. We all know that the oaths of fidelity he exacted were a safeguard for himself and his family. But they were more, as he points out in his emphatic, almost apostolic, way to the *missi* of 802.[28] In the first place, he says, his faithful men were bound to devote themselves utterly to God's service, remembering that the emperor could not personally watch over the faith of each individual. Moreover, they should in no way damage the interests of churches, widows, orphans or foreigners. A faithful man was bound by his oath never to hinder the emperor's orders or to impede his will or to deflect his justice. Halphen rightly says that 'the implications of the oath of fidelity were infinitely extendible'. They covered everything, because all actions—indeed, all thoughts, could be viewed in the light of their effect upon the aims of Christian society; and the ruler alone could judge of their effect. Any contravention of the Decalogue—theft, for example—ranked as *infidelitas*. The oath was, then, to something more than to the ruler: it was an oath to support the aim of Christian society as interpreted by the ruler. Any man who betrayed the interests of this society was therefore *infidelis*. The Merovingians and their contemporaries, though Christians, had known nothing like this.

His duties, as Charlemagne saw them, were moral duties; all his imperial activities, whether legislative or judicial or military, were an exercise in moral authority. We can see this clearly if we turn to the one composition of his mentor, Alcuin, that can fairly be termed a consistent statement of political theory, the *Disputatio de rhetorica et de virtutibus*.[29] Here and on other occasions, Alcuin was quite clear about his master's duties, which he derived in part from the seventh-century Irish treatise, *De duodecim abusivis saeculi*.[30] These were: to correct, to defend, to judge, not to oppress. He must rule, too (here following Isidore),[31] through terror; and this should save bloodshed because it would lead to the unresisting surrender of his natural prey, the pagan world upon his frontiers. His Christian duty was to follow the example of David and be a conqueror, a subjugator of peoples. More than this, he must be a *praedicator*, keeping his people free from heresy and converting the heathen, though never as a *sacerdos*. To these ends he is blessed by divine grace with the gifts of power and wisdom and *felicitas*. Let him but do his duty and the *felicitas regni* would be fulfilled in the beatitude of the eternal kingdom. Alcuin's interest was simply in his lord's moral responsibility, in the attainment of *stabilitas*, 'the enduring solidity of faith', and in his *morum nobilitas*. From this it followed, almost as a necessary myth, that the ruler must be the wisest and most moral man in his kingdom, an example to all. His moral duties hinged upon irreproachable personal behaviour, again as in the Old Testament; and here at once one sees the way to a formidable brake upon the exercise of sovereign authority. Alcuin's little lecture, however, was not concerned with brakes on sovereign authority but on its proper deployment towards the goal of salvation. He never troubled his head about how or when to get rid of unjust rulers. It was enough to point out to his readers that their emperor was replete with the virtues that alone could make his rule over them efficacious. A later generation had to face the practical problem of *reges iniusti*. As for Charlemagne, 'virtue he had, deserving to command', and that was enough. The peace of the Christian society he ruled was based on its unity of purpose, on its identification with its ruler, and of its ruler with God. Diversity of aim or divergence of any kind on the part of the individual was the evil most to be feared, and above all in the ruler. *Unanimitas*, society's pursuit of Christian peace, strongly suggests a resumption of interest in one of St. Augustine's themes, even if in new guise.[32] We are drawing near to what Arquillière termed 'augustinisme politique'. Charlemagne could command *unanimitas* of a kind, his aims seemed attainable because he himself was a *rex iustus;* and lest he were in any doubt about the precise personal qualifications of such, Cathwulf was at hand to list them for him. Cathwulf called them the eight columns of royal *iustitia.* Here they are:

> *Prima est veritas in rebus regalibus; secunda patientia in omni negotio; tertia largitas in muneribus; quarta persuadibilitas in verbis; quinta malorum correptio et districtio; sexta bonorum elevatio et exaltatio; septima levitas tributi in populo; octava aequitas iudicii inter divitem et pauperem.*[33]

There is nothing here to startle a man brought up in an older tradition. What is new is to regard so mixed a bag of virtues as the only road to efficiency in the office of ruler.

With what or with whose authority did Charlemagne imagine he ruled? Anointed, he ruled *gratia Dei*; and from this *gratia*, however God had bestowed it, his authority as a Christian ruler stemmed.[34] It was an effluence of God's grace, freely and revocably given. The ruler had no right to it, and without it he was no ruler. Again, earlier precedents could be cited: pre-Carolingian kings sometimes thought of divine aid or support as a desirable part of their armament. But this was not quite the same. Divine *gratia* had now become the very source of authority; it alone empowered the ruler to rule; for it was God's rule over God's people that was in question. The earthly ruler was therefore the channel, by grace, for the transmission of God's authority; and it also followed that, as the repository of that authority, the ruler must stand in a new relationship to his people. They were not the source of his authority; that was God; they were literally his *subditi*, his *subiecti*. Whatever of authority they exercised, they exercised by his concession or delegation, not of right. The gulf was widened between king and people. In the course of a remarkable analysis of this development, Dr. Ullmann writes: 'The king by the grace of God had effectively emancipated himself from the *populus* itself and on the other hand freely acknowledged God as the source of the royal power.' Emancipation is perhaps putting it rather strongly. Something depends on how we define *populus*; but I cannot easily picture the pre-Carolingian kings as conscious of being answerable to any *populus* for their authority or sovereignty; so that, if I am right, we have with the Carolingians not so much the substitution of a theory of descending delegation of authority for an ascending one, as the happy acceptance that what was already implicit had become explicit through looking harder at the Old Testament: it made sense to everyone—clergy, king and people—but nobody said, so far as I know, that a substitute had been found for a clearly-understood 'Germanic' theory of popularly-derived sovereignty.

I have said that the bishops of the ninth century saw themselves as and behaved as an *ordo* in a way that was new; and it is time to consider this further, in terms of its bearing on kingship.

Political upheavals must account for something of this revolution. The Carolingian bishops were often called upon to reach great political decisions; and in conclave they had a model of their own.[35] It was the Early Church. They saw themselves as the successors of the apostles grouped round St. Peter. For example, the synod of 829 was shot through with nostalgia for the Early Church, the bishops consciously imitating the council of Jerusalem of A.D. 50.[36] You could say that the model of the Old Testament momentarily yielded place to the New. And what duties will these pastors (for it is as pastors more than doctors or priests that they behave) allocate to themselves? They will correct sin, the social consequences of which were the obsession of the time; they will interpret that reign of justice which kings must establish; they will proclaim the *vita apostolica*, the way of life of the Christian community of Jerusalem, grouped round the apostles after Pentecost. It is the interpretation of a way of life that the bishops undertake; and one can hardly call this a deliberate infringement of royal prerogative.

We meet the *vita apostolica* in the pages of the treatise *De institutione regia*, put together in 831 from the acts of the Synod of Paris of 829 by Bishop Jonas of Orleans, for the guidance of Pippin of Aquitaine. It was a little lecture, addressed to his *domino nobilissimo prosapia, pulchritudine atque sapientia prestantissimo Pippino regi gloriosissimo*. The recent troubles of poor Louis the Pious have not tempted the bishop to take liberties, and we should be quite wrong to think of Louis' so-called deposition as some kind of Canossa. What had happened was this. Louis had threatened peace and unity, the conditions of salvation, because his partitions of the empire had threatened dislocation.[37] So the bishops, or some of them, intervened to convict him of sin; he was no longer *populo dux salutis et pacis*. There was nothing said of deposition. A penance was imposed on the emperor that made it no longer possible for him to rule because he would be shut off from the world. The office of ruler was therefore vacant. In terms of machinery for dealing with difficult kings we have not got much beyond the situation of 751, when the last Merovingian was packed off to a monastery. Machinery apart, however, we can now see 'augustinisme politique' in action. There is no secular state: there is only a secular power within the Church, a necessary weapon of ecclesiastical authority. To paraphrase Arquillière, Natural Law has become absorbed in supranatural justice, the Law of the State in that of the Church. The actions of the bishops matter less than their reasons, and their reasons are bound up with their feelings. Louis the Pious had shocked them in proportion as their feelings about the *vita apostolica* had become intensified. You can sense it, too, in the important letter of Pope Gregory IV to the bishops who had stood by Louis.[38] He also intervenes to rebuke sin: if the sinful emperor cannot ensure peace and unity, he, the Pope, must. Why, he inquires, had not the bishops shown to their emperor the portrait of the just ruler in *De civitate Dei*, V, 24?

To return for a moment to Jonas. There is so much that he does not say to King Pippin. He says nothing about unction, nothing about how divine authority reaches a king, nothing about any right of the subject to disobey a king, nothing about popes, nothing about deposition. But there is much about the king's moral attributes, his judgements and above all his justice, the characteristic and all-enveloping royal virtue. The atmosphere is that of the Old Testament. It might be Samuel speaking. What was the difference, then, between the virtues of the just man and those of the just king? It was a difference of scale, mostly; any man might imperil the salvation of Christian society by injustice, but the king was likeliest to do so because he had had entrusted to him a greater share of divine authority than had anyone else, and had the added responsibility of supervising authority delegated to those beneath him. This was *recta administratio* in action. So far Jonas went. He was a bishop. His whole emphasis, in the words of Delaruelle, was on conservation and morals—an unexpected goal, perhaps, for a member of an *ordo* whose irruption into politics had been revolutionary.

'During the reigns of Louis and Pious and his sons', writes Fritz Kern, 'kingship was more profoundly humbled before the Church than in any previous century.'[39] What would Jonas have made of this? Penance involving relinquishment of rule was humiliation

indeed; but humiliation of a man, not of his office. Others had done
penance without damage to their office—David, for example, and
the Emperor Theodosius. Kings were humbled, not kingship. The
troubles of the mid-ninth century brought into sharp relief the
importance of the personal suitability of rulers to fulfil a moral task,
so that for Christians the idea of kingship had become inseparable
from the idea of right. Carlyle claimed that the ninth-century
bishops saw their princes as barbarians.[40] But a sinner is not always
a barbarian; and a *rex iustus* seemed a possible kind of ruler. The
Carolingian age had no time for the impracticable. The duties of
the *rex iustus*, so clearly delineated for the Carolingians, were
realizable up to a point. If they were auxiliary duties, so also was
every function that God delegated within the hierarchies of Christian society. The pope was the embodiment of Christ, its head; that
was very clear; but within his kingdom and even among his clergy
the king was a man of godlike stature, whose person it was sacrilege
to conspire against: *Cor regis in manu Dei.*[41]

   The business of defining kingship was taken a step further through
the writings and the actions of Hincmar, archbishop of Rheims in
the mid-ninth century. Hincmar was a lawyer; and this is one
reason why kingship in relation to law is best looked at with his help.
Two of his treatises were written to help kings: *De regis persona*[42]
was addressed to Charles the Bald, and *De ordine palatii*[43] indirectly
to Carloman. The first was a collection of *sententiae*, but it was
Hincmar's own collection. Its tone is urgent. What he seemed to
want was an altogether more vigorous king, not afraid to correct,
punish or repress, and ready to fight. He has several chapters on
fighting, mostly from St. Augustine. Ruling he sees as a professional
job; indeed, his full title is *De regis persona et regio ministerio*. I
would say that the purpose of the treatise was to help Charles to be
more powerful in a useful way. *De ordine palatii* looks more
original, though Hincmar may be right to claim that most of it
came from an earlier book by Adalhard. It is an old man's work,
as it looks back to the age of Charlemagne, the imagined golden age
of a Christian society functioning as an organic unit under the priest-
hood and kingship of Christ. But there is something in the emphasis
of *De ordine palatii* that is fresh, something that goes a little beyond
St. Augustine even. I mean, the writer's preoccupation with the king
as creator and servant of law, and his conviction that the king is the
source of all human law made for the proper purpose of fulfilling

or complementing divine law.[44] Human law achieves this by its repressive character: by enforcing, that is, the conditions conducive to human salvation. He is fond of St. Paul's *lex propter transgressiones posita est*. If a man, including a king, were just, he would not feel the restraint of law. The majesty of human law lies, then, in its moral objective and in its power to interpret and enforce divine law, as revealed in the Scriptures; in a word, it is Christian. Hincmar does not state just how wide his definition of Christian law would be; certainly it would include the legislation of the Christian Roman emperors; but he does state that no Christian can plead ignorance of any law that is Christian. Precisely because all Christian law has a moral basis, the Christian ruler, imperfect as he is, must be the first to obey it, whether it be of his own promulgation or someone else's. If he does not, he is not a Christian. All Christian law is equally permanent in its binding effect, and therefore (and this perhaps is Hincmar's contribution) laws should be made accessible and intelligible by codification.[45] Multiplicity of laws leads to disorder. The essence of what he thinks about law is expressed in chapter viii, which runs as follows:

> And just as we have explained that no priest may plead ignorance of the canons of ecclesiastical law or do anything against the rules of the Fathers so also *leges sacrae* [that is, Roman Law] have been decreed that no man can plead ignorance of or dispute. Since it is declared that all men must know the laws and conform to their decisions, no layman, whatever his position, can claim exemption from their authority. Thus there are laws that kings and *ministri reipublicae* must enforce in the administration of their provinces; and there are also capitularies of Christian kings and of their predecessors legally promulgated by them with the general consent of their *fideles*; and these equally must be observed. St. Augustine says of these laws: 'It is right for men to debate them while they are being formulated but once they are agreed upon and accepted, judges no longer have the option to dispute them but only to implement them.'

Provided always that a law furthers the interests of Christian society, it must, then, be considered universally applicable to that society and immovable, whether in origin it be Roman Law, canon law, royal edicts or what we should call barbarian law. As to origin,

Hincmar clearly holds that the ruler is the source of law, whether consented to by others or not. Law is royal and should be royally enforced upon all, clergy and laity alike. The clergy in their persons are not exempt, any more than the king in his person is. Hincmar repeatedly distinguishes persons from their functions, and notably kings from kingship. This may seem obvious enough to us, but it was not so in the early Middle Ages. Once more, it emphasizes that what the Church had been doing to kingship was not to make it the lackey of the hierarchy but to strengthen it by freeing the office from the office-holder. Hincmar could be fairly unscrupulous at times; but he did not use his knowledge of law simply to gain his own ends. He had a firm grasp of its rightful place in an ordered society, and of the ruler's relationship to it. He had, too, for much of his career, to do with a ruler, Charles the Bald, who knew enough law to be personally acquainted with the Theodosian Code.[46] Dr. Ullmann means what Hincmar meant when he writes: 'the enforceable character of the laws was rooted not in the consent given by magnates, barons, etc., but in the royal *voluntas*. Hence the law of the theocratic king was a royal concession.'[47] It could even include royal interpretation of the Bible. Ullmann then goes on to distinguish this royal law from the popular or barbarian law-codes that seem to him to have been grounded in consent. No doubt they once were, but it is unlikely that, as they existed in writing in the eighth and ninth centuries, they were distinguished in this way. Their distinctiveness lay more in the fact that kings promulgated them and gave them the cover of their authority than in the general approval that once lay behind their acceptance. Not for nothing were the Burgundians called, as in Carolingian capitularies, *Guntbadingi*, 'followers of the law of King Gundobad'. The laws of the Bavarians would have been nowhere without repeated intervention of the Frankish kings.[48] No laws could have been royaller than King Alfred's. You will recall Fritz Kern's brilliant pages on 'the monarch and the law' where he writes: 'Law was the living conviction of the community, which, though not valid without the king, was yet so far above the king that he could not disregard the conviction of the community without degenerating into lawless tyranny.'[49] You cannot, however, cover the entire early Middle Ages in this way without being sure that 'community' has an invariable meaning. If Kern means that all new law was technically folk-law as that would have been understood in, say, the sixth century, then it seems to me to be untrue for the Carolingian age as a whole. It brings us, however, within range of the last big problem affecting kingship that I wish to draw your attention to: the problem, namely, of the *populus*. The Carolingians believed that they ruled a *populus*; not a *populus* of Franks, Lombards and others, though they were that, too, but a *populus christianus* whose members were equal in God's eyes and whose sovereign was God. Jonas of Orleans emphasized this equality: *cavendum his qui praesunt, ne sibi subiectos, sicut ordine ita natura, inferiores se esse putent*,[50] and Carlyle was right that the patristic theory of the natural conditions of human nature was one of the few which the ninth-century writers adopted 'with intelligence and conviction'.[51] This *populus*, then, was not the property of its earthly rulers: it was God's *populus*, which it was the ruler's duty to protect and to save. It embraced three *ordines*: laity, monks and clerics. They were ordained by God for the purpose of peace and salvation and were represented in the *Admonitio Generalis* of 789 as the supporting columns of the kingdom. Himself a member of the *ordo laicorum*, the king was master of all three. When all is said, one has the impression that *populus christianus* conveyed a clearer and more significant meaning than did *imperium christianum* to the men of the ninth century. The significance of *imperium christianum* is debatable to us because it was debatable to them.

Did this ordering of the *populus christianus* give it, or any part of it, a right to resist its ruler? The clergy could admonish a wicked ruler and the laity could assassinate him, but neither, as an *ordo*, could depose him. There was no machinery for doing so, and the want of it was not quickly felt. You could say that a bad king, a tyrant, unmade himself by the mere fact of contradicting the purpose of his office, but you really ought to endure him. This was Isidore's position in the seventh century,[52] and Hincmar acknowledged as much two centuries later after sad experience of royal inefficacy.[53] Running counter to this was the practice certainly, and the theory possibly, that men had a right to resist tyranny. If, in the last resort, as Kern says, a tyrant is one who interferes with another man's rights without his consent, then the times were rich in examples of resistance to tyranny of one kind and another; and we do not have to go back to Germanic tribal custom to find a reason for this: Greeks and Romans resisted, too; it is human nature. Rulers with their wits about them habitually did obtain what prior consent they could from

THE 'VIA REGIA' OF THE CAROLINGIAN AGE   197

those liable to be affected by their measures. When, therefore, we read that an eighth- or ninth-century king had decreed this or that in his court *consensu omnium* or words to that effect (including *consensu fidelium*) we should not assume that the consent was constitutive, though it may sometimes have been.[54] Hincmar is vague here. Nor, if it were so, need it have stemmed from a tribal past. 'Popular consent' may also have had religious overtones derived from the Old Testament. We must remember the Chosen Tribe behind the cohesive *populus*. We must remember that the *universus populus* that participated in the downfall of Louis the Pious was conceived in biblical and not in Germanic terms. (Some notion of the activity of the biblical *populus* can be had by referring to Dutripon's Concordance of the Bible, where the word occupies no less than twenty-five columns.) There was, too, the acclaiming voice of the *populus romanus*, liturgicized for the Carolingians by their bishops. *Consensus* may often have been no more than another word for convenience. Its corroborative effect, however derived, can only have been felt to strengthen the ruler's hand, not to weaken it. But still there was resistance of an untidy sort. I mean, that resistance was not a consequence of a clear sense of broken contract between ruler and people. Failure to keep coronation-oaths did not release a people from obedience to its ruler, nor was there any striving after a formalized procedure for expression of or implementation of resistance. What we actually find in the Carolingian age is practical resistance to kings and emperors without intention to limit the power of Christian kingship. There was a real problem here and no mere debating point; sooner or later, someone would want to limit kingship itself: Hincmar very nearly did. General recognition of it dawned, together with a theory of the right to resist, two centuries later. Unsatisfactory Carolingians were disposed of in a variety of ways. Would that we knew more of the circumstances of the so-called deposition of the Emperor Charles the Fat; but, if we did, we should probably find them peculiar to that occasion. So you chased away a bad king or tonsured him or murdered him, and then started again and hoped for the best.

Writing of the Carolingian age, Laistner says: 'It was a salutary thing, such as betokened a time of intellectual awakening, when men turned their minds to political theory, especially to the relation between Church and State.'[55] I am not positive that I know what this means. The state, at least as St. Augustine knew the state, came

hardly at all within the Carolingian purview, and it is certainly untrue if we think of Church and state in eleventh-century terms.
There is more to be said for Carlyle's opinion that 'when we study
the Carolingian writers, we feel at once that we are studying the
writings of men whose tradition of society and government is that out
of which our own has directly and immediately grown'.[56] We feel
this even while we recognize their incoherence and their capacity
for self-contradiction. Their purpose was to rethink, in their own
terms, the problem of authority in Christian society bequeathed to
them by the Fathers. The Church they knew was not the Church of
Gregory the Great, let alone of St. Augustine. The rulers they knew
were not Roman emperors or Byzantine emperors or Germanic
chieftains: they were Christian kings. To confuse the peoples of
Europe with the peoples of Israel was not, you will think, a very
practical first step, and the identification of Charlemagne with David
had no great future. So much of the Carolingian experiment was to
come to nothing, even if something of sacerdotal kingship did survive to bother later generations of students of Roman Law. Yet we
have to see that it was this, the *potestas* of biblical kingship, and not
the beginnings of theories of resistance, that penetrated the thought
of the age and reached down to touch action. This was their *via regia*.

NOTES

1 Migne, *Patrologia Latina*, 102, cols. 933–70. Alcuin also makes use of the
phrase in his correspondence and it is likely that other Carolingian writers
did the same.
2 This is also the view of F. Graus, *Volk, Herrscher und Heiliger im Reich
der Merowinger* (Prague, 1965), p. 347.
3 *Germania*, 7.
4 On what follows see H. Fichtenau, *Das karolingische Imperium*, ch. 2
(English trans., ch. 3). A good English example of the representation of
Christ and the apostles as ninth-century warriors is the beginning of Cyne-
wulf's *Fates of the apostles*.
5 See however A. Katzenellenbogen, 'The image of Christ in the early
middle ages', *Life and Thought in the Early Middle Ages*, ed. R. S. Hoyt
(Minneapolis, 1967), 66–84.
6 E. H. Kantorowicz, *The King's Two Bodies*, p. 77.
7 *MGH. Epist.* IV, p. 503.
8 See E. H. Kantorowicz, *Laudes Regiae. A study in liturgical acclamations
and medieval ruler worship.*
9 Ibid., p. 16.
10 1 Samuel VIII, 19 (*Corpus Christianorum*, CXIX, ii, 2, p. 75).

11 *Liber de reverentia filiorum erga patres et subditorum erga reges* (*M.G.H. Epist.*, V, pp. 406 ff.). See also appendix XXXII of Fritz Kern's *Gottesgnadentum u. Widerstandsrecht* (ed. R. Buchner, pp. 357–9).

12 Fichtenau seems to think that Alcuin borrowed the *nomen* 'David' for Charlemagne from Byzantium, but this is not proved and strikes me as less likely than direct borrowing from the Bible.

13 *M.G.H. Epist.*, III, p. 505. Pippin III is compared with David in at least four other letters, as Dümmler notes. See also the valuable observations of E. Ewig, 'Zum christlichen Königsgedanken im Frühmittelalter' (*Das Königtum*, Konstanz Vorträge III), esp. pp. 45 ff.

14 Cf. H. Schrörs, *Hinkmar, Erzbischof von Reims*, p. 384.

15 Ed. Jean Reviron, ch. 3, p. 139. Reviron's text should not be used, however, without reference to the critique of Dom Wilmart, *Revue bénédictine*, 45 (1933), pp. 214–33. On the date of composition of *De Inst. Regia* see J. Scharf, 'Studien zu Smaragdus und Jonas', *Deutsches Archiv*, 17 (1961), pp. 333–84.

16 Migne, P. L., 126, col. 22.

17 *Der König von Frankreich*, I, pp. 21 ff. See also Janet L. Nelson, 'National synods, kingship as office, and royal anointing: an early medieval syndrome', *Studies in Church History*, vol. 7 (1971), 41–59.

18 *Les rois thaumaturges*, p. 70.

19 Kantorowicz, *Laudes Regiae*, p. 78.

20 Cf. Schramm, op. cit., I, p. 71.

21 For example, by Smaragdus, loc. cit., col. 933.

22 Op. cit., pp. 70–1. Psalm 104 verse 15 reads 'nolite tangere christos meos et in prophetis meis nolite malignari'.

23 The suggestion is made by Kantorowicz, *Laudes Regia*, p. 56.

24 Schramm, op. cit., I, p. 23. See also Ernst H. Kantorowicz, *Selected Studies* (New York, 1965), 82–94, 'The Carolingian King in the Bible of San Paolo fuori le mura'.

25 This important point was well made by E. Delaruelle, 'En relisant le *De Institutione Regia* de Jonas d'Orléans', *Mélanges Halphen*, pp. 187 ff.

26 *Capitula tractanda cum comitibus, episcopis et abbatibus*, ch. 9 (*M.G.H. Capit.*, I, no. 71, p. 161). See also the excellent paper of F. L. Ganshof, 'L'église et le pouvoir royal dans la monarchie franque sous Pépin III et Charlemagne'. *Settimane di studio del centro italiano di studi sull' alto medioevo*, Spoleto, VII (1960), pp. 95–141.

27 For what follows see L. Halphen, 'L'idée d'état sous les Carolingiens', *Revue historique*, 185 (1939), pp. 59–70, and *Charlemagne et l'empire carolingien* (2nd ed., 1949), *passim*.

28 *Capitulare missorum generale*, chs. 3–9 (*M.G.H., Capit.*, I, no. 33, pp. 92–3).

29 Discussed by L. Wallach, *Alcuin and Charlemagne*, pp. 29–96.

30 Ed. S. Hellmann, *Pseudo-Cyprianus de XII abusivis saeculi, Texte u. Untersuchungen* (ed. Harnack and Schmidt), 34, i. See also L. Wallach, op. cit., pp. 8 ff., whom I follow.

31 *Sententiae*, 111, 47, 1 (Migne, P.L. 83).

32 The essential texts are cited by Ewig, loc. cit., pp. 68 ff. See also F. L. Ganshof, 'La *Paix* au très haut moyen âge', *Recueils de la société Jean Bodin*, XIV (1962).

33 *M.G.H., Epist.*, IV, p. 503.

34 The implications of *gratia* are fully examined by W. Ullmann, *Principles of Government and Politics in the Middle Ages*, pp. 117 ff., whom I here attempt to summarize, with slight differences of emphasis. See the same writer's discussion of Charlemagne's concept of rule in his *Growth of Papal Government in the Middle Ages* (2nd ed.), pp. 106 ff.

35 Cf. Delaruelle, loc. cit.

36 *M.G.H. Capit.*, II, pp. 6–7, 26 ff.; *M.G.H., Conc.*, II, pp. 596 ff.

37 The situation is best analysed by H. X. Arquillière, *L' augustinisme politique*, pp. 170 ff. See also Reviron, op. cit., pp. 99 ff.

38 *M.G.H., Epist.*, V, pp. 228–32.

39 *Gottesgnadentum*, p. 193 (English trans., p. 104).

40 R. W. and A. J. Carlyle, *A History of Mediaeval Political Theory in the West*, I, p. 220.

41 Proverbs xxi, 1.

42 Migne, P.L. 125, cols. 833–56.

43 ed. Maurice Prou, *Bibl. de l'école des hautes études*, 58 (1885), and by V. Krause, *M.G.H., Fontes iuris Germ. ant. in usum scholarum* (1894).

44 See the useful analysis of J. Devisse, *Hincmar et la loi* (Dakar, 1962), esp. p. 86.

45 As noted by Devisse, op. cit., p. 82.

46 Cf. *Expositiones pro ecclesiae libertatem defensione*, I (Migne, P.L. 125, col. 1039).

47 *Principles of Government*, p. 123.

48 The passage deserves quotation *in extenso*: 'Theodericus rex Francorum, cum esset Catalonis, elegit viros sapientes, qui in regno suo legibus antiquis eruditi erant. Ipso autem dictante iussit conscribere legem Francorum et Alamannorum et Baiowariorum unicuique genti, quae in eius potestate erant, secundum consuetudinem suam; addidit, quae addenda erant, et inprovisa et inconposita reservavit. Et quae erant secundum consuetudinem paganorum, mutavit secundum legem Christianorum. Et quicquid Theodericus rex propter vetustissimam paganorum consuetudinem emendare non potuit, post haec Hildibertus rex inchoavit, sed Clodherius rex perfecit. Haec omnia Dagobertus rex gloriosissimus per viris illustribus Claudio Chado Indo Magno et Agilolfo renovavit et omnia vetera legum in melius transtulit et unicuique genti scriptam tradidit, quae usque hodie perseverent' (ed. K. Beyerle, p. 8).

49 *Gottesgnadentum*, p. 127 (English trans., p. 73).

50 *De Institutione laicali*, II, ch. 22 (Migne, P.L., 106, col. 213).

51 Op. cit., I, p. 199.

52 Isidore's classic statement on kings and kingship is *Etymol.*, IX, 3.

53 For example, in *De fide Carolo regi servanda* (Migne, P.L. 125, cols. 961–84).

54 P. Classen, 'Die Verträge von Verdun und von Coulaines', *Hist Zeitschrift*, 196 (1963), shows how alert the *fideles* or magnates were to their political opportunities in the mid-ninth century.

55 *Thought and Letters in Western Europe* (2nd ed.), p. 315.

56 Op. cit., I, p. 197.

XI

The Franks
and the English in the ninth century:
some common historical interests[1]*

When Simon de Montfort turned on King Henry III with the words 'You ought to be locked up like Charles the Simple'—words which the king never forgave—he was drawing upon a stock of historical tradition accessible, in one form or another, to many gentlemen in western Europe. Englishmen and Frenchmen alike could be expected to know, and did know, something about Charles the Simple. They knew even more, of course, about other members of his family; about Charles the Bald, for example, and Charles the Great. How could it have been otherwise? The Carolingians had made the world in which the western seigneurial houses had taken root and grown up.

The evidence that much of this background was never forgotten, and suffered, not destruction, but embellishment, as the generations passed, is elusive and difficult to assemble, let alone to evaluate. It has not yet been properly worked out for France (despite the lead given by M. Fawtier[2]), much less for England, although here again a way has been shown by Mr. Ronald Walpole in his study of the two Middle English romances, *Roland and Vernagu* and *Otuel and Roland*.[3]

I wish now to consider only the very beginnings of this long process and to try to suggest some ways in which the political difficulties confronting the Carolingian kings affected historical writing (I use the term loosely) in eighth- and ninth-century France, and how comparable troubles in Anglo-Saxon England equally found their reflection in men's approach to, and use of, historical material. I am not going to speculate how this or that Frankish manuscript

* References for this chapter start on p. 215.

came to be known in England; nor, conversely, why this or that Frankish writer should have been able to draw on English sources. As and when this is worth doing, it should be done by an expert. Nor am I going to suggest that the writings I shall mention constituted a conscious body of propaganda, for plainly they did not.

I begin by looking at France.

We know, from the work of Levison, R. L. Poole and others, that, with certain great exceptions (for example, the *Histories* of Gregory of Tours), historical writing in Merovingian France owed much to English example. Behind the earliest Frankish annals lay Bede's chronology and English annals, or at the least English annalistic experience. (Sir Frank Stenton says bluntly that the Frankish annals 'were imitated from English models'.[4]) Yet my impression is that, despite Bede, the Franks and the English (I am thinking of the mid-eighth century and before) may not have had so very many historical interests in common. Anglo-Frankish trade there was, and Anglo-Frankish marriages, both affecting more of England than Kent; both, I do not doubt, as significant of friendly relations as we are told they were; though they were insufficient to evoke from Gregory of Tours the slightest interest in England, or from Bede much more than passing references to France (the history of which, admittedly, he was not writing), or from the hagiographers of the intervening century overmuch admission, Eddius alone excepted, so far as I can tell, that France and England were neighbours. Should we, I wonder, even be certain that the Franks and English continued, after the migration period, regularly to contribute to and to draw from a common reservoir of epic tradition? I am not convinced that *Beowulf* proves that they did, or *Widsith*. Even in the field of diplomatic, the theory of mutual indebtedness tends to disintegrate on careful examination: Levison, for example, demonstrates that the earliest Kentish charters were based, not upon Merovingian, but direct upon Roman models.[5] To call France, then, as Aldhelm does in a letter to the abbot of Péronne, *famosus* and *florigerus*[6] is perhaps more his good manners than an acknowledgement of England's direct debt to her.

Somewhere after the middle of the eighth century comes the beginning of a change; and the change is heralded, unless I am mistaken, by a development in the use of annals, so that they become full enough to have a narrative and a theme; and these annals are Frankish, not English. Their associations are with northern France and the Rhineland, and more particularly with the religious foundations over which the Carolingian family had influence. The nature of the development is, I suspect, implicit in the words of the last continuator of the chronicle of Fredegarius, when says, in a well-known passage, 'Up to this point the great Count Childebrand, uncle of King Pippin, caused this history or *Geste* of the Franks to be written down, with all possible care; and from now on the authority is Nibelung, the illustrious, the son and successor to Childebrand.'[7] In other words, we are dealing with family history, or something very like it. A great house, closely associated with the monastic missionary movement, appropriates one of that movement's most powerful weapons, the art of 'writing-up' the past, and turns it to its own use to justify and explain the eclipse of the royal dynasty of the Merovingians. In the eighth decade of the century, under Charlemagne, we reach the fully-collated *Royal Annals*, with the king as their central figure and his campaigns as their main matter; and they are our chief narrative source of information for his reign. I remind myself of two features of these annals. First, that their collation antedates Charlemagne's imperial coronation and thus cannot have been regarded by contemporaries as a new form of historical writing specially designed to bolster imperial pretensions. And, second, that war is their theme—war for the furtherance of Christianity, war for the keeping of good order, war for the defence of Frankish lands against attack from outside: especially the last two. It is well enough known that Charlemagne's final years were clouded by the growing Danish menace (and to this I shall return); but his whole career was, in a sense, a ceaseless campaign of defence—the defence of his house against enemies, within and without the limits of his kingdom.[8] To his successors, the most remarkable feature of his reign was the way he had had of curbing the fierce valour of the Franks themselves. This he had done by protecting their homelands and by finding them new lands and more plunder elsewhere. Like Ermanaric, the great Amal chieftain of the Goths, Charlemagne was *nobilissimus* to his followers and to their descendants because conquest made it possible for him to be lavish in his gifts, a generous ring-giver.

In the Frankish annals of the ninth century (the series is unbroken to the 880s), the continuous labour of the defence of Frankish Europe against the Danes and others ceases to be a royal and becomes an imperial duty. Those who interested themselves in the

Roman historians would have observed that defence of this sort always had been an imperial duty. An emperor ought to be a warrior. Further, they would have argued, an emperor's deeds ought to be chronicled in a form more worthy, more personal to himself, than the annalists could manage. And so Einhard, the Suetonius of his age, wrote his *Vita Karoli Magni*,[9] the first secular biography of the Middle Ages; and in his wake followed a remarkable succession of Frankish writers directly dependent on him. At certain of these I wish to look more closely.

Whether or not Einhard felt the need to leave a true picture of the master to whom he owed much, and whether or not he had the slightest interest in depicting Charlemagne as he really was, there can be no question that the *Vita* was written at a time of crisis, political and social. By the 830s, the Frankish chieftains, despite Danish and other raids, were behaving very much like their ancestors, long ago taken to task by Gregory of Tours for their *bella civilia*; with Charlemagne out of the way, they were reverting to type; and there was a need to remind them, vividly, that imperial subjects ought to have nobler employment than mere foraging about on each other's estates. What was more, the imperial family, the Carolingians themselves, needed a reminder that emperors were not just kings with exceptional opportunities—they were different in kind. The *Vita* provided the Franks with just such a vivid picture, perhaps inaccurate but certainly plausible, of how an emperor should live and how his subjects should behave. It does not seem to me to matter very much whether Charlemagne in fact lived as Einhard says he did; whether, for example, his concern for law-giving or for vernacular literature or for the liberal arts was as real as Einhard asks us to believe. Perhaps it was—it is possible; M. Halphen, as against M. Ganshof,[10] feels rather sceptical. What does matter is that the picture made sense to Einhard's readers and hearers. In general, it must have agreed with the historical facts, which men still remembered. If it had not done so, it would not now exist in nearly one hundred manuscripts, some of them very early in date. Einhard did not, I need hardly add, invent Charlemagne or his reputation; he simply gave the ninth century the Charlemagne it wanted—a Charlemagne fitted into a historical context that made him appear to be the end of a process and the crowning of an endeavour—the first Carolingian really to get away with not being a Merovingian. The fact that Einhard falsified the best-known annals made no difference;

annals and *Vita* could settle down quite happily together, even in the same manuscript, as we can see them doing in two Vienna MSS, and a Montpellier MS., all of the ninth century. The general picture was right, and Einhard's new *Geste*—which he says he feared might prove to be boring—was a complete success. Any doubt that might remain on that score may be removed by reading Walahfrid Strabo's preface to his own edition of the *Vita*, made in the 840s for a special home of the Carolingian cult, the monastery of Fulda.

Einhard's way of looking at Charlemagne was the way, also, of Charlemagne's grandson, Charles the Bald; and while we cannot be certain that Charlemagne deliberately modelled his rule, as Einhard alleges, upon this or that imperial precedent, we can be quite sure, because contemporaries leave us no room for doubt, that Charles the Bald saw himself as Einhard's Charlemagne, and was encouraged to do so by his advisers—chief among them, Hincmar of Reims. His reign has thus the pattern of deliberate and intricate archaism: *moribus antiquis res stat Romana virisque*. Various aspects of this archaism have been subjected to careful study. I am thinking of the work of E. H. Kantorowicz on the liturgical side,[11] and, with less enthusiasm perhaps, of that of Simon Stein on Charles's legal interests.[12] Of the latter, it is only fair to state that even if Stein is wrong, as against Krusch and the rest of the world, in acclaiming *Lex Salica* as a ninth-century forgery (complete with bogus glosses[13]), he is certainly right in emphasizing the great legalistic activity of the mid-ninth century. There *is* no manuscript of *Lex Salica*—and this holds also for the so-called *Lex Salica Emendata* of Charlemagne— that can be dated with any confidence earlier than the reign of Charles the Bald. Furthermore, our knowledge of Charlemagne's capitularies is based largely on the collections made by Charles the Bald; and whether or not Charles meant to deceive contemporaries, he plainly long misled posterity into thinking that *Karolus Magnus* at the head of a capitulary could refer only to his grandfather and never to himself. All the same, it was not, I suspect, Charles the Bald who started the myth (if myth it is) of Charlemagne the Legislator, but Einhard in his 29th chapter—itself based on Suetonius' *Life of Augustus*—for Einhard there says that Charlemagne, once emperor, realized that he ought to complete his people's laws, though as a matter of fact he only got as far as collecting them and committing them to writing. Yet this was enough.

However, it is with historical writings rather than with legal collections that I am concerned. I turn next to the *History of the Sons of Louis the Pious*,[14] composed between 841 and 844 by Nithard, son and successor to Angilbert, lay-abbot of S. Riquier, and thus grandson of Charlemagne. Nithard knew the *Vita Karoli Magni*; and he knew also the two *Lives* of Louis the Pious which may be said to constitute a continuation of it. To these he wished to add a *pièce justificative* on his kinsman, Charles the Bald; and he sat down more or less in the middle of battle to add it. The result attracted not too much attention at the time. Yet, here once more, it is the appeal to the golden age of Charlemagne that counts, the attempt to link Charles the Bald—at the expense, naturally, of his brothers—to the tradition of his grandfather.

What did Nithard think, or say, were the characteristics of Charlemagne's rule? 'I have not found it possible' he writes in his prologue addressed to Charles the Bald 'to pass over in silence the sacred memory of your grandfather, and so the beginning of my story will be with his reign.' Then he plunges straight into his subject: Charlemagne, full of wisdom and courage, terrible, lovable, admirable, glorious and very old (already '*Blanche ad la barbe e tut flurit le chef*'!), died leaving Europe full of felicity; and, what was more remarkable, he died having curbed the savagery of Franks and barbarians to such an extent that they no longer dared attempt anything, anywhere in the Empire, that was not in the public interest. Nithard is contrasting what is expected of Franks with what is expected of an imperial people, what happened under Charlemagne with what was happening in his own day. And he does it again in his last chapter: 'In Charlemagne's day peace and concord reigned, but now each man follows the path that pleases him best.'

May I notice one other feature of Nithard's book?—the introduction of the Strassburg oaths in the vernacular. Now, it may be that Charles the Bald and Louis the German did exchange these oaths in the forms given by Nithard. It may be that Nithard records them because he was himself their begetter, or because, in the vernacular, Charles could be made to sound as if he got a better deal than Louis. Possibly the original oaths were recorded in Latin. But these are surmises, and I tentatively add another: that they were included, quite simply, as a concession to the ninth-century Frankish taste for all vernacular, of which Einhard again is an early witness (Chap. 29: 'Charlemagne also had copied down the oldest barbaric poems in which the history and the wars of the original kings were sung. This he did to save them from destruction. And he started a grammar of the mother-tongue.' Then follows Einhard's account of the Frankish names for the months and for the winds). A greater than Einhard, Servatus Lupus, wrote, in September 847, to his friend Marcward: 'You have instructed our pupils in your native tongue, a knowledge of which is nowadays so necessary that only the idle are without it.' (The same Lupus, ten years earlier, had made a collection of barbaric laws for Evrard of Friuli.) This 'native tongue' was East, not West Frankish; the vernacular interests of the community of Fulda, notably under Hraban Maur, are of particular interest. I mention, in passing, this concern for the vernacular, about which a great deal more can be, and has been, said, because I think it may have some bearing upon a parallel concern in England.

Through all this occasional, biographical literature, sometimes drawing on the annals and sometimes not, runs a growing concern at the threat of the Danes. They are the god-given enemy against whom a good king, an emperor made in the classical mould, will wish to measure himself, and his people with him. It was the Danes, primarily, who made it necessary for Charles the Bald—long, of course, before he was emperor—and then Charles the Fat, to be like Einhard's Charlemagne. The invasions presented Charles the Bald with the necessity of buying-off some of his own magnates before they went over to the Danes, who knew when to make attractive offers. His kinsman Pippin II of Aquitaine closed with them in 857.[15] All that Charles could offer such followers was land he could ill afford to alienate and the reproach of his ancestors. What he feared was not outright defeat, but desertion and disintegration. Roughly speaking, the growth of the threat may be gauged from the mounting anxiety of Frankish writers to identify their rulers with Charlemagne. In the year 881, the Danes stabled their horses in the palace at Aix (or so the Fulda annalist reports) and shortly afterwards appeared Notker of St. Gall's *Gesta Karoli*, written at the request of Charles the Fat. In it occurs the famous passage describing Charlemagne in tears as he watched the Northmen in their longships manœuvring off the coast: *nimirum contristor quod me vivente ausi sunt litus istud attingere, et maximo dolore torqueor quia praevideo quanta mala posteris meis et eorum sunt facturi subjectis!* Few today would spend time arguing whether Charlemagne ever said anything of the sort, though phrases such as this (and, of course, Notker has others) were quite likely to have been cherished in oral tradition over the seventy intervening years. In fact, Notker was a simple fellow; he built on a foundation of Einhard and the annals, he used his childhood memories, he knew how to invent, and he knew the tastes of his contemporaries.[16] The *Gesta Karoli* is a tract, one effect of which must have been to sustain one of the most vigorous and most unhappy of the Carolingian kings in his subjects' esteem while he struggled to concentrate their energies upon the Danes. Notker prayed that Charles should have a son to undo the damage the Danes had done in his father's lifetime, but without success. The Carolingian call to resistance met with a weaker response at the turn of the century, though it cannot be proved altogether to have died out.

Soon after Notker comes Abbo, with his epic on the siege of Paris (in 885–6).[17] Contemporaries were agreed about this siege; it was the greatest trial of all. Fulk of Reims wrote to Charles the Fat that if Paris, head and key to the kingdoms of Neustria and Burgundy, were to fall to the Danish armies, it would be the end of France. The poem has no hero—not even, I think, Odo of Paris, on whom the real burden of the defence rested. In a sense, the Frankish people is the hero; but behind them stands the Carolingian emperor; he is 'the prince who is the subject of my song—*princeps de quo canitur*'. And this was to say very much, when one recalls (as the hearers of the poem would have done) that Charles was in the end deserted by his warriors and died, abandoned, far from Paris. His successor in France, Odo, owed his throne not to any general feeling that the Carolingians were effete, but simply to the temporary absence of a Carolingian of suitable age. Charles' son was a child: *et instante immanissima Nordmannorum persecutione periculosum erat tunc eum eligere*. That is what Fulk of Reims said, and I believe him.[18] Abbo finishes his poem by apostrophizing France, whom he takes to task for her vices; these, he thinks, would by themselves cost her her ancient kingdom. The poem was well received, to judge from the number of manuscripts of it that survive—one of which, at St. John's College, Oxford, though once at Durham, comprises part of Book III and a commentary in Anglo-Saxon.

Up to this point, I have tried to suggest no more than that the disintegration of Charlemagne's empire bred its own sort of defensive literature, the keynote of which was a harping upon the comparatively recent past. The men who wrote in Latin, and probably also those who recited the Frankish sagas, took refuge in the memory of the chieftain who had successfully defended his own;

and they decked him out, under Einhard's guidance, in Roman trappings that Alcuin might have found it hard to recognize him in. And the myth grew as the pressure increased.

Throughout much of the ninth century, Danish pressure on England was not less than that on France. One effect of this pressure was, I think, to draw the English and the Franks—or at any rate their rulers—closer together than they had ever been before. To some extent, of course, English kingship was already modelled on Frankish; Offa and Charlemagne, for example, had had many contacts (most of them carefully explored by Levison and Stenton); and while it may be the case that Offa considered himself, on dynastic grounds, at least the equal of Charlemagne, on every other ground Mercian kingship had stood to learn and to gain from the contact. The Franks had provided the types for Mercian monetary reform; and the Franks had evolved the style *Rex Francorum* somewhat before Offa, by analogy, first called himself *Rex Anglorum* in his charters. These are familiar examples of Frankish influence on Anglo-Saxon kingship, and I press them no further than to say that, against such a background, and given a common enemy, Frankish and English kingship might readily come to conform to a single historical pattern in the minds of men of letters.

Danish raids on England first became really serious in the fourth and fifth decades of the ninth century. In 850 and 854 the Danes wintered in England, and in 855 some appear to have settled in Shropshire, round the Wrekin. In the same year King Aethelwulf, their opponent, crossed to the Continent, and, after visiting Rome, spent several months at the court of Charles the Bald. Here he married Charles's small daughter Judith, in order, no doubt, to complete the Anglo-Frankish alliance against the Danes. (Conceivably at the same time he acquired his Frankish secretary, Felix.) So important was the match considered in England that when Aethelwulf died, Judith was married, despite ecclesiastical opposition, to Aethelbald, his eldest surviving son. At any time, therefore, after 856 it may be assumed that contact between the two courts would have been fairly regular, especially as the years of crisis approached. These years were the years of Alfred; and it is then, I believe, that the full force of Frankish example hit England.

First, we have the *Anglo-Saxon Chronicle*, of which Sir Frank Stenton has recently written: 'When compared with the great Frankish annals of the ninth century, which seem to descend from an official record, the *Chronicle* has definitely the character of private work.' I do not quite understand the grounds for this distinction between official (that is, royally sponsored) and unofficial, or aristocratic, chronicles. It seems to me that the Frankish and Anglo-Saxon chronicles are generally comparable in inspiration, wherever they were written. It is believed that the first portion of the *Anglo-Saxon Chronicle*, as we now have it, was compiled from earlier annals and from lists of kings, during the reign of Alfred; and it has quite reasonably been supposed that its compilation, or at the very least its dissemination, had the approval of the king himself, because of the magnitude of the undertaking and because it appears to reflect the interests of the house of Wessex rather than those of any other family, identifiable or not. Perhaps a further reason for advancing this supposition presents itself: why should a king, the records of whose reign make him look almost as much like a Charlemagne as Charles the Bald did, fail to provide himself with so obvious and so well-tried a means of literary support? However much the earliest Frankish annals may have owed to English example, it seems to me that the debt could be the other way round when we reach Alfred. It may be worth observing that a St. Bertin MS. (now at Corpus Christi College, Cambridge) containing a list of Frankish kings, reached England in Alfred's reign; but I am not only thinking of specifically Frankish material that could have come from France only, as, for instance, the Latin entries on Charlemagne and his wars from the Rouen annals, that figure in the Peterborough MS. of the *Chronicle* (Laud. MS. 636), nor of the Frankish entries for the years 714, 715, and 840 inserted in the later St. Augustine's Canterbury MS. (Cotton Domit. A. viii).[19] Much more to the point is the general shape of the *Chronicle*. At its best, it is a record of a people at war; and when it treats of war it finds what Plummer[20] called its 'sense of subject', the struggle against the Danes. It comes to life. Compare any of the great passages of the *Chronicle* from the reigns of Alfred or Edward the Elder with the work of, say, Hincmar or Prudentius in the St. Bertin continuation of the Frankish annals, and I do not see how the conclusion can be avoided that the two were built against the background of common experience. This background, I would say, was experience of war against the *pagani*, the sea-raiders, the land-seizers, whose exploits did not always move all the English, or all the Franks, to that pitch of resistance their kings demanded.[21] There is something artificial, then, about the *Chronicle*,

as about the *Royal Annals*. Whatever its source-material, it reads like
a reflection of an urgent political need—the need, not of a people
but of a dynasty, the House of Wessex, for historical background in
the form of a prose *Geste*. (Precisely because it is a *Geste*, Geoffrey
Gaimar found it so easy to adapt to his own purposes, and, as it were,
to bring up to date, in the twelfth century.) Wherever the work of
collation and composition was done, sooner or later the results would
be diffused among the *scriptoria* of the religious houses that were the
mainstay of late Old English kingship, and would there be drawn
upon by whatever writers were interested in the story. Whatever
force it was that disseminated manuscripts of the Frankish annals
among the *scriptoria* of Northern France in the ninth century also
disseminated the *Chronicle* among the English houses.

Standing on the shoulders of the chroniclers and of the annalists is
Asser, to whose indebtedness to the Franks W. H. Stevenson long
ago drew attention. The question of the authenticity of Asser's *Life*
has been much disputed. The case against authenticity has been put
by J. W. Adamson and by V. H. Galbraith, but to my mind most of
their arguments were long ago met by Stevenson in his introduction
and more recently by Professor Whitelock. The fact—if, indeed, it
matters—that no manuscripts of Asser's *Life* survive may be taken as
an argument for authenticity; Asser failed precisely where Einhard
succeeded, and, unlike Einhard, did not complete his work. Alfred's
immediate successors were not particularly interested in him and did
not even make use of his name for their children (an exception is
the son of Aethelred and Emma, the Confessor's younger brother,
killed in 1036); he is not mentioned by name in the dooms of Edgar,
Aethelred or Cnut; and his dynasty, when it catches the attention of
the Anglo-Norman historians, is the dynasty of Cerdic, or of
Edward the Confessor, and not that of Alfred. Even Aethelweard, a
member of the family, addressing a direct descendant of Alfred, is
less enthusiastic about the great king than is, for example, Florence
of Worcester.[22]

Frankish-Latin usage came naturally to Asser's pen: *graphia*,
pagus, *cambra*, *fasellus*, *capellanus*, *ministeriales* and plenty more.
That he had access to Frankish sources of information is shown,
among other things, in his account of how Charles the Bald had his
daughter Judith crowned before she left with Aethelwulf for
England, because he knew that the English usage in coronations
was less generous to queens. The St. Bertin annals (at this stage the

work of Prudentius of Troyes) could have been one such source; and the West Saxon court had a link with Reims, where the St. Bertin annals were almost certainly written, in Grimbald, one of the learned foreigners in Alfred's entourage. Again, Asser's account of Alfred's crowning or investiture with the rank of consul at Rome agrees very closely with the Frankish annals on the Roman anointing of Carloman and Louis, Charlemagne's sons, in 781. And then, clearly, Asser knows the two biographies of Louis the Pious, and he uses Einhard quite freely. In chapter 73, Asser returns from a digression to his main theme, *de vita et moribus et aequa conversatione, atque ex parte non modica, res gestas domini mei Aelfredi*: Einhard, in his preface, had spoken of his work on the *vitam et conversationem et ex parte non modica res gestas domini et nutritoris mei Karoli*. The inspiration of the chapter on Alfred as poet and hunter can scarcely not be the *Vita Karoli Magni*, directly or indirectly. (It would have been indirect if, as is very possible, Alfred himself and not Asser was the first user of Einhard.) Alfred, like Aethelwulf, had seen with his own eyes the Carolingian court and court school, and had known Charles the Bald. He was able, apparently, to tell Asser a story about the reception of Offa's daughter, Eadburh, by Charlemagne. His friend Grimbald had spent years at Reims, one of the great centres of Carolingian power. Finally, Alfred had married a daughter to Baldwin II of Flanders, another enemy of the Danes and a grandson of Charles the Bald. It was this Baldwin who first extended the power of his house from the area round Bruges to the rich Carolingian fiefs in the Tournai–Lille region. He became lay-abbot of St. Bertin, and was the first count of Flanders to show an unmistakable interest in the Carolingians. I should infer this from the name of Arnulf, which he chose for his eldest son; it was the name of one of the founders of the Carolingian dynasty, and, by the close of the ninth century, was beginning to find its way into genealogies and collections of saints' lives, especially in northern France and the Rhineland. To this Baldwin, Alfred married his daughter. Contacts of such a kind tempt one to suspect Carolingian influence upon Alfred in almost every direction; military, liturgical, educational, literary, artistic. The Alfred Jewel is witness to the introduction of Carolingian enamelling technique into England;[23] in his coinage alone does Alfred appear to have owed nothing to the Continent.[24] How does Alfred's preoccupation with the vernacular make sense, except against the wider background of European interest?

I cannot even persuade myself that the legal collections of his reign can be fully understood without reference to the Continent; collections incorporating material as old as the Kentish laws, written down, as Bede says, in English, at Aethelberht's command: *decreta illi iudiciorum, iuxta exempla Romanorum, cum consilio sapientium constituit, quae conscripta Anglorum sermone hactenus habentur;*[25] though *what* laws, is not at all clear. One comparative lawyer[26] has recently put forward the view (for which I know of no linguistic support) that, for all practical purposes, there is very little that is pre-Alfredian about the Kentish laws, either in substance or in format. 'In brief, then,' he writes, 'our text of the laws of Aethelberht is a collection, made no earlier than Alfred's time, of old laws of various dates, all attributed to Aethelberht.' He thinks that the Kentish scribes, watching the independence of their kingdom disappear, salvaged what they could of their customs and attributed them to their great kings, Aethelberht, Hlothhere, Eadric and Wihtred. This is certainly going too far; though, on the other hand, even if very little had survived in writing from the past, Alfred must often have pondered the sense of Bede's words about law—for the *Ecclesiastical History* was one of the books translated from Latin into English in the circle of his learned friends. But my point is that, language apart, the incentive to collect and collate laws was not peculiar to Alfred. Can we really suppose that the great ninth-century collections of Germanic, and especially of Frankish, law can have had no effect on a king whose debt to the Continent was in other respects so considerable?

What appears to me to lie behind all this vigorous archaism (if I may still call it that) is a profound sense of dynastic insecurity. We hold that Alfred was a great and glorious king in part because he rightly implies this. (In fact, of course, he was telling his contemporaries, precisely as Charles the Bald told his.) But there was nothing secure about Old English kingship, or about the position of the house of Cerdic, in the ninth century; its great days were still ahead, waiting not least upon the help it was to have from the continental monastic reform movements. There was nothing secure about the rule of the king who decreed that 'if anyone plots against the life of the king, either on his own account or by harbouring outlaws, or men belonging to the king himself, he shall forfeit his life and all that he possesses'.[27] Lists of kings, and genealogies showing descent from the gods, can be interpreted as signs of weakness, quite as easily as of strength. What Mr. Philip Grierson[28] has recently written about comparable literary activity concerning the alleged dynasties of the Ostrogothic Amals, the Lombard Lethings and the Visigothic Balts applies equally forcibly to the Carolingian descendants of St. Arnulf of Metz and to the West Saxon heirs of Cerdic; all, when threatened, turned for help to a past which they proceeded to elaborate. The western kings of the ninth century were threatened with external dangers that only united peoples could effectively have met. But instead of commanding unity, they risked, as a rule, disruption and rebellion every time they moved from their ancestral estates. They lived still in the war-world of the heroic age, where private vengeance alone secured law and order and where national interests mattered not at all, since there were none. 'Centripetal forces' may have been at work in ninth-century England; but they were hidden from Alfred. He recognized and vigorously faced the threat to his dynasty implicit in the Danish invasions; and the Danes were dangerous not only because they really were destructive in their lust for plunder,[29] but also because they were occasionally attractive. That motives other than plunder—e.g. a desire to share in trade—may sometimes have been operative is suggested by Renée Doehaerd in an article on the wine trade of Northern France:[30] or again, they could be generous lords, as the Franks had sometimes found—the Franks, to whose vendetta-ridden society even the Arabs had not always seemed repulsive. And so Alfred turned for help to the experts on kingship —Charlemagne's descendants, whose would-be supplanters, twenty-seven years after Alfred's death, could think of no gift more fitting for his grandson than Charlemagne's own lance.

POSTSCRIPT

It would be possible, and even desirable, to add a large bibliography to this paper, affecting both its Anglo-Saxon and continental parts. I confine myself to drawing attention to one important work: that of Professor Dorothy Whitelock on the Anglo-Saxon Chronicle, and in particular to her view of its Alfredian aspect (*The Anglo-Saxon Chronicle*, 1961, pp. xxii ff.). Like Sir Frank Stenton, she maintains that 'the confident attribution of the work to Alfred's instigation cannot be upheld', in part because he would not have 'mistaken the ceremony that took place at Rome when he was a child'.[31] But she goes on to add that 'the rapid dissemination of the work may owe something to his encouragement', and that 'the Chronicle does not stand entirely apart from the works produced by Alfred'. I do not think that this is very far removed from my own view, which is still that the dissemination of the Chronicle had the king's approval, though I add that its compilation also may possibly have been with his knowledge. Certainly I should not go so far as Professor R. H. C. Davis, 'Alfred the Great: propaganda and truth' (*History*, June 1971, p. 177), who holds that 'there seems to be no difficulty in believing that in a general sense [Alfred] wrote it'. For this I should need proof; and I know of none. All the same, were I to look for a birthplace for the Chronicle, I should look to Winchester.

NOTES

1 A paper read to the Anglo-French Historical Conference, Oxford, 21 September 1949. I have to thank Miss Dorothy Whitelock for criticism of this paper; it expresses my views, not hers. Subsequently published in *History*, vol. 35 (1950), 202–218.
2 *Les Capétiens et la France* (Paris, 1942).
3 *Charlemagne and Roland* (University of California Publications in Modern Philology, vol. xxi, 1944).
4 *Anglo-Saxon England*, p. 16. See also p. 172. This view of annalistic origins is rejected, for cogent reasons, by C. W. Jones, *Saints' Lives and chronicles in early England* (New York, 1947), pp. 10 ff., and elsewhere.
5 *England and the Continent in the Eighth Century*, Appendix 1.
6 *Monumenta Germaniae Historica* (= M.G.H.), *Auctores Antiquissimi*, XV, 499.
7 M.G.H., *Scriptores Rerum Merovingicarum*, ii, 182.
8 On deserters from Charlemagne's host, see Heinrich Fichtenau, *Das Karolingische Imperium* (Zurich, 1949), p. 188; and M.G.H., *Leges, Capitularia regum Francorum*, i, 161.
9 A convenient edition, with a French translation, is that of Louis Halphen, in the series *Les Classiques de l'histoire de France au moyen âge* (3rd edition, revised 1947).
10 Cf. M. Ganshof's admirable summary of his views in his review of A. Kleinclausz, *Eginard* (*Revue belge de Philologie et d'Histoire*, 1943).
11 *Laudes Regiae* (*University of California Publications in History*, vol. xxxiii, 1946).
12 *Speculum* (April and July 1947), and *Le Moyen Âge* (January 1941).
13 The Malberg Glosses are, incidentally, perfectly good evidence that the ninth century compiler of *Lex Salica* considered vernacular to have been, in the time of Clovis, the proper vehicle for the transmission of written custom. England was not quite so isolated, in this respect, as is commonly believed.
14 Edited and translated by P. Lauer, *Les Classiques de l'histoire de France au moyen âge* (1926).

15 *Annales Bertiniani*, s.a. 857. Cf. J. Dhondt, *Etudes sur la naissance des principautés territoriales en France* (Bruges, 1948), p. 28; and Stenton, *Anglo-Saxon England*, p. 317, for the comparable desertion to the Danes, with most serious consequences, of Aethelwold, cousin of King Edward the Elder, between 899 and 902.

16 His reliance on Einhard is discussed by Margarethe Wevers, *Einhards 'Vita Karoli Magni' in der mittelalterlichen Geschichtsschreibung und Helden-sage* (Marburg, 1929).

17 Edited and translated by H. Waquet, *Les Classiques de l'histoire de France au moyen âge* (1942).

18 Flodoard, *Historia Ecclesiae Remensis*, iv, c. 5 (*M.G.H.*, *Scriptores*, xiii, 563).

19 Sir Frank Stenton describes the manuscripts of the chronicle in *Anglo-Saxon England*, pp. 679 ff. See also his important paper, 'The south-western element in the Old English Chronicle', in *Essays in Mediaeval History presented to Thomas Frederick Tout* (Manchester, 1925). It should be emphasized that much work still remains to be done on the chronicle, and that the leading part in this work should be taken, and is being taken, by linguists rather than historians.

20 Earle and Plummer, *Two Saxon Chronicles*, ii, cxvi.

21 Note also R. W. Chambers, *Widsith*, p. 77; 'Every reference to the Danes in Old English verse is couched in the most friendly and respectful tone.'

22 For a probable early use of Asser, see A. Campbell, *Encomium Emmae Reginae* (1949), pp. xxxv–xxxvii.

23 On this, and on Alfred's indebtedness in other artistic respects to the Carolingian renaissance, see T. D. Kendrick, *Anglo-Saxon Art to 900* (Methuen, 1938), chaps. 11 and 14.

24 Cf. G. C. Brooke, *English Coins* (third edition), chap. iv.

25 *Historia Ecclesiastica* (ed. Plummer), book 2, chap. 5.

26 A. S. Diamond, *Primitive Law* (1st Edition), pp. 63 ff.

27 Laws of Alfred, cl. 4.

28 'Election and Inheritance in Early Germanic Kingship', *Cambridge Historical Journal* (1941).

29 Cf. H. Shetelig, *Viking Antiquities in Great Britain and Ireland*, Part 1 (Oslo, 1940), *passim*.

30 'Ce qu'on vendait et comment on le vendait dans le Bassin parisien' (*Annales*, July–Sept., 1947).

31 Eric John, *Orbis Britanniae* (1966), pp. 37 ff. looks to continental parallels and suggests one possible explanation of this difficult passage in the Chronicle and Asser.

XII

The Vikings in Francia*†

It seems fitting that a lecture bearing the name of the man who, more than any other historian, has enabled us to understand the English Danelaw, should be devoted to the Vikings in a neighbouring area. Sir Frank Stenton was wonderfully at home with Danish settlers and their problems while at the same time recognizing the full extent of the terror they inspired and the destruction they caused in the earlier phases of their English career. As to the terror and destruction, King Alfred was a contemporary witness. He remarks in his Will that 'we were all harassed by the heathen army' and in the preface to the *Cura Pastoralis* must refer to the Vikings when he says 'remember what temporal punishments came upon us'. 'I remembered', he says, ' . . . before everything was ravaged and burnt.' And he was not alone in his opinion.[1] But there is a second reason why this might be a favourable moment for looking briefly at the Vikings in Francia. Modern study of the Vikings in England has developed swiftly; not, indeed, so swiftly as the study of them in their native Scandinavia, but certainly more swiftly than that of the Vikings in Francia. We must bear in mind, too, that it was sometimes (I would not say often) the same Vikings who attacked the Franks and the Anglo-Saxons. For this reason it may not be inappropriate to look at the Frankish Vikings through English eyes.

But first it is right to give some account of the present state of study of the Frankish Vikings, so that we may be quite clear how much we know and how much we do not know. What we do have is a fairly sound knowledge of what a modern Belgian scholar calls

* References for this chapter start on p. 233.
† Stenton Lecture, University of Reading, 1974.

P

the 'histoire événementielle' of the Viking attacks on Francia;[2] that is to say, the chronology of the attacks and their immediate local effects. This we owe primarily to the labours of a German scholar, Walther Vogel, whose book, *Die Normannen und das Fränkische Reich*, published in 1906, remains fundamental for the period 799 to 911. It is indeed 'histoire événementielle', firmly based on the annals and accepting their approach to events. Subsequent scholars followed in his path—notably Ferdinand Lot, who published a number of important studies on Francia and the Vikings.[3] Their synthesis, like their sources, long remained unchallenged, except for a general but undeveloped doubt raised by Marc Bloch who first, to my knowledge, suggested that *we* were in a better position to assess the significance of the Viking assault than were the watchers on the sea-coast and the monks in their scriptoria.[4] However that may be, the suggestion bore fruit, as Bloch's suggestions often did. The present generation has taken a new look at the Vikings, and has probed behind the literary sources into the evidence of archaeology, numismatics, place-name study, liturgy, and the witness of later medieval writers, to mention only the most obvious. This has been all to the good. The outcome, so far, has been twofold. First, we have had new attempts at general synthesis, as for example from Professor Peter Sawyer (largely for England)[5] and from M. Lucien Musset, who has ranged masterfully over the whole field.[6] Secondly the evidence at the regional and local levels has begun to be re-assessed. To this we owe valuable studies, such as those of Albert D'Haenens on Belgium,[7] Musset on Normandy[8] and W. C. Braat on Frisia;[9] and there have been studies of special aspects, like Fernand Vercauteren on the Carolingian policy of defence[10] and Herbert Jankuhn on trade.[11] From these and comparable studies we have begun in a modest way to think afresh of what it meant when one civilization confronted another, and what the extremely difficult and diffuse evidence can really be made to yield at this place or that.

How, then, do we now approach the study of the Vikings and Francia? There could be no better starting-point than M. D'Haenens' splendid survey, published in the Spoleto *Settimane* for 1969[12]—a survey that has the additional merit of reflecting the way in which his co-workers now look at things. His position is that we know less than we thought we knew about the impact of the Vikings on Francia, though overall more than contemporaries knew. All the

same, the evidence for every locality has still to be gathered and
assessed. To take one point only, there is no full inventory of the
material remains of the Vikings in Francia, nor yet of their victims.
At least it seems clear that these remains, where we know about
them, will not contradict the impression most powerfully left on us
by the literary evidence: namely that the invasions were to the
Franks a traumatic experience. Without saying that it was all in the
mind, D'Haenens emphasizes the mood of panic. How *could* one
expect panic-stricken clergy to give accurate accounts, let alone
detached assessments, of the thing that scared them? Monastic
chroniclers and annalists, and still more the writers of saints' Lives,
exaggerated. Probably they did, and in the matter of figures it has
long been suspected that they must have done so. Who now would
suppose that the Vikings went up the Elbe in 600 boats,[13] containing perhaps 30,000 men, to attack Hamburg, which cannot have
had more than a few hundred inhabitants? Would some watcher on
the river bank have counted 600 boats? What he saw was clearly an
alarming number of boats and men. It is reasonable to accept
Professor Sawyer's case for scaling down the reported numbers of
Viking attackers generally,[14] so long as we also remember to scale
down the numbers of those who opposed them. On the other hand,
reported numbers are sometimes convincingly low: I cannot, for
instance, imagine that when Abbo describes small detachments of
warriors venturing forth on their exploits during the siege of
Paris,[15] he is simply employing a literary device to highlight their
heroism. In short, numbers are sometimes exaggerated and sometimes not. We thus reach the heart of the position taken up by
D'Haenens, which is, if I do not misrepresent him, that proved
cases of a spirit of panic make a general case for literary exaggeration
and cast a general air of doubt on the literary evidence as at present
understood. This in turn makes it easier to give greater weight to
what one might call the constructive side of the Viking venture,
characterized as it was by trading as well as raiding and culminating
as it did in colonization. Who, looking at their magnificent achievements in boat-building, could doubt that the Vikings would scarcely
ever have been content to be mere robbers? If one carries this argument along its way, with however many cautions, it must happen
that someone will eventually ask, as has M. Ménager, 'je me suis
senti porté à reviser [aussi] la triste réputation des wikings, au point
de me demander par quelle aberration leur fut donné ce nom même

de *viking* qui, dans leur langage, signifiait "pirate".'[16] Or, to put it another way, should we view the Vikings as little more than groups of long-haired tourists who occasionally roughed up the natives? I must not be unfair to M. D'Haenens, who is well aware that the Vikings did enormous damage: but still I confess that such is the impression left on my mind by his survey. In a word, he would have it that the more we understand the Vikings the more there is to excuse and extenuate in their actions, and the less reason, consequently, is there to accept at face-value the accounts of them left by the natives.

I have said enough about the question of numbers, on which my conclusion is that it forms no very secure basis on which to cast general doubt on what Franks say about Vikings. I come now to a more vexed question, which may be called the question of clichés, or topoi. We have been very conscious, perhaps over-conscious, of these trying literary devices ever since the publication of E. R. Curtius' great book.[17] What medieval writer was free of them? Or, come to that, which of us does not cast his thoughts in accepted moulds that are often literary in origin? It does not follow that, doing so, we cease to speak the truth; nor does it follow for men of the ninth century. The problem is surely not clichés but the meaning of apparently straightforward words and phrases, like *desertus et incultus locus*.[18] M. D'Haenens counters the claim of M. Hubert that Carolingian buildings suffered severely from the Vikings[19] with the remark, 'pour l'interprétation des sources matérielles on recourt aussi à une série de clichés'.[20] No doubt, and one must always be careful. But how often can we be sure that a ninth-century report of Viking depredations is imaginary or untrue? At times we certainly can. For example, Alcuin writes a poem on the sack of Lindisfarne.[21] He had been very far from Lindisfarne in June 793, the time of the Viking attack, and knew no more about its details than he could have had from one letter; but this does not prevent him from composing an elegant poem full of recollected images and themes.[22] It comes from the heart: the sacking was a terrible event for Alcuin as for all who heard of it; but no one would dream of turning to the poem for an account of the incident. But things are not always so easy. Pirenne is taken to task by D'Haenens for inferring from the use of the biblical phrase *potestas tenebrarum*, by one writer, a monk of Stavelot, that the Vikings habitually attacked by night.[23] Habitually they may not have done so; but sometimes they apparently did, as for instance at Bordeaux in 848[24] and at Chartres in 858.[25] I should infer from this no more than that the Stavelot writer's mind may have pounced on the biblical phrase as suggestive of one characteristic of Viking attack. I do not recall that it is often used by other writers. It is a doubtful case; Pirenne may not have been entirely wrong.

But let us look at more solid accounts of Viking attacks and campaigns. First, the Annals of St. Bertin, as compiled between 835 and 882 by Bishops Prudentius and Hincmar.[26] Their value for Viking studies is judiciously summarized by Professor Sawyer who adds, however, that 'far less space and attention is paid [to Viking raids] than to other matters which must, in the view of the writers, have been as or more important'.[27] I would not quarrel with this, but it needs explanation. The Annals are not a panic-account of anything but a record of events as they occur or become known. The annalists (and particularly Hincmar) betray personal feelings from time to time, but their aim is not to assess the importance of the events they record, let alone to place the events in any order of importance. We cannot, then, weigh up one sort of event against another and decide that it is more or less significant because it occupies more or less space. Indeed, the most impressive aspect of the Annals is their cool spirit (I do not say of detachment, since that would have been impossible). Their language is measured and their details for the most part carefully weighed. Thus, if they record a Viking attack when a town is raided, one is disposed to assume that it was raided and not necessarily razed or burnt. The last thing I should assume from the Annals is that, to the annalists, the Viking raids were no more than an aggravation of a situation of civil war. Hincmar knew better than that: sick and old, he fled from his own city in 882 before just such a raid: *villulas quasdam incenderunt sed civitatem, Dei potentia et sanctorum merita defenderunt*; a quiet statement of fact, as the archbishop sees it. His province had suffered terribly. Compare this with another account that ranks high in Viking historiography: the account by the monk Ermentarius of the translation of the relics of St. Philibert from Noirmoutier,[28] first to Déas, then to Cunault and Messay and finally to Tournus. Here there is more of a feeling of personal involvement and of the sufferings of Christians at the hands of pagans (to which I shall revert). It is Christians who to him are the victims of Viking massacres, pillages, devastations and burnings. The tone is also patriotic, and we are left in no doubt that ordinary people suffer. However, the point I would make here still concerns the matter of accuracy, or trustworthiness: the city of Rouen is attacked, pillaged and burnt; Paris, Beauvais and Meaux are taken; the stronghold of Melun is razed; Chartres is occupied; Evreux and Bayeux are pillaged, and other cities are successively attacked. It seems that the words are carefully chosen to indicate the differing fates of these places as reported to the monk. He may have been wrong, but at least he seems to want to give an objective account; and this is not what one would expect from the author of a book of miracles. It is certainly not what one always finds in the general run of monastic accounts of Viking attacks, though even so one should not approach any of them in a spirit of resistant scepticism. The chronicle of St. Wandrille, for example, records more than a series of wild guesses, though it makes its mistakes.[29] *Numquam tale exterminium in his territoriis auditum est.* How shall we say that this is a wrong judgement on the raid of 851–2 from Bordeaux to the Seine basin? In sum, I believe that the literary sources exaggerate when I can catch them out, but otherwise I give them the benefit of the doubt.

To the Frankish clerics who recorded the Viking attacks the Vikings were, as often as not, best described as *pagani*, heathen. The Anglo-Saxons agreed that this—*haethene men*—was the appropriate word, and so too did the Arabs of Spain, who called them *al-Majus* (fire-worshipper, wizard, heathen).[30] The Franks did not use this word of their own kind whose rebellions they also recorded. In short, the difference between a Frankish count in revolt against his king and laying waste the countryside, and a Viking whose depredations were not dissimilar in effect, was best expressed as a difference in religion. I do not say that that was the only difference, nor that Vikings at work were indistinguishable from counts on the rampage either in the ninth century or earlier; but only that it summed up the difference. The Vikings were heathen, a divine judgement on a Christian society rent by strife and dissension. Of course it has been urged that this is precisely how one *would* have expected the clerics to judge the ravagers of churches and monasteries; yet the critical word was not applied by them to other ravagers. Therefore it may be well to reconsider the impact of Viking paganism on Frankish society.

One cannot briefly summarize the content of Scandinavian paganism in the ninth century.[31] It is enough to say that it was a

tenaciously-held polytheism easily adaptable to the purposes of warfare. It certainly involved sacrifice. The fact that it was polytheistic
made it, in the end, easier for the Vikings to accept Christianity, as
Marc Bloch observed.[32] But Bloch also observed that the resistance
of the Vikings to conversion was a prolonged one. Lucien Musset
holds that Viking paganism reacted in a positive and hostile way to
Christianity; in a word, it was consciously anti-Christian. Thor's
hammer became a symbol in opposition to the Cross, immersion a
riposte to baptism, funerary rites suggested renewed devotion to the
old gods, Genesis excited comparable speculations eventually collected in the Edda, runic writing enjoyed a renaissance.[33] It may be
that some of the later Odin-bracteates, the inspiration of which
stemmed from that area of Denmark which was probably the home
of Ragnar and his sons, bear witness to the same reaction. Now it is
impossible to know what all this meant to a Viking band operating
in Frankish waters, at any one place or time. The most we can say
is that Viking paganism was a positive force, easily identifiable as
such by men of a different religion; and it is the reaction of these
men that matters in the present context.

What was it that made clerics look upon pagan Vikings as men
apart? Their witness is unanimous and comes from places widely
separated that had no connection with each other. As to pillage, they
were used to that: in 878 Pope John VIII excommunicated ravagers
of church property, and he did not mean Vikings but men like
Count Bernard II of Toulouse.[34] But it seemed to churchmen that
there was something deliberately anti-Christian about the Vikings,
that had little to do with pillage in a general sense. How could they
have thought otherwise when attacks fell on sacristies, altars, and
reliquaries? Particularly reliquaries: again and again we read that
saints' relics were hidden or removed to safety; and it was the safety
of these, and not any treasure as such, that was the chief concern
of monks and priests. Moreover, sacristies housed wine for the
celebration of mass. To the Vikings it was just wine, but to the
clergy it was wine with a difference. Thus at Redon the *pagani* broke
in: *biberuntque de vino quod illic positum erat ad missas. Mox ut
gustaverunt, in rabiem omnes sunt conversi.*[35] In a word, you do not
drink mass-wine without incurring special penalties. The abbey of
St. Denis became very anxious about its supply of mass-wine.[36]
Relics, then, and mass-wine were special objects of plunder. Churches,
as a matter of course, were burnt and destroyed, or partially

so, though they could rise again in a comparatively short time. Some of the monasteries that suffered severely were able to continue their literary work without much, or any, break,[37] though it is not always certain where exactly the work was executed. In the ninth century St. Martin's of Tours was producing some fine manuscripts, as were also Fleury, Ferrières, Auxerre, St. Denis, St. Germain, Corbie and other houses. But in this context one would need to know more precisely *when*; for a century is a long time. For example, St. Martin's was certainly busy in the first half of the ninth century. In 862, however, Charles the Bald was offering the monks the nearby *villa* of Léré as a refuge; in 869 he was suggesting not only Léré but Marsat in the Auvergne for the same purpose; and in fact the refuge the monks preferred was their own purchase of Chablis in Burgundy.[38] But if we mean to assess the impact of the Vikings on monasteries we must make allowance not only for what was being written—and men's minds will work in surprisingly adverse circumstances—but also for what perished. Monks were murdered for no very clear reason. Failure to hand over treasure or to find ransom-money is not always stated as an explanation. Even M. D'Haenens allows that men may have been tortured and martyred.[39] Undoubtedly they were. Four monks who refused to flee from St. Bertin in 860 were tortured, of whom one survived the experience. Not surprisingly, the other three were looked upon as martyrs. Their names were recorded in the *Miracula sancti Bertini*.[40] Viking slaughter at Paris was preceded and encouraged, according to Abbo, by a *visum cruentum*, a bloody vision—or possibly a sacrifice?[41] What happened to Duke Seguin in 845, when he was captured and put to death? *Occisus est*.[42] Or Archbishop Madalbert of Bourges in 910?[43] Dr. Alfred Smyth[44] has advanced some reasons for holding that as late as the eleventh century the Vikings practised ritual sacrifice of important victims to Odin, in the form of the blood-eagle. That is, the victim, after being a target for javelins or arrows, was stretched face-downwards over a stone, so that his ribs could be torn upwards from the spine in a shape suggestive of an eagle's wings. Finally he was beheaded. Examples of this practice may have included: King Ælla of Northumbria, Halfdan son of King Haraldr Harfagri of Norway, King Edmund (a victim, like Ælla, of the great Danish Viking Ívarr), King Maelgualai of Munster, and just possibly Archbishop Ælfheah if Thietmar is to be trusted. It may also be noted that where one source will report little more than *occisus est,* or will concentrate on some aspect of the torture reminiscent of earlier Christian martyrdom (as, use of arrows), another will betray the essentially complex procedure of the sacrifice. It happened in Scandinavia, in Ireland and in England. I am presuming that Francia was not exempt. The witness of Anglo-Saxon England is perfectly relevant to the Frankish scene. Some Viking kings of York were resolute pagans: we have their coins, stamped with Thor's hammer, to prove it, to say nothing of place-names that betray the cults of Thor and Odin. Nor is there any reason to restrict certain religious practices to certain strains of Viking, as for example Norwegians or Danes. If Musset is right, no expedition was likely to be purely Danish or Norwegian:[45] that is to say, we do not know that it was. Can we lay the blame for atrocities exclusively at the door of the berserkir, the young warriors specially vowed to Odin and to bloodshed? If we do, we may find ourselves in the awkward position of M. Musset, who on one page decides that the berserkir were chiefly a literary theme of the later saga-writers but on the next page concludes that tales of Viking murder and wild barbarism must be rejected as a cliché, 'sauf dans le cas des *berserkir*'.[46] What he is really saying is that where we meet with an atrocity that cannot be dismissed we should attribute it to a posse of wild men with whom the larger body of Vikings shared none of the characteristics. As I read the sources, there is no justification for any such division, nor for arguing that men whose real objective was booty should not at the same time make appropriate gestures to the gods who saw them through.[47] Once more, the Anglo-Saxon witness is relevant. Archbishop Wulfstan writes thus in the early eleventh century, the lateness of the date making his words the more impressive: 'Among the heathen no one dares to withhold anything great or small from the prescribed worship of idols . . . among the heathen no one dares to diminish inside or outside their temples any of the things that are brought to the idols and given as sacrifices . . . among the heathen no one dares to do any harm to the priests of the idols.'[48] In a word, the Danes were more careful about their religious practices than were the Christians addressed by the archbishop. And never a word about berserkir!

Now, it is perfectly clear that the Franks did not resist the Vikings to a man and were ready on occasion to buy them off sooner than fight and, rarely, to join forces with them against other Franks, as Æthelwold joined them in England. But it does not follow that the

Franks were unclear about the nature of Viking paganism. Consider Charles the Bald, who personally defended his abbey of St. Denis against Ragnar and the Vikings. He turned St. Denis into a *castrum*. And not only St. Denis—St. Omer and St. Vaast were also fortified. Indeed, the fortifying of monasteries goes back to 830, when Louis the Pious gave permission to Noirmoutier to build a *castrum*. One might expect this in the case of threatened monasteries. But many royal residences that had no religious purpose were also fortified in the ninth century, both by Louis the Pious and by Charles the Bald.[49] In other words, the Vikings were not judged to confine their attentions to monasteries and churches. In 862 at Pîtres the bishops asserted that Charles needed the spiritual gifts conferred by consecration to fight the Vikings on the spiritual and physical levels, and this he acknowledged.[50] He needed the military virtues of strength and prudence from the Church, which in its turn was clear about the military duties of an anointed king. Charles and his bishops knew the nature of the enemy they faced. The great pronouncement of Pîtres, to say nothing of the evidence scattered throughout the king's extensive *Acta*, need more careful study before we can pronounce on his will or ability to resist the Vikings. He was prepared to take the daring step, disapproved of by some, of permitting the Loire Vikings to winter in his territory on condition that when spring came they should depart if still pagans, and only remain to be absorbed if they had accepted Christianity.[51] Their religion struck him as crucial. Or consider a well-known case of apostasy. In 864 Pippin II of Aquitaine went over to the Vikings, as some others did in even less excusable circumstances.[52] But he did more. Already a monk, he renounced his vows and accepted the religion of the pagans.[53] Later in the same year he was captured, brought to trial and condemned to death, *ut patriae et christianitatis proditor*.[54] In the event he was allowed to die a natural death in close custody at Senlis. Some have doubted whether *apostata* need mean more than that he was a renegade monk.[55] But Hincmar, our main informant, is very specific: *et ritum eorum servat*. This cannot be dismissed on the ground that Hincmar can hardly have known what went on between Pippin and the Vikings, because he can have known very well what was reported at the trial. Surely there can be no doubt about what actually happened: to secure Pippin's loyalty, the Vikings insisted on his apostasy—which was no more than what the Franks required of Vikings who were prepared to accept peace-terms and settle. And the interest of the story lies in this positive Viking reaction rather than in the fact of Pippin's desertion to their side. Later in the St. Bertin annals, under the year 869, we read of another apostate monk who joined the Vikings and practised their religion, *et nimis christianis infestissimus erat*.[56] But he was less lucky than Pippin. After capture he was executed. Such things did happen. Archbishop Fulk of Reims, writing to Charles III in 885/6, remarked that apostasy to the Vikings was not uncommon,[57] and Hincmar in his *Consilium de poenitentia Pippini regis* cites a letter of Pope Leo I which contains a ruling about penance for those who worship idols.[58] I can only conclude that we should take Viking paganism seriously at any time before the eleventh century, when conversion was general and permanent. Moreover, we should allow that the Vikings themselves could take seriously, and as a threat, a religion to which many of their fathers and neighbours had been forcibly converted by Charlemagne. In their earliest encounters with them, the Franks could well dismiss a few boatloads of Vikings as *pyratae*; but by the middle of the ninth century they had learnt better: they were dealing with *daemonum cultoribus*.[59]

I turn now to a second aspect of Viking impact on the Franks, which may help to explain the terror they were said to inspire: namely, their treatment of towns, countryside and people. It is easy to lump together the Viking attacks with the civil wars of the ninth century and regard the former as merely complicating the latter; or, again, to point to examples of local magnates feathering their own nests at the expense of their neighbours because the Vikings provided the opportunity, or, finally, to take the long view and show how medieval France benefited from the Vikings. It benefited in the sense that the rigidity of domanial structures was shaken; that labour, always scarce, became more fluid; that conditions eventually improved for the peasant on domanial land. But this is how the economic historian views the matter.[60] A contemporary peasant, suddenly deprived of the rigidity that protected him, may not fully have appreciated these hidden fruits—hidden, indeed, for another century. There remains good reason to isolate, when we can, the destruction and desolation caused directly by the Vikings and to form some opinion as to whether or not contemporary writers had got it out of focus.

But first it is right to emphasize a point that certainly did not escape the Vikings: Western Francia—by which I mean the western half of Francia from Frisia to the Pyrenees—was on the whole a prosperous and developing area in the early ninth century. We can see this most clearly in the growth of ecclesiastical communities of every kind under the early Carolingians. Whether the destruction of the Frisian state by Charles Martel was advantageous to Francia is an open question;[61] it depends on whether one gives greater weight to political or economic considerations. Similarly, the condition of southern Aquitaine, constantly threatened by Gascons, remained delicate. But from Flanders in the north to Bordeaux in the south, rising prosperity was the order of the day, even if the peasant knew little about it. Many monasteries and churches greatly extended their estates in the half-century between 750 and 800: for example, Corbie, St. Bertin and St. Denis. The whole area of the Parisis saw a rapid growth of ecclesiastical domains, mostly at the expense of the Merovingian *saltus* and *fundi*. *Coloni* and serfs were established on these new properties, assarting began, and cultivated land began to extend over ancient forest.[62] This in turn necessitated new parochial arrangements, and not only in the Parisis. There is plenty of evidence of Carolingian resolve to divide up big parishes into smaller units. However, Hincmar advised caution. Though he paid much attention to the smaller sub-divisions of his province, he judged the times unpropitious for further advance, at least without careful inquiry. The St. Bertin polypticon of 850 shows the kind of information that he and others wanted.[63] It is difficult to date, let alone to quantify, information of this kind; but no one will question that if western Francia was easy to pillage in the early ninth century, it was equally well worth pillaging.

Now, to take the easier problem first, how did the Vikings affect town-life? The evidence is plentiful and for the most part, in my opinion, incontrovertible. Take Bordeaux, capital of the critical marcher-territory separating Gascons from Franks. Its history, up to the ninth century, was one of increasing prosperity, which the barbarian incursions of the fifth century and the wars of the eighth did little to interrupt. But in the opinion of a scholar who has studied its early history closely, the ninth century was a disaster without parallel in its entire history. The *mid*-ninth century saw its nadir. Ancient Burdigala disappeared. And this was due neither to Gascons nor to Franks: 'les ravages des Normands ont été meurtriers et dévastateurs.[64] Further north, the cities of the Loire suffered scarcely less and took long to recover. Those of the Seine and yet further north seem to have recovered more quickly. But the story is the same everywhere. M. Musset may exaggerate when he writes that *every* town attacked by the Vikings was burnt,[65] but one can certainly accept his further conclusion that material losses were immense. Some towns were burnt more than once, and even exposed trading-posts like Quentovic and Doorstad took a long time a-dying. One suspects that the whole of a town did not as a rule go up in flames all at once. However, this is only one side of the picture. More interesting, and less easy to determine, is what happened to the inhabitants. Something may be learnt from the fate of the Gallic townsmen whose enemies were not Vikings but Arabs; milder enemies, by and large. In the years between 890 and 975 the episcopal cities of Embrun, Gap, Grenoble and Toulon lost something like two-thirds of their inhabitants,[66] even though the Arabs did not even enter all of them. We do not know where the townsmen went or whether any of them ever returned, or when. Moreover, there was a close relationship between town and countryside. If the lands round towns were devastated—and they were—what inducement was there for townsmen to remain within the walls (if there were walls) and starve? Sometimes our sources are precise in what they report. For example, the Annals of St. Bertin inform us that Rouen was not only burnt but that *reliquumque vulgum* were killed or carried off;[67] at Quentovic all were killed;[68] at Nantes, men and women were killed;[69] Bordeaux was burnt and depopulated;[70] the Seine towns were attacked *etiam procul positis*;[71] Orléans and its surrounding countryside were burnt;[72] the Vikings in Angers depopulated the nearby towns,[73] and so on. I should not wish to make too much of the economic importance of any Frankish town of the ninth century. Nevertheless, there were a lot of them; they were centres of exploitation, sheltering more than churches and monasteries; and the aggregate of their populations would have numbered many thousands. It is a matter of people, not of economic prosperity. It is odd that M. Duby should hold that on the whole the towns benefited from the influx of what he calls 'les fuyards de la campagne et leurs richesses'.[74] We do not know how often these 'fuyards' did take refuge in towns, nor what, if any, 'richesses' they were likely to bring with them; nor even if towns were likely to welcome additional mouths to feed. It is all guesswork.

But it is especially the fate of the population of the countryside that merits attention. If Bordeaux was ruined, so too was Aquitaine.[75]

The population of the Périgord, and perhaps also of the Limousin, fled for refuge to Turenne in the Haut-Limousin.[76] We do not know if or when they returned. Charles the Bald wrote to Pope Nicholas I on the condition of Aquitaine generally and of Bourges in particular, referring both to Viking devastations and to *malorum Christianorum infestatio*, concluding with an assurance that his messenger would tell the pope more.[77] The king's mind is not confused about the enemies of Aquitaine. They are two in number, Vikings and 'bad Christians', in that order. An outsider, Andreas of Bergamo, sums the matter up thus: *unde usque hodie sic dissipata est nobilitas Aquitanorum, quae etiam Nortemanni eorum possederunt terrae.*[78] This is confirmed by Pope John VIII's letter to the bishops of the province of Bourges in 876: *Burdegalensem urbem, sed et totam paene provinciam ... diversis cladibus, sed praecipue incursibus Nortmannorum deletam, et in solitudinem partim gladiis partimque captivitate deductam.*[79] But look at the situation further north. We have seen that ecclesiastical estates had greatly expanded. Some of these lay far from their mother-churches and monasteries, yet depended on them. St. Wandrille was a case in point. Not only the monastery but its *villae* were destroyed, to the extent that medieval St. Wandrille, when it finally emerged, depended upon a different kind of economy.[80] Many large-scale proprietors like monasteries went under, and the great lay estates that we associate with the late tenth and eleventh centuries did not emerge to take their place overnight. It is a question, moreover, of the organization of the countryside, vast areas of which depended for the control of their exploitation upon distant monasteries. What happened to the peasantry dependent upon Corbie or St. Bertin when their mother-houses went up in flames and the monks were scattered?[81] We do not yet know, but we can at least suppose that insecurity such as this may have had as unnerving an effect on rural communities as did actual destruction. Of course there was disruption of cultivated land and dispersion of peasantry—which can only mean the movement of population, whether temporary or permanent.[82] Now, the opinion of M. D'Haenens, who has made a special study of Belgium, is that Viking destruction was less than has been supposed.[83] I am not sure how much *was* supposed to have been destroyed, though I accept his conclusion. The Picard charters of the period—and there are something over fifty of them—hardly ever refer to the effects of Viking attack.[84] Yet why should they? And does it in any degree affect the conclusion, based on much evidence, that no region of Francia endured more terrible assaults? With it we must take southern Frisia. Years ago, I ventured the opinion that 'the Carolingians seem to have curbed Frisian sea-power' so that Viking warbands found no resistance in Frisian waters.[85] Professor Sawyer questioned this, though I still think the Frisians had more sea-power than he allows. I note, too, that M. Duby believes that the Vikings made it easier for Frisian shipping to be absorbed by the Franks.[86] But whatever the extent of Frisian sea-power, the direct confrontation of Carolingian with Danish authority in the Frisian and Saxon regions must surely be connected with the *timing* of the earliest Viking raids on the Empire. The Danes found a Frisian overlord who brought wealth with him, gathering it conveniently into *portus* (or trading depots), and who furthermore was aggressive. There was something worth raiding quite near home, and no particular reason why raiding should not be indulged. The Frisians were paying tribute to the Vikings as early as 819, Doorstad and Antwerp were attacked and burnt in 834, and Quentovic and Rouen a few years later. But destruction is not the same as disruption, and movement caused by a sense of danger and lack of protection; nor can we tell how typical the results obtained for Belgium are likely to prove. It was not destruction that ruined the great fair of St. Denis but insecurity,[87] and the known fate of merchants who had risked themselves on the Seine.[88] I do not see that we have good grounds for deciding that the countryside was not deserted,[89] and *no* region depopulated.[90] The survival of institutions, whether urban or rural, proves nothing, and in any event there is no agreement as to what is meant by depopulation, still less what is meant, over a wide area, by dispossession and disruption. Charles the Bald at least thought that something ought to be done for peasants driven from their homes by the Vikings, and did it at Pîtres,[91] by ordering that all those who fled from the *persecutio* of the Northmen should not be oppressed by any *census* or *exactio*, perhaps believing that they had no 'richesses' with them. The whole of clause 31 of the Edict reads as if movement of population had become a serious matter. It reveals, also, a widespread concern about who was going to sow and harvest crops.

We know a little more than this about the movement of the West Frankish population. I have already referred to the flight into the Haut-Limousin. Others went further afield to regions which, if not always free from Viking attack, were comparatively safe. In general we can speak of Burgundy as a place of refuge, and M. Latouche associated the rise of Burgundy with the influx of refugees.[92] In other words, not all those who found a home there chose to go back if the opportunity occurred. The Ardennes and the Auvergne were also places of refuge,[93] from which some monks and some peasants returned, and some not. It is a matter requiring further research, of the kind that M. Fournier has devoted to the Basse-Auvergne.[94] It may be thought strange that peasant-communities should uproot themselves and move off into the unknown; and indeed it is, unless one makes allowance for the threat that hung over them and for the welcome extended to agricultural labourers in a world chronically short of that commodity. The *castella* provided for them as places of refuge near their own homes were a temporary solution only: you could not work the fields and spend half your time in a fortification, supposing that the king allowed your lord to maintain so dangerous an asset. I think, then, that if one allows that there was a 'bouleversement foncier' one must accept the consequences and allow also a major displacement of population which probably benefited other parts of Francia. The extent of it and the nature of it remain undetermined.

One final point. We know that in Francia, as elsewhere, the Vikings amassed large quantities of booty from Danegeld, and we know in particular how Charles the Bald dealt with their demands. But they showed an equally steady interest in another form of loot: they took captives from towns, countryside and monasteries. Some were ransomed and may have been taken with ransom in mind. But this will only have applied to captives of rank. Others, and probably the majority, were destined for the slave market. Wherever the Vikings struck, they reduced captives to slavery, of whom a proportion—particularly women—reached Scandinavia. The rest were sold further afield. The Dublin Norsemen (mostly Norwegians but with a Danish element) were great slave-traders, and carried out raids for this purpose. It looks very much as if they regularly milked certain monasteries of their inmates, taking care not to do permanent damage to the monasteries.[95] The capacity for survival of some Frankish monasteries may be attributable to the same policy. At least it is clear that one factor in the depopulation of western Francia was the Viking appetite for slaves.

What I have been saying may look like the beating of a dead horse. I am afraid it is not. Much recent work on the Vikings in

Francia and elsewhere has focused our attention on the general setting and on long-term results; and it is right that we should give proper consideration to the fact of civil disturbance of a major kind for which the Vikings were not directly responsible and also to the fact that the Vikings were not always out for blood nor invariably unattractive as allies to Frankish landowners on the make. Let us add that economic recovery did, slowly, occur and that some of the patterns of Antique life did survive in the substructure of medieval France. Having said that, we have not said all. Contemporary witness clearly distinguished the Vikings, their religion, their depredations, aims and methods from dissident magnates and warring kings; and it accords them a degree of fear that is lacking in any account of what Franks did to each other. If we say that this witness is exaggerated we have to prove it over a time-span of at least a century and for several regions of Francia. Perhaps, as detailed work in these regions comes to completion, we shall be in a position to do so. But, as things are at present, the witness stands: *numquam tale exterminum in his territoriis*.[96]

NOTES

1 I am grateful to Professor Whitelock for advice on King Alfred's attitude.
2 Albert D'Haenens, 'Les Invasions normandes dans l'empire franc au ixe siècle', *Settimane di Studio del Centro Italiano di Studi Sull'Alto Medioevo*, XVI (Spoleto, 1969), p. 235.
3 These are reprinted in Lot's *Recueil des Travaux Historiques*, 2 (Geneva-Paris, 1970) and 3 (1973).
4 *La Société Féodale*, I (Paris, 1939), p. 30.
5 *The Age of the Vikings*, 2nd edn. (London, 1971).
6 *Les Peuples Scandinaves au Moyen Age* (Paris, 1951). There is much, too, from the archaeological angle, in J. Brøndsted, *The Vikings* (London, 1960) and H. Arbman, *The Vikings* (London, 1961), and from the literary in G. Turville-Petre, *The Heroic Age in Scandinavia* (London, 1951). A. R. Lewis, *The Northern Seas* (Princeton, 1958) should be used with caution.
7 *Les Invasions normandes en Belgique au ixe siècle* (Louvain, 1967).
8 'Naissance de la Normandie', in *Histoire de la Normandie*, ed. M. de Bouard (Toulouse, 1970), pp. 75-130.
9 'Les Vikings au pays de Frise', *Annales de Normandie*, iv (1954), pp. 219-227.
10 'Comment s'est-on défendu, au ixe siècle, dans l'empire franc, contre les invasions normandes?' *Annales du xxxe congrès de la Fédération Archéologique de Belgique* (Brussels, 1936) pp. 117-32.

Q

11 'Der fränkisch-friesische Handel zur Ostsee im frühen Mittelalter', *Viertel-jahrschrift für Social- und Wirtschaftgeschichte*, xl (1953), pp. 193–243.

12 Loc. cit., pp. 233–98.

13 *Annales de Saint-Bertin*, ed. F. Grat, J. Vielliard and S. Clémencet (Paris, 1964), p. 49 (s.a. 845).

14 Op. cit., ch. 6.

15 *Le Siège de Paris par les Normands*, ed. H. Waquet (Paris, 1942), *passim*.

16 *Settimane di Spoleto*, XVI, p. 725.

17 *European Literature and the Latin Middle Ages* (London, 1953), ch. 5.

18 See Pierre David, *Etudes historiques sur la Galice et le Portugal du VIe au XIIe siècle* (Lisbon–Paris, 1947), 172; and D'Haenens, loc. cit., p. 255.

19 'L'abbaye de Déols et les constructions monastiques à la fin de l'époque carolingienne', *Cahiers Archéologiques*, ix (1957).

20 Loc. cit., p. 583.

21 *De clade Lindisfarnensis monasterii*, Mon. Germ. Hist., *Poet. Caro. Aevi*, I, 229.

22 These are discussed by P. J. Frankis, 'The thematic significance of *enta geweorc* in *The Wanderer*', *Anglo-Saxon England*, ii (Cambridge, 1973), p. 267.

23 Loc. cit., p. 294. H. Pirenne, 'Sedulius de Liège', *Mém. de l'Acad. royale de Belgique, classe des lettres*, 23 (1882), p. 5.

24 *Gesta sanctorum patrum Fontanellensis coenobii*, ed. F. Lohier and J. Laporte (Rouen–Paris, 1936), s.a. 848.

25 Cf. F. Lot, *Recueil*, ii, pp. 771–80.

26 See above, note 13.

27 Op. cit., p. 30.

28 *Monuments de l'histoire des abbayes de Saint-Philibert*, ed. R. Poupardin (Paris, 1905), pp. 60–3.

29 Cf. F. Lot, *Etudes critiques sur l'abbaye de Saint-Wandrille* (Paris, 1913), pp. xxx–xlvi.

30 See Arbman, op. cit., p. 85.

31 The best survey is that of Jan de Vries, *Altgermanische Religionsgeschichte* (3rd ed., repr., Berlin, 1970).

32 Op. cit., i, p. 55.

33 See L. Musset, *Les invasions: le second assaut contre l'Europe chrétienne (viie–xie siècles)* (Paris, 1965), p. 227; E. Marold, *Frühmitt. Stud.*, 8 (1974) pp. 204, 214, 217–18.

34 *Ann. Bert.*, pp. 224–7.

35 *Gesta Conwoionis abbatis Rotonensis*, 3, 9. Mon. Germ. Hist., *Script.*, 15, 459. Raiders of Saint-Denis were also reported to have fallen sick, *vario modo* (*Ann. Bert.*, s.a. 865, p. 125).

36 Lupus of Ferrières, *Correspondance*, ed. L. Levillain (Paris, 1935), ii, p. 144, letter 107. See also Levillain, 'Etudes sur l'abbaye de Saint-Denis à l'époque mérovingienne', *Bibliothèque de l'école des Chartes*, xci (1930), p. 35.

37 See Pierre Riché, 'Conséquences des invasions Normandes sur la culture monastique dans l'occident Franc', *Settimane di Studio*, xvi, pp. 706 ff.

38 See G. Devailly, *Le Berry du xe siècle au milieu du xiiie* (Paris, 1973), pp. 111–12.

39 Loc. cit., p. 263.
40 *Mon. Germ. Hist.*, *Script.*, XV, 1, p. 509.
41 *Le Siège de Paris*, lines 196–7, p. 30.
42 Ademar de Chabannes, *Historia*, ed. J. Lair, *Etudes critiques sur divers textes des xe et xie siècles*, ii (Paris, 1899), iii, 17. See the comments of L. Auzias, *L'Aquitaine carolingienne* (Toulouse–Paris, 1937), p. 246.
43 *Annales Masciacenses*, *Mon. Germ. Hist.*, *Script.*, III, p. 170.
44 *The common origins of the Scandinavian kingdoms of York and Dublin* (Oxford, forthcoming).
45 *Les Invasions*, p. 217.
46 Ibid., pp. 213–14.
47 Cf. D'Haenens, loc. cit., p. 281.
48 *Sermo Lupi ad Anglos*, ed. D. Whitelock (2nd ed., London, 1952), p. 25. I am indebted to my wife for the translation.
49 See Vercauteren, loc. cit., esp. pp. 129–30, and C. Brühl, *Fodrum, Gistum, Servitium Regis*, i (Cologne–Graz, 1968), p. 90.
50 *Mon. Germ. Hist.*, *Capit.* II, 2, pp. 303 ff.
51 *Ann. Bert.*, s.a. 873, p. 194.
52 For examples see Auzias, op. cit., p. 324.
53 *Ann. Bert.*, s.a. 864, p. 105.
54 Ibid., p. 113.
55 W. Kienast, *Studien über die französischen Volksstämme des Frühmittelalters* (Stuttgart, 1968), pp. 64–5, n. 73, summarizes these views.
56 *Ann. Bert.*, s.a. 869, p. 166.
57 Flodoard, *Hist. Eccl. Remensis*, IV, 5 (*Pat. Lat.* 135, col. 273): 'multi, Christianam deserentes religionem, paganorum se societati coniunxerant ac tuitioni subdiderant'.
58 *Pat. Lat.* 125, col. 1121. This is the document that Hincmar was asked to draw up to help the judges to decide how to deal with a prince charged with many crimes, including apostasy.
59 *Ann. Bert.*, s.a. 841, p. 39.
60 Cf. Georges Duby, *Guerriers et paysans* (Paris, 1973), p. 135.
61 See Musset, *Invasions*, p. 207.
62 See Michel Roblin, *Le Terroir de Paris aux époques gallo-romaine et franque* (2nd ed. Paris, 1971), pp. 342 ff.
63 Cf. J.-F. Lemarignier, 'Quelques remarques sur l'organisation ecclésiastique de la Gaule du VIIe à la fin du IXe siècle principalement au nord de la Loire', *Settimane di Studio* XIII (1966), pp. 478 ff.
64 Charles Higounet, *Bordeaux pendant le haut moyen âge* (Bordeaux, 1963), p. 41.
65 R. Folz, A. Guillou, L. Musset and D. Sourdel, *De l'Antiquité au monde médiéval* (Paris, 1972), p. 503.
66 David, op. cit., p. 171.
67 *Ann. Bert.* s.a. 841, p. 37.
68 Ibid., s.a. 842, p. 42.
69 Ibid., s.a. 843, p. 44.
70 Ibid., s.a. 848, p. 55.
71 Ibid., s.a. 856, p. 72.

72 Ibid., s.a. 865, p. 117.
73 Ibid., s.a. 873, p. 192.
74 Op. cit., p. 134.
75 See Auzias, op. cit., pp. 244, 332.
76 Ibid., p. 323; Lot, *Recueil*, 2, p. 794.
77 *Pat. Lat.* 124, col. 874.
78 *Script. Rer. Langobard.*, ed. G. Waitz, p. 226.
79 *Pat. Lat.* 126, col. 689.
80 Lot, *Etudes*, pp. lxv ff. Cf. the sermon of Lupus, ed. W. Levison, see p. 111, above note 2, op. cit., p. 563.
81 See Lemarignier, loc. cit., pp. 463–5.
82 As Bloch saw, op. cit., pp. 39 ff.
83 Loc. cit., p. 290.
84 Cf. Duby, op. cit., p. 133.
85 *The Barbarian West* (3rd ed. London, 1967), p. 152; Sawyer, op. cit., p. 201 and note 20 in first edition; the matter seems to have been dropped in the second edition. My opinion was also that of Sir Frank Stenton, *Anglo-Saxon England* (3rd ed., Oxford, 1971), p. 240.
86 Op. cit., p. 130.
87 Levillain, *Etudes*, p. 35.
88 *Ann. Bert.*, s.a. 861, p. 84.
89 Though Musset thinks that we have (*Invasions*, p. 238), generalizing, if cautiously, from the opinion of H. Platelle, *Le temporel de l'abbaye de Saint-Amand des origines à 1340* (Paris, 1962), p. 83.
90 Again, the opinion of Musset, *De l'Antiquité*, p. 525.
91 *Capit.* II, 2, p. 323.
92 *The birth of western economy* (London, 1961), p. 221. Also Lorraine, according to Hincmar, *Pat. Lat.* 126, col. 13.
93 As noted by D'Haenens, loc. cit., p. 278.
94 Gabriel Fournier, *Le peuplement rural en Basse-Auvergne durant le haut moyen âge* (Paris, 1962), esp. pp. 552–63.
95 Cf. Alfred Smyth, note 44 above.
96 *Gesta S. P. Font.*, s.a. 851; Lot, *Saint-Wandrille*, p. xxx.

Index